AF663774

State and Economy in Pre-Colonial Manipur

State and Economy in Pre-Colonial Manipur

Edited by

J. B. Bhattacharjee

AKANSHA PUBLISHING HOUSE

NEW DELHI • GUWAHATI • VISAKHAPATNAM

AKANSHA PUBLISHING HOUSE
4649-B/21, Ansari Road
Darya Ganj, New Delhi - 110 002
Ph.: 23263193 / 9811582579 / 09435116718
Fax: 011-23263193
Email: ektabooks@yahoo.com
Visit us at: www.akanshapublishinghouse.com

State and Economy in Pre-Colonial Manipur

© Institute of Northeast India Studies, Kolkata

First Published 2010

ISBN 978-81-8370-241-6

All rights reserved. No part of this publication may be reproduced or transmitted, in any form or by any means, without prior permission of the author. Any person who does any unauthorized act in relation to this publication may be liable to criminal prosecution and civil claims for damages.

[The responsibility for the facts stated, conclusions reached etc., is entirely that of the author. The publisher is not responsible for them, whatsoever.]

PRINTED IN INDIA

Published by Akansha Publishing House, New Delhi and Printed at Harmain Offset Press, Delhi.

Contents

Preface

The Meitei Kingdom in Manipur came into existence in the ancient period and flourished as an independent political entity till the beginning of the nineteenth century; it became a protected state under the British after the First Anglo-Burmese War (1824-26) and a princely state after the Anglo-Manipur War of 1891. The state emerged from the Meitei ethnic society through a unique process of social integration and consolidation. It is said that the large number of ethnic proto-Meitei clans that had migrated to the Manipur valley from Southeast Asia in different waves at different points of time were regrouped into seven clans, namely, Ningthouja, Angom, Luwang, Khuman, Khaba-Aganba, Chenglei, and Moirang. Each of the seven clans had settled exclusively in different parts of the valley and those settlements eventually developed into autonomous principalities or chiefdoms. The pre-Meitei autochthonous groups, namely, Loi, Chakpa, and few other minor ethnic groups, who were in possession of the valley, were gradually pushed by the Meiteis to the marshy and less fertile foothill regions. These autochthonous groups also gradually came to be identified as one, called Loi. In course of time, the entire valley became divided between the seven Meitei clan-principalities, but the scramble for expansion and occupation of more fertile lands dragged them into mutual conflicts in which the Ningthoujas emerged as the victors. These Ningthoujas were the first to immigrate, their principality included the most fertile central valley, and a legend that the first Ningthouja ruler, Nongda Lairen Pakhangba, was a god in the human form deified the royal clan and strengthened their position among the Meitei chiefdoms. The Ningthouja chiefs defeated the Angom, Luwang, Khaba-Aganba, Chenglei and the Khuman chiefs one by one in sporadic wars which continued till thirteenth century. Thereafter, the Ningthouja king was proclaimed as the king of the Meiteis, and the institution of Meitei kingship came to be established in Manipur. Kangla, the original seat of authority of the Ningthouja chiefs, became the capital. Moirang, the last surviving Meitei chieftaincy, was defeated and forced to accept the suzerainty of the Ningthoujas. Eventually this principality was also absorbed into the Meitei kingdom, thus completing the process of Meitei integration and state formation The pre-Meitei autochthonous groups (i.e. the Lois) as well as other ethnic groups, including some of the tribal clans from the neighbouring hills, who immigrated into the Manipur valley till about the fifteenth century AD were integrated into the Meitei lineage structure through a unique process of Metei-ization. They adopted the Meitei language and immensely contributed to the social, cultural and economic growth of the kingdom. The Meiteis followed their traditional religion, called *Sanamahi*, in which the ancestor worship predominated, but in the medieval period the entire community embraced *Vaisnava* faith at the initiative of the kings who endowed Vaisnavism with the status of the state religion. The Meitei king was first called *Lainingthou*, but the title was changed to *Maharaja* in 1724 AD (1646 *Saka*) and the kingdom came to be known as Manipur.

The Meitei kingdom in Manipur, if the claim of the royal chronicle can be accepted, is one of the longest surviving early states in the Indian subcontinent, while the emergence of the state through a process of cultural integration and assimilation of a large number of ethnic societies into a single-fold (Meitei) was indeed unique to this kingdom. This massive integration and assimilation seems to have been possible because the king was in complete control of the economy in the kingdom. Whereas some scholarly works on the political, social and cultural history of Manipur are available for the enthusiastic readers, the role of material culture in the emergence, growth and sustenance of the erstwhile kingdom are yet to be fully explored. Therefore, with the singular objective to empirically explore the source materials as well as to gain insights on the economic contents of the Meitei State in Pre-Colonial Manipur, the Institute of Northeast India Studies, in collaboration with the Department of History, Manipur University, organized a workshop on 'Economy of the Early Meitei State' at the Department of History, Manipur University, Imphal, on 24th September 2007. Professor N. Joykumar Singh, Head, Department of History, Manipur University and his colleagues in the department took the initiative and provided logistic support for the workshop. Life Members of the Institute in Manipur, faculty members and research scholars in the Department of History, Manipur University and a good number of local scholars participated in the workshop, the memory of which shall be cherished for long by the participants as a serious academic discourse to probe absorbingly into the subject. Professor Gangmumei Kamei, a well known historian of Manipur and a Life Member of the Institute, initiated the deliberations by his keynote address. Twelve themes were presented and discussed. One of the major findings of the workshop was that the society and economy in pre-colonial Manipur was under total control of the state. The land, forests, mines and minerals, agriculture, industry and craft, including dress and ornaments for various sections of the people, were absolutely regulated by the kings. As a result, natural and human resources were not fully explored, technology remained backward and the economy could not develop to its full potentials. The presenters were then asked to re-look their drafts in light of the comments and suggestions and to submit the papers for publication. This, unfortunately, took a very long time, despite intermittent twinkles and bells, and explains the delay in bringing out the book. *State and Economy in Pre-Colonial Manipur*, a title decided at the workshop, is a collection of those papers which we could at the long last recover from the authors. As per consensus of the workshop, some fillers have also been included in the collection. All said, what emerges between the themes in the collection is the 'state, society and economy interface in pre-colonial Manipur'.

I am sorry to those who submitted their papers in reasonably good time, but I had to hold them on while waiting for the others. A few more themes, originally presented in the workshop, could perhaps be added, had we been able to wait longer; but sorry, the human patience and tenacity cannot be without some limit and somewhere, one has to say, 'this far and no farther'. I am indeed thankful to my friends in the Department of History, Manipur University, who organized the workshop, to all participants of the workshop, and to the authors whose contributions have made this publication possible. Hope, it will generate some fresh interest in the study of Pre-Colonial Manipur. Finally, thanks to my friend Shri M. P. Misra of the Akansha Publishing House, New Delhi, who patiently waited for the manuscript for two years and did his part at the shortest possible call.

Institute of Northeast India Studies
Kolkata - 700129

(J. B. Bhattacharjee)

Our Contributors

Prof. Gangmumei Kamei, former Professor of History, Manipur University, Imphal

Dr. N. Joykumar Singh, Professor, Department of History, Manipur University, Imphal

Dr. O. Ranjit Singh, Guest Lecturer, Department of History, Manipur University, Imphal

Dr. L. Kunjeswori Devi, Associate Professor, Department of History, Manipur University, Imphal

Mr. N. G. Rhodes, Numismatist, 28 Napier Gardens, Hythe, Kent, UK

Mr. S. K. Bose, Numismatist, BF 70, Sector I, Salt Lake City, Kolkata

Dr. S. Amal Singh, Research Associate, Centre for Manipur Studies, Manipur University, Imphal

Dr. L. Basanti Devi, Lecturer in History, Standard College, Imphal

Dr. M. Jitendra Singh, Professor of History & Dean, School of Social Sciences,, Manipur University, Imphal

Dr. K. Ruhinikumar Sharma, Lecturer in History, Ideal Girls' College, Imphal

Mr. H. Sudhir, Assistant Professor, Department of History, Manipur University, Imphal

Ms Jayati Bhattacharjee, Lecturer in History, Women's College, Shillong

Ms Sarbani Bhattacharjee, ICHR Junior Research Fellow, Department of History, North-Eastern Hill University, Shillong

1

Evolution of the Meitei State The Formation of Early State in Manipur

Gangmumei Kamei

State and State Formation

The state, as a political institution, has been looked upon by the social scientists from various angles. A section of the classical political thinkers considered it as a definitive territory, having a government with external sovereign relations. To the sociologists, the state is a social organization which has given expression to the existing relations in a society and to the idea pertaining to power, authority, force, justice, property and the laws. The ancient Greek and Roman thinkers thought that the state was coterminous with the society. On the other hand, the great German philosopher, Hegel, described state as the 'March of God on Earth'. To the Marxists, the state was a political structure created by the propertied class to manage the complex social relationship and to protect the interests of the rich and the powerful. This facial of the state emerges from Frederick (Friedrich) Engels, according to whom, the distinguishing features of the state are the territory, establishment of the public power, imposition of taxes, introduction of public debts and the authority of the bureaucracy. Therefore, the state is the highest form of - or the most powerful – human institution ever created by the human. These views are indeed so well known that one and everyone can go on repeating them. However, all these perceptions put together, the state is essentially a social institution with the basic features, such as, population, territoriality, legitimacy (power and authority), and sovereignty.[1]

The historical understanding of the state formation processes in different parts of the world calls for specific set of evidences in all specific cases. In history - and for that matter, in all social sciences - the state formation is the process of evolution of a people or a social group occupying a territory into a political society through different stages of social and economic functions. This political society is the state. However, there seem to be no single paradigm to explain the process of state formation. This is evident from the seminal work of Ronald Cohen and E. R. Service[2] who observed that there is no clear cut or simple set of causal statement that explains the phenomenon of the state. In fact, Cohen in an earlier work had asserted, "The formation of state is a funnel like progression of interactions in which a variety of pre-state structures responding to the different determinants of change are bound by other unresolvable conflicts to choose additional and more complex laws of political hierarchy. Once a particular solution is hit upon, the structural features of the adaptation and benefits cause these polities to converge culturally and socially to the early states."[3] In the ancient Indian context, Romila Thapar observed that there is no single factor of state formation, that the state formation is a complex process in which a range of factors may be crucial to apply to varying situations, and that the form of the state would vary according to the nature of its origin.[4] Henri J. M.

Claessen and Peter Skalnik, in their monumental work,[5] encountered (i) the population growth and population pressure, (ii) war, threat of war or conquest, raids, (iii) conquest, (iv) progress in production and the promotion of surplus, tribute, affluence, (v) ideology and legitimization, and (vi) the influence of already existing states as the major factors of state formation. J. B. Bhattacharjee[6] observed that all those factors, as enumerated by Claessen and Skalnik, were relevant in the context of the formation of early states from the ethnic social base in Northeast India, although he emphasized social stratification – caused by economic differentiation and ritual status - and legitimacy to be more important factors than others in this region.

Although for the present purpose of studying the evolution of the Meitei State it is not proposed to go into the origin of the state as speculated by the political philosophers and the sociologists, it is certainly necessary to understand the state and the typology of states for a clearer perception of the processes of state formation.

Typology of the States

Morton M. Fried classified the states into (i) pristine state and (ii) secondary state. The pristine state is also called primary state. The pristine or primary states, like the primitive societies, are simple, early, original, primary and lacking in development, while the secondary states, which are founded due to the external pressure from the existing states, are sponsored by the existing developing states which impose their own model on the formation of the new state.[7] Henri J. M. Claessen and Peter Skalnik also classified the states into two, namely, (i) early and (ii) modern. According to them, the early states are simple, non-industrialized and pre-capitalistic, while the modern states are complex, industrialized and developing.[8]

The formation of the pristine or early states has been explained by two theoretical formulations; namely, the 'conflict process' as propounded by Frederick Engels and the 'evolutionary process' as proposed by Morton H. Fried. Frederick Engels, whose formulations eventually became the basis of the Marxian Theory of State,[9] explained the formation of the states on the basis of intra-societal conflicts and the forms of class struggle through four stages of social and political development, namely, (i) primitive communism, (ii) emergence of private property, (iii) formation of social and economic classes, and (iv) emergence of the state.[10] According to Engels, the primitive communism was the first stage of social formation in which there was no property, no trade and commerce, no class of rich or poor, and no despotic ruler. In course of time, the individuals started acquiring things from the common or community's pool of resources, and the property so acquired by the individuals emerged as private property of those individuals. The creation of the private property led to the concentration of property or wealth in the hands of the few and resulted in the formation of a powerful social and economic class which possessed wealth. The more dominant ones within this class then articulated themselves to expand the size of their respective individual private property and to establish control over the resources in the territory through concerted policies and actions. This dominant class then created a military power in order to protect its interests. In the process, a structure of productivity, based on surplus production due to the technological development, was also created. The trade in surplus commodities resulted in the change in the nature of economy from consumption or subsistence level to that of production of commodities for exchange. The new type of economy invariably facilitated the emergence and growth of middlemen, entrepreneurs and capital. The class structure so evolved was perpetuated through the state.[11]

Fried's perception of the evolution of the pristine states passed through three stages with corresponding social and political formations, as shown below:[12]

Stages	Form of Social Formation	Polity Formation
Stage I	Egalitarianism [Primitive Society]	Band and Tribal Polity
Stage II	Ranked Society [Diversified Society]	Chiefdom
Stage III	Stratified Society	State

Claessen and Skalnik also identified three stages in the evolution of the early states as they classified the early states into (i) inchoate early state, (ii) typical early state, and (iii) transitional early state, on the basis of the levels of social and economic development. Thus, in the inchoate states the kinship ties are still very dominant, in typical states such ties are counter-balanced by the territorial ones, and in transitional states the kinship ties have already been marginalized by the dominance of the appointed officials.[13]

It may not be wrong to observe that 'evolution' is the common dominant theme between the analyses of Engels, Fried and Claessen-Skalnik. There is also some continuity in the formulations of all analysts of state formations, beginning with Frederick Engels to whom the origin of the state formation studies and the Marxian theory of state are unanimously attributed.[14] Engels' emphasis was on 'conflict'. However, the Marxian model, in which Engels' formulation is pre-eminent, has been found by many scholars to be Eurocentric and inappropriate to explain the evolution of states in the Indian subcontinent. In the Indian context, Romila Thapar explained the evolution of the pristine states in the Vedic period as the transformation of the lineage society. According to this explanation, the lineage, which was a corporate group of unilinial kins with a formalized system of authority as the binding force, gradually transformed into a combined lineage and territorial group. The stratification led to the emergence of chieftainship, and a sharper stratification of the chieftainship was germinal to the state formation. Thus, according to Thapar, the lineage society had gradually transformed into the state. [15]

In the context of the Meitei state formation in early Manipur, the formulations of Romila Thapar and of Claessen and Skalnik seem to be very relevant. As we proceed, we shall see that there was an evolution of a pristine state over a long period of time in ancient and medieval Manipur. The process of state formation was evolutionary in character. The evolution of the state was through a transformation of the lineage-based clan-chiefdom of the Meiteis to the state. The state formation was also a process of cultural evolution. The creation of culture was a great human achievement by the use of which the society tamed and governed its members, and created and maintained the complex social organization. Culture had technological, economic, religious, artistic and recreational functions. All these depended on the ability of the political aspects of culture to integrate and protect the society. The society grew and declined depending on the ability to preserve the authority. The growth and decline of the culture also depended on the ability of the state to preserve its culture and civilization. As regards the pristine state, our focus is on the factors contributing to the emergence of the pristine society and state. The major factors of state formation enumerated by Claessen and Skalnik, namely, growth of population and population pressure, war, war machine, threat of war, conquest, progress in production and creation of surplus, imposition of tribute, affluence, ideology and legitimization and the influence of the existing states, are all meaningful in variable degrees in case of the evolution of the Meitei State in Manipur.[16]

Emergence of the Meitei Clan-Chiefdoms

The Meiteis in ancient Manipur had developed a lineage based social system, and the polities, which as they ultimately emerged, were clan-chiefdoms and clan-principalities. Historical texts and literary works refer to the presence of a large number of ethnic and social groups in ancient Manipur valley. These were the proto-Meitei social groups, like the Mangang, Angom, Luwang, Khaba, Nganba, Khuman, Moirang, Sarang, Leishangthem, Heiram Khunjam, Chenglei, Haorok Konthou, Manting Mara, Lera Khongang, Thanga, Kambong, Ulok Ushai, Haokha-Lokkha, Ningol Latam, Phantek Khuyon, Chakpa, etc. There were also hill tribal communities like the Anal, Tangkhul and Kabui (Rongmei). These tribes and social groups, except the hill tribes, were socially organized into seven clans of the Meiteis during the reign of King Nongda Lairen Pakhangba who founded the Ningthouja dynasty. The clan genealogies give the account of the origin and genealogical trees of the concerned clans showing their historicity. Myths were created to provide the background of the origin of the clans which were constituted into the Meitei social fold.[17]

Pre-Pakhangba Polity

The historical texts make references to a large number of pre-Pakhangba chiefs and rulers who ruled in different periods of the traditional 'Meitei Age' (Era), known as the *Chak* (viz., *Hayi Chak*, *Haya Chak*, *Langba Chak* and *Konna Chak*). Of these accounts, *Kangbalon*, a chronicle which is supposed have been compiled during the reign of Khuyoi Tompak, the son and successor of Pakhangba, gives a brief account of several rulers and chiefs. Kangba was the first chief of the Meiteis. His successors were Maliya Phambalcha (founder of the Era of *Maliya Phambacha*), Nongdamhan and Taohuireng (who faced a slave rebellion), Kaksuba, Tonkonba (discoverer of the wild paddy), Pitingkoi, Lambicha,

Sopaiba, Puthiba (inventor of the plough), Kuptreng, and Sentreng.[18] The accounts of these rulers present a picture of the emerging chieftainship, although we cannot establish the historicity of their rule in a chronological frame.

The Clan-Chiefdoms

The clan was both a social and a political institution among the ancient Meiteis. This duality in the nature and function of the clan is a unique feature of the Meitei lineage system. The clan is known as the *Salai*, which literally means ancestor god of the lineage (*Sa* = *Sagei*, *Lai* = God). There was no *salai* system in the legendary period, though there are references to the *sagei* (lineage or families). It was during the reign of King Pakhangba that the clans were regrouped into seven and recognized as parts of the Meitei social system. The seven clans were Ningthouja (the royal clan, Mangang), Angom, Luwang, Kha-Nganba (combination of Khaba and Nganba), Sarang Leishangthem (combination of Sarang, Leishangthem and Changlei), Khuman and Moirang. Each of the original clans had a territorial region under its occupation and control. Smaller groups were absorbed into the seven clans along with their territory. Pakhangba is thus credited with the creation of the Meitei *Salai* system which became the cornerstone of the Meitei society and state.[19]

The clan (*Salai*) in the Meitei society became both a social category and a political organization when the seven clans were created. Each clan had a delineated territory which became the political space of the clan chiefdom. The name of the clan was identical to the name of the territory in possession of the particular clan. The clan was also a linguistic identity, because the members of a clan spoke in the same dialect. In course of time, all the clans spoke the Meitei language which was an outcome of political hegemony of the Ningthoujas who called themselves as the Meiteis. However, in a clan territory the people of other clans also could migrate and settle down permanently.

The chief of a clan was called *Piba*, who was also the social head of the clan. He was originally the head of the lineage (*sagei*) and head of the village inhabited by his kinsmen. The *Piba* was expected by his clansmen to be the protector of the clan lands, including the agricultural lands, forests, rivers and lakes. The chief of the clan by his moral and social authority and physical prowess organized a group of armed kinsmen for the defence of the land and the protection of life and community. The *Piba* became ultimately the protector of the land and people within the clan territory. So the *Piba*, the social head of the clan, became the political authority with his command over the armed militias which were raised and looked after by him for the protection of the people of his clan and its territory. With this authority the *Piba* became a *Ningthou* (chief or ruler or king) of the clan within the clan territory which ultimately grew into a principality or chiefdom.

As the concept of clan territory emerged, the clan land was considered as communal land of the clan with the collective responsibility of the community to protect the land. The land within the clan chiefdom was owned by the clan in common where the individual families were allowed individual land holdings. They also enjoyed the right to use the common land like the forests, rivers and lakes. The *Ningthou*'s foremost duty was the protection of the people and the territory. He exercised his authority over the military force for the performance of this duty. The members of the clan, and later on all the inhabitants of the principality, were to render military service under the command of the *Ningthou*. It was the beginning of the compulsory military service to the ruler, known as the *Lallup* system. The chief also established his individual ownership over portions of lands out of the common lands of the clan. He compelled his kinsmen and other subjects to render manorial service to him for agricultural production. Thus, he acquired enough food grains for the maintenance of the royal households and for the administrative establishment of the principality. He asked the subjects to cut timber from the forests for building houses in the royal palace and for manufacturing boats. He also asked those among the subjects who possessed the required skill and experience for different types of specialized activities to render such services to him. In return of the services rendered by the people, the chief was endowed with the responsibility of performing the religious rites and rituals for the well being of the entire clan and the chiefdom with the help of the priest. Thus, he combined in himself the role of the *Piba* (social head), *Ningthou* (ruler) and the *Maiba* (high priest). However, the chief was the *Piba* in respect of his own clan only. Ultimately, he was the *Ningthou*, i.e., the political head or ruler or the chief of the clan-principality or chiefdom (which might have included several original clans), and in that capacity he was the ruler of all within the principality, including the immigrants from other Meitei clans and other ethnic groups who have been allowed to settle in his principality.

The clan genealogies give the list of chiefs of the clans who ruled in succession, whereas the clan chronicles give brief historical accounts of the respective clans. However, the Moirang and the Khuman chronicles are important for their political history and the account of their polity as well. The reason may be that these two chiefdoms offered resistance to the Ningthouja supremacy for a long time. They were the last two among the chiefdoms to accept the suzerainty of the Ningthouja chiefs. The Angom, Khaba, Nganba, Sarang and Leishangthem polity did not develop beyond rudimentary chiefship (*Ningthou*), the heads of those clans having accepted feudatory status in the court of the Nigthouja chief much earlier than the Moirang and the Khuman chiefs. The *Angam Ningthou* and the *Luwang Ningthou* are frequently mentioned in the chronicles among the feudatories in the

Ningthouja court. The income to the chief or chiefdom came in the form of tributes from the people, including the lesser clans and ethnic groups at the village levels who came under the hegemony or control of the respective chiefs. As the *Piba* of the clan, the chief got financial support from the heads of the sub-clans or sub-lineages (*sagei*) of his clan (*salai*) and the kinsmen of the clan as a whole.[20]

The Meitei State: Foundation of the Ningthouja Dynasty

The establishment of the Ningthouja kingdom with the seat of authority at Kangla in the heartland of the Manipur valley by Nongda Lairen Pakhangba marked the beginning of the Meitei State. The emergence of the Ningthouja dynasty was an outcome of the struggle between the various ethnic groups and the clan chiefdoms. There were also other ethnic groups who attained the status of clan or sub-clan within the Meitei society. There was indeed a perpetual conflict for a very long time among the clans for the occupation of Kangla which was the seat of political power, religion and culture of the Meiteis. In the Meitei psyche, Kangla was regarded as the navel of the earth and the centre of the Meitei worldview and universe.

Pakhangba occupied Kangla after defeating the Khabas. He also defeated Poireiton, a leader of the colonizers to the Manipur valley. This event is attributed by some chronicles to the first century AD. Pakhangba was supported by several clans, viz. Angom, Luwang, Mangang, Khuman, Moirang and Chakpa. The royal chronicles described him as the founding monarch of the ruling family. Thus, the *Pakhangba Phambal*[21] recorded that Pakhangba was given the title of *Meidingu*, a corruption of *Meitei-Ngu*, i.e., Lord of the Meiteis. He was the first monarch to have performed the coronation ceremony. His reign saw the reorganization and improvement of the Meitei social and political structure. It was he who organized the proto-Meitei ethnic groups into seven clans of the Meiteis. He became the head of the Meitei social confederacy and the head of the Meitei polity. The fact that Pakhangba was crowned as the king of the Meiteis (*Meidingu* or *Meitei-Ngu*) might lead to a query whether the ancient Meiteis had already developed the institution of monarchy or kingship or whether Pakhangba just declared himself as the monarch of the Meiteis. If we are to accept the proto-historical accounts of political formations before the emergence of the Ningthouja dynasty, it becomes clear that the Meiteis had already developed the concept of monarchy. There are also references to Yaibirok, the mother of Pakhangba, who made serious attempts to make her son assume the kingship of the Meiteis at Kangla. However, we are short of historical evidence to trace the details of the Meitei polity before the accession of Pakhangba to the throne of Kangla. In any case, he created the administrative machinery of a state which was followed by his successors. As a matter of fact, all the kings of the Ningthouja dynasty who ruled in Manipur after Pakhangba claimed their decent directly from Pakhangba.[22]

Growth of the Meitei State

The Meitei kings ruled from Kangla. They gradually established their complete control over the forest rich plain areas of the basin of the Imphal and Iril rivers in northern Manipur valley, which was a part of the Ningthouja clan-principality. The forests were cleared and agriculture was practiced in the upper valleys of the two rivers. In the early stage, the broadcasting and shifting cultivation (*Pamlou*) were practiced. Later on, they took to wet rice cultivation. In the central part of the valley, there were swampy areas with large number of lakes and marshes which were required to be drained continuously. The water from the swampy areas was drained through three rivers – Imphal, Iril and Nambul. The kings employed the labour of the people through the

Lallup system in dredging the rivers and correcting or changing the courses of the rivers. Irrigation was undertaken directly by the state. These rivers also provided the waterways. The swampy areas and lakes were traversed by waterways in which the canoes were used in large number. The state penetrated into the thickly forested Nongmaijing hills and the Kaubru mountain for the supply of timber, collection of forest products, and catching of wild elephants for the royal stable and the armed forces.

With absolute control over the fertile plains of northern Imphal valley and the forests of the surrounding mountains, the Meitei rulers had acquired enough resources to strengthen and expand the boundary of the state. In the meantime, there was already enough population for engagement in state sponsored irrigation works and for the development of agriculture. The dredging of the rivers and the draining out of water was also resulting in land reclamation in the marshy regions making new areas available for agriculture and settlement of the immigrants. The rulers organized the militias as the Meiteis were a martial race. The state also minimized the menace of ravages caused by the wild animals, like tiger, leopard and boar in the foothill regions. The thinly populated areas in the valley and the foothills were opened up for the settlement of the immigrants who contributed to the increase of population, productivity, revenue and wealth of the state.[23]

State under Naothingkhong

The Meitei state seems to have gradually expanded till about the eighth century AD. The *Naothingkhong Phambal Khaba,* a historical text dealing with the adventures and coronation of King Naothingkhong, presents a portrait of a well developed state structure in the eighth century. His kingdom came into contact with the Shans of the kingdom of Pong in Upper Burma. Samlung, a prince and a brother of the Pong king Sukhampha, visited Manipur valley and stayed for ten years at a place which came to be called Pong Ingkhol (homestead of the Pong) on bank of the Iril river in Manipur. The contact with the Shans was a significant development in the expanding relations of the Meitei kings with a foreign country, namely, the kingdom of Pong in Upper Burma. Naothingkhong married a Bengali princess, named Chingngurembi, who was said be a princess from the west.*

---

*'West' occurs frequently in the literary sources and historical writings on pre-colonial Manipur in connection with migrations as well as political and commercial contacts. The Brahmins, Bisnupriyas and the Pangans immigrated into Manipur from that direction. The holy men and the *Vaisnava* preachers also came from the West. The territory immediately on the west of Manipur is the Cachar plains or the modern Barak Valley of Assam. In the later part of the British rule, the two districts in the area, namely, Cachar and Sylhet, formed the Surma Valley Division under a Commissioner. These two districts were transferred from the Dacca Division of Bengal to Assam in 1874 when Assam was constituted into a province under a Chief Commissioner. Cachar district then included the present North Cachar Hills district. R.B. Pamberton in his Report of 1835 mentioned about the Jiri route through which migrations and trade took place between Cachar and Manipur since early times. Since the British time, 'Cachar Road' is the highway between the two. In the medieval period, the Cachar plains and the North Cachar Hills together made the Heramba Kingdom. The *Cheitharol Kumbaba* mentions of the relations between the rulers of Manipur and Heramba. It appears that at some point of time in the medieval period the boundary of Tripura Kingdom extended up to the borders of Manipur. An Assamese *Buranji* of the Ahom time, called *Tripura Buranji*, mentions a big market at a place called Rungrang where the people of Manipur, Heramba and Tripura regularly traded. However, the Cachar-Sylhet region is historically a part of ancient Bengal which consisted of the sub-regions like Raḍha, Gauḍa, Puṇḍravardhana, Vanga, Herikela, Samaṭaṭa, etc. from time to time. Srihatta, or the Cachar-Sylhet area, seems to have been generally a part of Harikela as attributed by the literary and numismatic sources.

(Contd...)

The *Naothingkhong Phambal Khaba* also recorded some interesting information on the agricultural development in Manipur. It is said that the people belonging to the Ningthouja, Khuman and Luwang clans were devoted to wet rice cultivation. The hill tribes, like the Shelloi Langmais, among whom Naothingkhong took shelter and married a

---

(Contd...)

According to two Panchakhanda inscriptions, dated to c. 5th century AD and 12th century AD respectively, the Tripuri king Adidharma-pha granted land to some Brahmins in Sylhet. The Tipperah Copper-plate inscription of 7th century AD mentions the grant of land by Samanta ruler Lokanatha of Samatata for a temple and for the settlement of Brahmins in Jayatungavarsa, which has been identified with the Jatinga valley of Cachar-North Cachar area. According to the Nidhanpur Copper-plates of 7th century AD, King Bhaskaravarman of Kamarupa granted land to some Brahmins in the Chandrapuri *Visaya*, which is identified with western Sylhet. The Paschimbhag Copper-plate of 10th century AD recorded the grant of land to four *mathas* in Chandrapura *Visaya* within Srihatta-*mandala* of the Pundravardhana-*bhukti* by Sricandra who was the king of Vanga-Harikela. Finally, there are two Bhatera Copper-plate inscription of the 11th-12th century AD which recorded the existence of the sovereign Srihatta Kingdom (Srihattarajya) that included Cachar, Sylhet and the adjoining areas. The area, therefore, formed part of the different kingdoms that came into existence in eastern regions of Bengal in different times. The parts of Srihatta also later on came to be known under different names. Nonetheless, the people in the Cachar-Sylhet area do share a common geographical space and a common dialect and culture. Barrie M. Morrison in his *Political Centres and Cultural Regions in Early Bengal* (New York, 1976; Indian Reprint, Rawat Publishing House, Delhi, 1980, p. 9) called this division 'Sylhet Basin' and described it as one of the five cultural regions of Bengal. Geographically, it forms the north-eastern corner of the Bengal Delta. Therefore, some scholars refer to this division as Northeast Bengal. This Northeast Bengal or Sylhet Basin is situated immediately on the west of Manipur. For details see J. B. Bhattacharjee, "The Ancient Political Structure of Barak Valley", *The NEHU Journal of Social Sciences and Humanities*, vol. X, no. 2, April-June 1992, pp. 1-38.

tribal girl named Petangba, practiced shifting cultivation or *pamlou*. There were plentiful harvests in the kingdom. The historical text also gives the impression that there was a surplus in the production of food grains. Fishing was another means of livelihood for many. There were conflicts and quarrels over the exercise of fishing rights in the streams and rivers.

The state machinery had considerably been developed in the mean time. The coronation ceremony, the gorgeous coronation costumes and participation of the members of the royalty and nobility in the ceremony, as known from *Naothingkhong Phambal Khaba*, show that there was an elaborate administrative hierarchy and rituals which were the symbols of a developed state. The military system was well organized. It consisted of cavalry, foot soldiers and riverine navy. The weapons were sword, spear and shield. The *Lallup* system was also mentioned, but it seems to have been in a rudimentary stage.[24]

Loiyamba Shilyen (Shinyen): The first written constitution

Naothingkhong's great initiatives in state-building were carried further by his successors. However, the Meitei State attained a more consolidated status, two hundred years after Naothingkhong, under King Loiyamba. In fact, Loiyamba (1094-1122 AD) was a remarkable Meitei king. The formation of the Meitei state was almost completed during his reign. In 1110 AD, he issued a royal edict, popularly called *Loiyamba Shilyen*, which is believed to be the first written constitution in the history of Manipur. It deals with the working of the Meitei monarchy, privileges of the royalty and nobility, working of the different administrative departments, functions of the various state officials, and the distribution of economic occupations and functions to different social groups or lineages among the subjects, the maintenance of the abodes of the deities, functions and duties of the priestly class, etc. In short, it gives a picture of a fully developed Meitei state system. The royal chronicle, *Cheitharol Kumbaba* refers to the creation of six administrative divisions during the reign of Loiyamba, which were the precursors of the *Pana* system of district administration. The six administrative divisions created by Loiyamba were Khongchalup, Khogbilup, Angoubalup, Nongmailup, Khurailup and Khongjenglup. The *Loiyamba Shilyen* also mentions four *panas*.[25]

Lallup System

The royal chronicle, *Cheitharol Kumbaba* mentions the existence of the *Lallup* system for the first time during the reign of Loiyamba. This *Lallup* was the compulsory feudal service rendered to the state by the male subjects between the age of 16 and 60 years. Under this system each able bodied male subject had to render to the state labour for ten days out of each forty days. The *Lallup* covered both military and non-military development works. The word *Lallup* literally means 'war organization'. Perhaps, it was originally a military service which was gradually extended to non-military activities of the state. The development of the elaborate *Lallup* system was the manifestation of the emergence of feudalism in the social, political and administrative structure of the Meitei Kingdom.

The *Loiyamba Shilyen* projected a well organized state, society and economy in Manipur. The agrarian economy was supplemented by the growing cottage industries – handloom and handicrafts. It was so extensive that the state had to regulate these activities. The edict also shows the presence of the artisan class. The monarchy was fully entrenched in the life of the subjects and the king was becoming very powerful. The nobility was strengthened over the years and the hierarchy of the nobility was formalized. The court etiquette had become very elaborate. The edict mentions the duties and functions of the king and the members of the royal family. The duty of the priestly class was also regulated by the state. The king assumed the social and religious stewardship over and above his royal functions. The state is projected as the regulator of the economy in which the *Lallup* system played the role of the facilitator.[26]

Emergence of the Nation-State

Almost four centuries after King Loiyamba, the Meitei state under King Kyamba (1467-1506 AD) attained the status of a nation-state. The power of the Meitei state was reflected in the military aggrandizement and territorial expansion. The entire valley of Manipur, covering all the erstwhile regional principalities, was brought under the direct rule of the Ningthouja dynasty. The Khuman and the Moirang principalities offered resistance to the Ningthouja expansionism for a long time. However, the Khuman autonomy could not survive for long and in the fourteenth century the principality was absorbed in the Meitei state. Moirang maintained its independence for many centuries. The rulers of Moirang could do so due to the resources available in the neighbouring hills and their control over the Loktak lake. Nonetheless, King Ningthoukhomba (1432-1467 AD) defeated the Moirangs in the fifteenth century and forced them to accept the suzerainty of the Ningthoujas. This principality was also eventually absorbed in the Meitei state. The hill tribes in the foothills were gradually brought under control. Finally, the Meitei kings established their political control over the chiefs in the hill areas between Manipur valley and Kabaw valley, though they did not directly rule in the hills.

The most significant achievement of King Kyamba was the conquest of Kabaw (Kabo) valley. Kyamba made a joint military expedition in the Chindwin basin in Upper Burma along with King Khekhomba of the Mau Shan Kingdom of

Pong. The two kings made conquests in two banks of the Chindwin river. Kyamba conquered Kabaw valley and several other principalities in the west bank of the river, while Khekhomba conquered the territories to the east of the Chindwin. The *Pong Meitei Lamyen Lairik* (Treaty fixing the boundary between Meitei and Pong) is an account of the treaty made between King Kyamba of Manipur and King Khekhomba of Pong. This was an agreement made between the two kings to the effect that the Kabaw valley in the west of Chindwin was given to Kyamba. This treaty between the two independent states (Manipur and Pong) was the confirmation of the conquest of territories by a Meitei King outside Manipur and the recognition of the international entity of the Meitei state by a powerful king of Upper Burma in the fifteenth century. The *Cheitharol Kumbaba* also recorded the event. It further mentioned that King Kyamba introduced some internal reforms in Manipur after his return from Burma. Of these reforms, most important was the streamlining of the *Pana* system. He established two new *Panas* – Ahallup and Naharup. It is conjectured that the *Pana* is a Shan word. However, *Loiyamba Shilyen* had earlier mentioned the existence of some *Panas* during the reign of King Loiyamba.[27]

Chronicle and Calender

Kyamba introduced the practice of recording the royal chronicle, known as the *Cheitharol Kumbaba*, and the *Cheithaba* system of counting years from 1485 AD. The peaceful reign of Kyamba at home witnessed the expansion of the territory of Manipur, and the incorporation of the Kabaw valley and the Shan population of the valley to the population of Manipur. The kingdom attracted immigrants from mainland India, particularly the Brahmins and the Muslims.[28]

Resume

The evolution of the Meitei state over a long period of

about one thousand five hundred years (first to fifteenth century AD) is the story of the formation of a pristine (primary) state. The Meiteis were organized by King Pakhangba into a single society in the first century AD and this society became a nationality by the time King Kyamba reigned in the state in the fifteenth century AD. The Meitei language was the symbol of the Meitei nationality and on the basis of its unilingual character the Meitei kingdom became a nation state. Meitei was the nation, and the state was called Kangleipak which was renamed as Manipur in the eighteenth century AD.

NOTES & REFERENCES

1. *International Encyclopedia of Social Sciences*, vol. 15, p. 150.
2. Ronald Cohen & E. R. Service (ed.), *Origin of the State : the Anthropology of Political Evolution*, Philadelphia, 1978.
3. Ronald Cohen, *Anthropology of Political Evolution*, Philadelphia, 1975, p. 7.
4. Romila Thapar, *From Lineage to State*, Oxford University Press, Bombay, 1984, pp. 3-14.
5. Henri J. M. Claessen & Peter Skalnik (ed.), *The Early State*, Mounton Publishers, The Hague, 1978, p. 62.
6. J. B. Bhattacharjee, *Bhauma-Naraka Legend and State Formation in Pragjyotisa -Kamarupa*, NEIHA, Shillong, 2004, pp. 61-67.
7. Morton H. Fried, *Evolution of the Political Society*, New York, 1967, p. 17.
8. Henri J. M. Claessen & Peter Skalnik, *op.cit.*, p. 21.
9. Sherman H. M. Chang, *Marxian Theory of State*, New York, 1931.
10. Frederick Engels, *Origin of Family, Private Property and the State*, Moscow, 1977, p. 7.
11. *ibid*, pp. 7-12.
12. Morton H. Fried, *op.cit.*
13. Henri J. M. Claessen & Peter Skalnik, *op.cit.*
14. J. B. Bhattacharjee, *op.cit.*, pp. 59-65.

15. Romila Thapar, op.cit., pp. 155-73.
16. Gangmumei Kamei, "State Formation in North East India: A Review", Presidential Address, *Proceedings of North East India History Association*, VIIIth Session, Kohima, 1987, pp. 1-16.
17. L. Ibongohal Singh & N. Khelchandra Singh (ed.), *Cheitharol Kumbaba* (Royal Chronicle of the Meitei Kings), Manipuri Sahitya Parishad, Imphal, 1967.
18. Kh. Yaima (ed.), *Pakhangba Phambal*, Imphal, 1967; *Cheitharol Kumbaba, op.cit.* For references to *Kangbalon* see N. Khelchandra Singh, *Ariba Manipuri Sahityagi Itihaas*, Manipuri Sahitya Parishad, Imphal, 1969.
19. *Cheitharol Kumbaba, op.cit.*
20. For details see Gangmumei Kabui (Kamei), *History of Manipur*, Vol. I (Pre-Colonial Period), National Publishing House, Delhi, 1991.
21. *ibid*; Also see *Pakhangba Phambal, op.cit.*
22. *ibid.*
23. *ibid.*
24. Ch. Manihar Singh (tr. & ed.), *Naothingkhong Phamban Khaba* (English translation), Imphal, 1986.
25. Kh. Chandrasekhar Singh (ed.), *Loiyamba Shinyen*, Imphal, 1984; *Cheitharol Kumbaba, op.cit.*
26. *ibid.*
27. *Pong Meitei Lamyen Lairik*, manuscript in collection of B. Kullachandra Sharma of Imphal. Extracts available in N. Khelchandra Singh, *Ariba Manipuri Sahityagi Itihaas, op..cit..* For further details see Gangmumei Kabui, *History of Manipur*, Vol. I (Pre-Colonial Period), National Publishing House, Delhi, 1991.
28. For details, see Gangmumei Kabui, *History of Manipur*, Vol. I, *op.cit.*

2

Glimpses of Literary Sources for Studying Pre-Colonial Economy of Manipur

N. Joykumar Singh

A tiny border state of the Indian Union, Manipur has a small population of about twenty five lakhs,[1] but one of its precious assets is the rich historical traditions which uphold her distinct cultural identity. It is because of the fascinating historical processes that were particular to Manipur that the scholars in recent times have been taking keen interest in studying the uniqueness of the traditions of the state. The efforts of these scholars have been significantly rewarded by the unfolding of the historical past and the cultural heritage of Manipur as the seat of an ancient civilization. One may now come across a good number of scholarly works on the political and cultural history of Manipur. However, the economic life of the people of Manipur in the earlier periods has not yet been fully explored, despite the fact that this is absolutely necessary for a systematic understanding of the evolution of the Meitei Kingdom as well as other aspects of life and conditions in early Manipur.

The study of the economic history of Manipur during the colonial and post-colonial periods should not be very problematic, since the basic source materials are available in the form of archival, official and non-official records to reasonably satisfy the inquisitiveness of researchers. But such a study of the pre-colonial phase, particularly the ancient and medieval times, is extremely problematic due to the fact that the dearth of the required and reliable source materials is a serious predicament for research in the economic history of early Manipur. The pre-historic artefects and the archaeological, numismatic and epigraphic sources are either non-existant or these are too scanty for reconstructing the material life of the people. The only alternative is the literary source. Fortunately, Manipur has a large number of local chronicles, since the medieval period, which give us significant information about the natural resources, agriculture, indigenous art and crafts, occupations of the people, trade and commerce, etc. Although written in the medieval period, the local chronicles do reflect on the earlier periods as well. The information on the past that came down in the form of oral traditions, myths and legends found place in the chronicles. These literary works are known in the local language (Meitei) as '*Puya*', some of which have in the meantime been edited and publishied by the scholars, while others are preserved in manuscript form by various institutions as well as in private collections. The glimpses of some of these *Puyas* may be useful for an understanding of the importance of the literary sources for studying the economic conditions and material life in pre-colonial Manipur.

1. ***Hidaklon***[2] – In Manipuri, '*hidak*' means medicine and '*lon*' means account. The *Puya*, entitled '*Hidaklon*' is, therefore, an account of the indigenous medicines. In fact, this *Puya* gives a very detailed account of the various types of medicinal plants available in Manipur. It also gives valuable information about the techniques

and methods of preparation of some of the traditional medicines and the names of the medicines for the treatment of different types of ailments and diseases. The traditional medical practitioners in Manipur are locally known as '*Maiba*'. Before the penetration of the modern medicinal system in Manipur, these *Maibas* took care of the medical needs of the people by applying traditional medicines or herbal drugs as well as by ritual practices to treat the patients and to expel the diseases. These *Maibas* excercised considerable influence in the society as they were respected as the savers or protectors of life of the people. The *Hidaklon* is thus a very important literary source for studying the healthcare system and the secrets of healthy life of the people in pre-colonial Manipur.

2. ***Yellon***[3] - This *Puya* is an account of the edible plants of Manipur. Although written in the format of a directory of the various types of herbs, plants and fruits from which the edibles could be extracted, the *Puya* also deals with the food processing activities or food technology that were prevalent in Manipur in early times. The source is, therefore, important for an understanding of the quality of the material life as it provides clues to the food habits and callory intake as well as the cleanliness and hygienic sense of the people in Manipur.

3. ***Uron***[4] - .It deals with the varieties of commercially important and economically valuable trees available in Manipur and their uses for various purposes. Besides listing the trees and describing their uses, the manuscript also mentions about the shrubs and canes that were widely used for fire wood and timber, for making furniture and for the construction of houses. The quality trees formed an important local resource and contributed to the betterment of life style and comfort of the people.

4. ***Waron***[5] – This *Puya* is an account of the bamboos of Manipur. Besides enumerating the varieties of bamboo in the forests of Manipur and those grown domestically, the *Puya* deals with the role of bamboo in everyday life of the people, its ritual relevance and the social and economic importance of the bamboo craft like basketry. The baskets were manufactured in Manipur on commercial scale.

5. ***Leiron***[6] – '*Lei*' means flower, and '*ron*' means account. This *Puya* is indeed a detailed account of the flowers of Manipur. It informs that, besides offerings in religious rites and rituals, the flowers were widely used by the people for ornamental and decorative purposes. Some of the flowers were also valued for their high mecidinal contents. Men and women were involved in flower business. A guide to floriculture in early Manipur, the *Leiron* is an important source of history.

6. ***Thumkhonglon***[7] – This *Puya* is an important source for the study of the indigenous salt manufacturing industry of Manipur. The salt was manufactured in Manipur in the early times from the local salt springs through indigenously developed technology. The locally manufactured salt is used till today for cooking and for traduitional religious ceremonies. The *Puya* contains a list of salt springs in Manipur, the local communities involved in salt-manufacturing and the indigenous methods of manufacture of salt. It is indeed an important source of economic history as the taxt deals with a traditionally important manufacturing industry of Manipur in which a large number of people, particularly in the Loi area, were involved and they met the requirement of the people in the entire state for an essential item of daily use.

7. ***Nunglon***[8] – It is an account of the precious stones locally available within Manipur. '*Nung*' means stone and '*lon*'

means account. It provides the details of the stones, the sites of extractions, and their uses. The text is also a clue to the fondness of the people for the precious stones.

8. ***Sading***[9] – Like *Nunglon*, the *Sading* is also an account of the precious stones and other valuable metals of Manipur. It is important to learn from the *Puya*s that the stone-carving and metal-casting had become important enterprises in early Manipur and some of the local clans had attained professional specialization in those crafts.

9. ***Loiyamba Shinyen***[10] – The *Loiyamba Shinyen* (*Shilyen*) is a royal edict or charter issued by King Loiyamba of Manipur in the beginning of the twelfth century AD assigning or distributing social and econonomic functions to specific families, lineages or sub-clans (*yumnak*) and held selected families responsible for maintenance of the shrines of the traditional deities (*umanglai*). As many as thirty families were identified for weaving and eight families were given the duty of dying, fifty-five families were allotted the duty of maintenance of the religious shrines, the selected families of priests were made responsible for worship of various deities, one hundred and one families of priests and priestesses were allotted the duty to cure diseases by herbal medicines and ritual sacrifices, a state department was created for propitiating the guardian spirits of the kingdom for protection of the king, and ten officials were appointed for the management of land. The edict divided the common people in the kingdom into four *Panas* (divisions) and made it compulsory for every able bodied male in the kingdom between 16 and 60 years of age to render manual service (*Lallup*) to the king for ten days in every forty days by rotation. This *Lallup* system eventually became the backbone of economy in the Meitei Kingdom.

10. ***Cheitharol Kumbaba***[11] – The celebrated royal chronicle of the Meitei kings of Manipur, the *Cheitharol Kumbaba* is considered as the most important literary source for reconstruction of the history of Manipur. Besides being an authenticated record of the day-to-day events of political, administrative and social relevance throughout the rule of the Meitei kings, this chronicle informs about the water management, land reclamation, agrarian settlements, construction of dykes and canals for irrigation, taxes and tributes, the technological inventions and innovations, the agricultural and industrial practices, the useful crafts like salt manufacturing, sericulture, weaving and dyeing, trade and markets, and many other such aspects that are essential for studying the material life and economic conditions of the people of Manipur since early times.

The *Puyas* mentioned above are only to give some examples and intended to draw the attention of the researchers to the treasure of literary sources of the economic history of early Manipur. The forest resources – plants, cane, bamboo and timber, the carpentry, basketry and cane industry, indigenous tradition of medicinal or herbal treatment, salt-manufacturing, precious stones curving, etc. are some of the very important areas of the economic history of Manipur in the pre-colonial period. Therefore, the literary sources on those areas have been referred to on a very selective basis in this paper with the objective to highlight the importance of the *Puyas* for research in economic history. Of the ten *Puyas* discussed in this paper, the *Cheitharol Kumbaba* is well known and has been extensively used by the scholars. The *Loiyamba Shinyen* has also been referred to by some historians. As regards the eight other *Puyas*, the historical importance of those has not yet been explored adequately. Therefore, it is felt that there is a need to highlight the contents of these lesser known *Puyas*. However, the contents discussed in this brief paper are only to provide glimpses of the subject-matter of the each individual *Puya*. These are synoptic, and far from being detailing. It is also important to note that the *Puyas* of Manipur are very large in number. Indeed, they are innumerable. Many of the *Puyas* might have been lost under the stretches and strains of time and circumstances. Some of those which survived the odds also might have been ruined due to the absence of timely protection and preservation. There have been some cataloguing[12] of the available *Puyas* in recent times, but the attempted surveys to list the extant ones might have missed a few more. It is true that a good number of the *Puyas* have been edited and published during last two to three decades, but many are still manuscripts, preserved in libraries, archives and private collections. Those should also be transcribed and published before it is too late. The scientifice preservation of the manuscripts as cultural heritage of the people should be considered as equally important as the content analysis and use of the *Puyas* as the indigenous sources of the history of Manipur. The scholars of political, social and cultural history of Manipur have already focused on the importance of these literary sources in their works, but the economic contents are in no way insignificant. This is precisely the objective of the instant attempt at a brief presentation.

NOTES & REFERENCES

1. Area of Manipur is 22,327 square kilometers and it returned a population of 23,88,634 souls in the Census of 2001. See *Basic Statistics of North East Region, 2002*, NEC Secretariat, Shillong, 2002, pp. 9, 1.
2. An unpublished manuscript. The original text of *Hidaklon* is in the collection of Padmasree N. Khelchandra Singh of Imphal.
3. P. Chandrasekhar (ed.), *Yellon*, Imphal, 1998.

4. An unpublished manuscript. The original text of *Uron* is in the collection Shri B Kullachandra Sharma of Imphal.
5. An unpublished manuscript. The original text of *Waron* is in the collection of Dr Birachandra Singh of Imphal.
6. Chitrasen (ed.), *Leiron Tengtha*, Imphal, 1996.
7. C. Hemchandra (ed.), *Thunkhonglon*, Imphal, 2004.
8. Irom Amubi Singh (ed), *Nunglon*, Ningthoumacha Manisana Keibung, Imphal, n.d.
9. Ng. Kullachandra Singh (ed.), *Sading*, Imphal, 1982.
10. Kh. Chandrashekhar Singh (ed.), *Loiyamba Shinyen*, All Manipur Umanglai Haraoba Committee, Uripok Naoremthong, 1982. For observations on the importance of this *Shinyen/Shilyen* as a source for state and economy in early Manipur and the Meitei State Formation see Gangmumei Kabui (Kamei), "A brief note on *Loiyamba Shilyen* : A Royal Edict on social distribution of economic and administrative functions", *PNEIHA*, IIIrd Session, Imphal, 1982, pp. 31-36; J B Bhattacharjee, "*Loiyamba Shinyen* : A Landmark in Meitei State Formation in Medieval Manipur', *Proceedings of the Indian History Congress*, 64th Session, Mysore, 2003, pp. 362-68.
11. The *Cheitharol Kumbaba* or the royal chronicle of the Meitei kings is said to have been maintained in the court from the time of King Pakhangba in the first century AD. As Rena Laisram writes : "By far the most important source for the study of Meitei history is the royal chronicle called *Cheitharol Kumbaba*. These state chronicles were recorded in Meitei *mayek* in the courts by the learned *Maichous*. *Cheitharol Kumbaba* records the historical events of nearly two thousand years covering the reign of seventy eight kings from Nongda Lairen Pakhangba (33-154 A.D.) to Bodhachandra Singh (1941-1955 A.D.). This chronicle which runs to about eight hundred pages is a voluminous one. When exactly this chronicle began to be recorded has been debated by many scholars. The chronicle itself mentions that it was King Kyamba who introduced the system of *cheithaba* or counting of years in the year 1485 A.D. The accounts before this is sketchy and scholars believe that it must have been constructed out of available source materials. E. Nilakanta quoting the chronicle brings out the event of 1780 A.D. when the king Bhagyachandra is said to

have ordered the re-compiling of the lost *Cheitharol*. The incident implies that the chronicle was already in existence before the reign of this king. The language and style of the text has made scholars to conclude that the chronicle must have started the recording of historical events from the 15th century A.D." – Rena Laisram, *Early Meitei History – Religion, Society & The Manipur Puyas*, Akansha Publishing House, New Delhi, 2009, p.20. However, no one does deny the fact that the *Cheitharol Kumbaba* is the most detailed and systematic account of early Manipur and it is being widely used by the historians as a source of the history of Manipur. The chronicle is available in print, see, for example, Th. Madhob Singh (ed.), *Cheitharol Kumbaba*, Imphal, 1939; L. Ibungohal Singh & N. Khelchandra Singh (ed.), *Cheitharol Kumbaba*, Manipuri Sahitya Parishad, Imphal, 1967. The contents of the chronicle are also available in parts in English translation. Immediately after the British occupation of Manipur in 1891, the government commissioned one Bama Charan Mukherjee to translate *Cheitharol Kumbaba* into English. Mukherjee completed the work in 1897 with the help of 14 Meitei *Pandits*. The translated text was thereafter accessioned in the India Office Library and Records, London. L. Joychandra Singh of Imphal obtained a copy of the translation and published it under the title *The Lost Kingdom – Royal Chronicle of Manipur*. See L. Joychandra Singh, *The Lost Kingdom – Royal Chronicle of Manipur*, Prajatantra Publishing House, Imphal, 1995. The most recent translation from the original is by Saroj Nalini Arambam Parratt. See Saroj Nalini Arambam Parratt (tr. & ed.), *The Court Chronicle of the Kings of Manipur: The Cheitharon Kumpapa*, Routledge, New York, 2005.

12. See, for example, N. Khelchandra Singh (ed.), *A Catalogue of Manipuri Manuscripts*, Manipuri Sahitya Parishad, Imphal, 1984.

3

Contextualizing Pre-historic Sites of Manipur

O. Ranjit Singh

The studying of the pre-historic archaeology of any part of the earth begins on the cognizance of the fact that our earth is nearly 4,600 million years old and the evolution of the earth's crust shows four stages, known as 'quaternary', which is divided into two – (i) Pleistocene (Ice age) and (ii) Holocene (Post-Ice age). The former lasted from 2 million BC to 12,000 BC, and the latter beginning in about 12,000 BC continues to our day. The human is supposed to have appeared on the earth in the early Pleistocene, which has a special significance in prehistoric archaeology as this period witnessed the evolution and development of the humankind and the human cultures. The answer to the question - how old is the human and its culture in Manipur (?) can be given, as any where else, with the 'help of the spade and shovel of the archaeologists.'[1] Manipur was an ancient kingdom. The people of this land have undergone several ordeals in the course of its long drawn civilisational history. It is generally believed that the history of Manipur begins from 33 AD. However, as H D Sankalia told us, "History of a country or region commences from the time its written records are available, and the period which precedes this is called pre-history."[2] Sankalia further told us that the prehistory deals with a period when writing was unknown to the particular country or region or the people whom we are studying.[3] Therefore, the history or story of the humankind before the existence of written records is known as 'pre-history'. The early man who lived before the invention of writing are called 'pre-historic man'. As they did not leave behind any written account of their existence, the story of their life and society is reconstructed on the basis of evidences found in the forms of fossils, skeletons and the relics like stone, bone tools and weapons, paintings, potteries, etc. Some of those pre-historic cultural objects have been discovered and collected from different parts of Manipur, though these are yet to be scientifically dated.

Khangkhui Caves

Paleolithic tools have been discovered from the hilly areas of Manipur. The caves of Khangkhui in Manipur, the number of which is three, are considered to be the most important pre-historic sites in Northeast India. These caves are located near Khangkhui Khullen, at a distance of eleven kilometers to the south-east of Ukhrul town in the Ukhrul district of Manipur.[4] Khangkhui caves are limestone caves. In 1969, excavation was carried out by O. K. Singh and many stone artifacts, bone tools and faunal remains were discovered in these caves, which show habitation of Stone Age men in the caves of Khangkhui.[5] A chopper, which according to O. K. Singh is of Southeast Asian type, hand axe, spear heads, scrapper of different types, blades, borers, flakes, point, knife, tabular flakes and large fluted core of sandstone were collected. Along with these tools, the animal bones and teeth of herbivorous animal were also found.[6] It is observed by T. C. Sharma that on the basis of cultural materials consisting of stone and bone tools in addition to faunal remains, it can be argued that Khangkhui caves yielded some evidence of upper or late Paleolithic period.[7] He further stated that the first evidence of the Pleistocene man in Manipur dated back to about 30,000 BP or Upper Paleolithic period.[8] L. Kunjeswori Devi observed that "this type of cave is one of the most interesting among the caves of North-Eastern India with which both bone and stone tools are associated and the antiquity of Khangkhui caves goes back to that of Late Quaternary."[9] The findings like tools, points, scrapers, chisels, a big chopping tool, etc. suggest that the chief occupation of the people of that time was hunting and they lived on hunting. According to H. D. Sankalia, from the time of Mesolithic or late Stone Age phase, the people did hunting and they knew how to grow the crops and also they had the knowledge of technology in the field of making tools.[10]

In Khangkhui caves, it is suggested that there were two shelters of wet phases and a long dry phase which are supported by the discovery of tools of herbivorous bone and teeth in the first and third layers. Most of the tools are flakes without plate form, and in some cases the flakes exhibit longitudinal mid-ridge and cortex on them.[11] The stone tool industry discovered in Manipur is closely comparable with that of late Choukoutien culture of China. Both the industries are based on the manufacture of core and flake implements, with a few blades in addition to a small series of microliths. It is significant to note that the blades with mid-ridges on both the surface and flakes with a beveled edge of Khangkhui Caves are not found anywhere else. These types might have been a local development while others are of foreign origin.[12]

Tharon Caves

The site of Tharon Caves is situated at 93.32′ longitude and 25.3′ latitude in the midst of thickly forested Reyangling hills, about 5 kilometers towards the north of Tharon village in the Tamelong district of Manipur. The altitude of the cave site is 976 meters above sea level. The cave is locally called Kalemki (*Kalem* = bat and *Ki* = house), meaning 'bat house' or the 'house of bat'. According to Gangmumei Kabui, "The Tharon Caves, believed as the house of the ancestors of the Laingmei Nagas, dwelt by the spirits, is the subject of many legends and traditions of the Zeliangrong people of Tamelong."[13]

There are five caves at this site and this is considered as an important pre-historic site of Manipur. A stream, known as Kalem-Ki-Magu, runs near these caves. In 1979 archeological work was done at this site by the Department of State Archaeology, Government of Manipur. In 1981 the said department and another team, including L. Kunjeswori Devi, jointly explored the site and a lot of pre-historic materials were collected. The explorations revealed that,

> Out of the five caves of Tharon, one is very long and has branches in fourteen bifurcated passages and open towards the stream. Upstream from this cave opening, there is another underground passage, on the right side of the stream which connected the entrance cave. There also existed another cave towards the downstream facing the main stream. While exploring near the stream running around the cave area, edge ground pebble tools including a flake tools and elliptical with grinding faces were discovered on the northern side of the entrance cave at a little higher altitude, there is a rock shelter facing north west and in front of which is a narrow plateau just opposite to the rock shelter across the plateau, there are two other rock shelters which are facing towards south east. The floor of these caves or rock shelters are filled with sandstone slabs that fall from the roofs and walls of the caves, as a result, sometimes, caves become narrow and shallow and no artifact could be collected from inside the cave. The collected artifacts from that site have a close similarity

with those of the Thailand, Burma, Malaysia and Vietnam.[14]

Gangmumei Kabui also observed that the Tharons have distinct affinity with the Haobinhian culture.[15] According to L. Kunjeswaori Devi, the Tharon site has a pre-Neolithic character and traits of Hoabinhian culture.[16] Incidentally, the Hoabinhian culture is of Mesolithic cultural pattern of Southeast Asia, as observed on the basis of the historic finds in the village of Hoabinhi in North Vietnam. The similar relics are found in many other places of Southeast Asia. The Tharon caves were probably occupied by the proto-Austroloids before the advent of the present Tibeto-Burman inhabitants of the area. The proposed date is around 5,000-4,000 BC.[17]

Napachik

Napachik, another Stone Age site of second millennium BC,[18] is a hillock in the northern part of Wangoo village of Manipur, lying on the right bank of the Imphal river. Under the supervision of O. K. Singh, an archaeological work was done at Napachik in 1981. The whole deposit is essentially of hill washed sediments and has seven layers in structure. Each and every layer has preserved cultural materials belonging to either Hoabinhian or Neolithic or both. The cultural materials collected from this site included choppers, scraper, flakes, edged ground knife, grinding stone, ground and polish celts and potsherds, tripod leg wares, plain and carded wares. Artifacts which consist of lithic contents, particularly microliths and potsherds, have also been found in the south-eastern foothill. According to O. K. Singh,

> Typo-technologically the cultural materials from Napachik may be divided into two phases. The small chipped pebble tools with inclined plain striking ... ... platform and edge ground knife as convex flake which are of the Hoabinhian character may represent the earliest phase, while the latter phase represented by

> the fully ground celt and the hand made cord marked pottery and tripod vase. The materials of these two phases have been mixed up due to the redepositing in the slope wash. However, this is subject to confirmation with future wares.[19]

O.K. Singh further observed, "As the materials at Napachik being found in the slope wash it is a difficult task to establish a definite chronological sequence of the cultural materials. However, it is quite likely that while a culture that has affinity with the Hoabinhian tool complex of South East Asia continued, a full Neolithic culture equipped with ground and polished celts and handmade corded tripod wares which have similarity with the Chinese Neolithic culture arrived at Napachik around second millennium BC".[20] Gangmumei Kabui opined that the valley of Manipur was already settled or inhabited by the Neolithic people in or around 2,000 BC.[21]

Nongpok Keithelmanbi

Nongpok Keithelmanbi is another pre-historic site of Manipur. It is situated at a distance of 15 kilometers to the north-east of Yairipok and on the bank of Thoubal river. The pre-historic materials like chopper, scrapers, blades, flakes pebble graver, cores split pebbles and ordinary pebbles have also been yielded from this site. The raw materials of the artifacts are sandstone and chart. The core tool consists of pebble, chopper, scraper and engraver. Hammer technique seems to have been applied in manufacturing blocks of pebble. Localities 2 and 3, out of the three localities,[22] indicate the existence of Neolithic culture and Locality 1 shows Neolithic-cum-Hoabinhian culture.[23]

Machi

Machi is the village of the Marings, who are believed to be the oldest of the tribes of Manipur. The village is situated in the Chandel district of Manipur. In this pre-historic site O. K. Singh found a pebble chopper tool on a hill top of Machi.

It perhaps confirms that Manipur was inhabited by the Stone Age man since the Early Stone Age or the Lower Paleolithic period.[24]

Megalithic sites

Some notable megalithic sites in Manipur are Mao, Maram, Uilong, Maring areas, Salangthel, Ukhrul, Tharon, Khoupum, Keithelmanbi, etc. The stone megaliths are found among the tribes of Manipur like Mao, Maram, Zemei, Liangmei, Rongmei, Tangkhul, Maring, Anal and others. The megalithic monuments of Manipur are not burials or tombs but merely memorials to the dead and they throw light on the art and technology of the people of the region.[24] According to Gangmumei Kabui, "Stone Megaliths are victory memorials, ceremonial status stone and memorial for the dead."[25] T. C. Hudson described the stone megaliths of Uilong village as the stone-hedge of the Nagas. At Uilong and Keithelmanbi stone megaliths belonging to the Tangkhuls and Koirengs are found. Megalithic remains are also there at Tharon Khullen. Salangthel is also an important megalithic site. It is located on the hill range overlooking the Loktak Lake, about 50 kms. south-west of Imphal. The megalithic monuments at Salangthel of Mehir type were, supposedly, built by the Kom tribes. Rengam, a Kom hero, could turn many huge stones into pebbles which he used to carry in his pocket and planted them on the hilltops of Arakan, Lushai and Manipur hills.[26] The stones at Makhel and Kezakenoma are memorials, which point to the dispersal of the migrating Naga tribes.[27]

Rock Engravings

Pre-historic men of Manipur seem to have been proficient in painting and engraving. Relics of engravings have been found at different pre-historic sites like Tharon, Khoupum and Salangthel. During the exploration along the stream Fiyangu, which flows towards the south-west of the Tharon caves, the rock engravings of different designs on the bed are found at five different places depicting animals, human beings, human hands and a number of different signs and symbols. Some of the figures are geometrical. The first engraving includes a composite representation of both animals and anthropomorphic figures. Of the three rows of animal figures that are found at the same site, the first consists of fifteen heads of Mithun, while the second and third contain thirty four and four heads of pigs respectively. Above the first row three figures of houses are there. Above and below these three rows there are two anthropomorphic figures, one above and another below the rows. The paintings indicate the historic deeds of the chiefs of the villages. The second, third and fourth engravings include figures of thirty men in a row with trumpets in their mouths, a couple of human figurines, and the human figurines inside a big circle of 2.65 meters in diameter. The fifth bears three straight lines segmented with small lines at equal intervals throughout.[28]

Another rock engraving site on a peak is Khoupum, which is located 1454.55 meters above sea level to the south of Cachar road. The peak forms the western wall of the Khoupum plateau and lies on the left bank of the Irang river. There are more than fifty engraved stones on the hill ranges. These engravings include footprint of children and adults, some in pair and some single, game board, wine jar, sword, counting lines, measuring figures, symbol of female genital organ, a variety of flowers, fish, bird, etc.[29]

Salangthel is another site situated on the hill range overlooking the Loktak Lake at a short distance towards the west of the Thamnapokpi village, near Moirang, with an altitude of about 1400 meters above sea level. There is an engraved symbol of a female genital organ on a flat horizontal stone. Some flat horizontal stones with foot prints are also found in the same site.[30]

Summing up

The pre-historic sites and cultural objects found in different parts of Manipur are by no means insignificant. The challenge is to collate and correlate the recovered cultural materials for reconstruction of history of the early societies in the region and to focus on the historical linkages between the societies and the elements of continuity and change in the region. As a matter fact, the importance of studying the pre-historic sites and objects is being more and more appreciated as a dependable key to an understanding of the social and polity formation processes in early times in all parts of the world. In case of Manipur, the beginning of pre-historic archeological research is relatively very recent. The systematic exploration and excavation started only about a couple of decades ago by O. K. Singh and few other local young archeologists. Nonetheless, the pre-history and archeological studies have, in the mean time, begun to reveal that Manipur was at some point of time the home of the Paleolithic, Hoabinhian and Neolithic peoples. The tools recovered from Khangkhui caves, Machi and Nongpok Keithelmanbi typo-technologically belong to the upper Paleolithic period of pre-history. Thus, Manipur can be proud of its rich pre-historic cultural remains. These pre-historic cultural materials may be divided into four groups, viz. stone tools, potsherds, megalithic monuments and metal objects. It is very true that in the absence of any positive evidence and scientific dating it is not desirable to conjecture on the exact dates of the available antiquities. On the other hand, the scientific dating of the extant artifacts and the study of the remaining unexplored objects and pre-historic sites in Manipur are likely to enable the scholars to relate those objects and sites to the communities who might have created them for an understanding of the origins and nature of state and economy in pre-historic and early Manipur.

It is not unlikely that the pre-historic human and the cave dwellers of Manipur - Paleolithics, Hoabinhians and Neolithics or Austroloids or something else - were the predecessors or precursors of the present-day inhabitants in the hills and plains of Manipur, since it is historically established on the basis of the literary sources that the Meiteis immigrated into the Manipur valley from outside the region in different waves over a long period of time and they established seven clan-principalities in the valley which were eventually integrated into the Meitei Kingdom. Before the emergence of the Meitei kingdom or state there was a phenomenal social process of integration of all the indigenous and immigrant ethnic groups towards the formation of a larger Meitei or Manipuri society.[31] The possibility of the pre-historic humans and the cave-dwellers merging into the pre-Meitei aborigines of the valley and, in turn, assimilating with the immigrants from the east and west – the Indo-Mongoloids and the Indo-Aryans respectively – to form the larger Manipuri society also should not be ruled out without scientific analysis of all the possibilities. The human movements from plains to hills and *vice verse*, during the hunting and food-gathering days of the migrating hoards or thereafter while domesticating the plants and animals and settling down in huts and hearths as villages and communities, are not uncommon in the history of the humans.[32] Therefore, investigating the possible continuation of the cultural and material traits and practices of the pre-historic human and cave-dwellers in the social and biological texture and the way of life of the contemporary ethnic societies in Manipur may be a crucial area for scientific social research to reach the closest approximation of historical truth.

NOTES & REFERENCES

1. T. C. Sharma, "Pre-historical finds as Source of History of Manipur", Paper presented at the seminar on Sources of

History of Manipur and Adjoining Areas, Department of History, Manipur University, 1983.

2. H.D. Sankalia, *Indian Archaeology Today*, Delhi, 1979, p.3.
3. *ibid.*, p.2.
4. O.K. Singh, "Archaeological Research in Manipur", *East Himalayas*, 1970, p.150.
5. A.B. Sharma, *Pakhangba*, Imphal, 1952, p.243.
6. O. K. Singh, *op.cit.*
7. T.C. Sharma, *op.cit*, p.3, based on O.K. Singh's paper, *op.cit.*
8. *ibid.*
9. L. Kunjeswori Devi, *Archaeology in Manipur*, Rajesh Book Depot, Delhi, 2003, p.7.
10. H.D. Sankalia, *Pre and Proto history of India and Pakistan*, Pune, 1974, p. 9.
11. L. Kunjeswori Devi, *op.cit.* p.7.
12. *ibid.* While making the observation L. Kunjeswori Devi referred to Zia Lan-Po's *The Cave Home of Peking Man*, pp. 38-44.
13. Gangmumei Kabui, *History of Manipur*, vol.I, National Publishing House, New Delhi, 1991, p.51.
14. L.Kunjeswori Devi, "Archaeological Study of Pre-historic Monuments at Tharon, Tamelong District, based on My Field Work", a paper read in the UGC sponsored Seminar on Pre-Colonial and Colonial History of Manipur and Adjoining Areas, Department of History, Manipur University, Imphal, 1984. Also see O.K. Singh, *Indian Archaeology, a Review* (hereinafter IAR), Imphal, 1981, p.44; *Report of the State Archaeology Department*, Govt. of Manipur, 1983 (hereinafter RASD), pp. 3-5.
15. Gangmumei Kabui, *op.cit.* p. 51.
16. L. Kunjeswori Devi, "Archaeological Study of Pre-historic Monuments at Tharon, Tamelong District, based on My Field Work", *op.cit.*; Also see O.K. Singh, IAR, p.44; RASD, pp.3-5. Manipur; O.K. Singh, *Manipurgi Meihourol*, Yeningtha, Imphal, 1980.
17. O.K. Singh, "Toll Gazing at Tharon: Did Austroloids once Inhabit Manipur?", *Resistance*, Imphal, 30 Dec. 1980; *Press Note on the Archaeological survey of Tharon*, Deptt. of Archaeology, Govt. of Manipur; O.K. Singh, *Manipurigi Meihourol*, Yeningtha, Imphal, 1980

18. O. K. Singh,*Archaeology in Manipur (series-1): Napachik, A Stone Age Site in Manipur valley*,Imphal, 1984.
19. O.K. Singh, *Archaeology in Manipur*, *op.cit.*,p.13.
20. *ibid.*
21. Gangmumei Kabui, *op.cit.*, p.53.
22. O.K. Singh, *Pre-historic Archaeology of Nongpok Keithelmanbi*, Imphal, 1986, p. 5.
23. T.C. Sharma, *op.cit*; RASD, 1983.
24. L. Kunjeswori Devi, *op.cit.* p. 21.
25. Gangmumei Kabui, *op.cit.* p. 54.
26. K.B. Singh (ed), *An Introduction to Tribal Language and Culture of Manipur*, Manipur State Kala Academy, Imphal, 1993, p. 65.
27. Gangmumei Kabui, *op.cit.*
28. L. Kunjeswori Devi, *op.cit.* p. 23.
29. *ibid*, p. 24.
30. *ibid.*
31. Gangmumei Kabui, *op.cit.*, pp. 69-74; J. B. Bhattacharjee, "Economic Dimension of the Meitei State Formation" in F. A. Qadri (ed.), *Society and Economy in North-East India*, Volume 2, Regency Publications, New Delhi, 2006, pp. 58-76..
32. B. D. Sharma, C. L. Anand & J. B. Bhattacharjee (ed.), *History of Science*, NEHU Publications, Shillong, 1984, pp. 15-30.

4

Archaeology of Early State in Manipur

L. Kunjeswori Devi

The structural remains and the extant monuments of royal heritage are said to be accepted as useful evidence in the state formation studies as they do authentically testify the economic resources at the command of the rulers and the level of technological advancement at various points of time in the history of the concerned state. In the context of the Meitei state formation in Manipur, J. B. Bhattacharjee observed that the palaces, buildings and temples, roads and bridges, dams, dykes and canals constructed by the kings indicated the wealth and prosperity of the state and its technological development and the pomp and grandeurs of the royalty, on one hand, and the redistributive welfare measures to ensure continued loyalty and support of the common people to the state in return of the royal dispensation, on the other.[1] As a matter of fact, the palaces, buildings, temples, etc. might have come into existence in Manipur after the fifteenth century AD when the Meitei Kingdom had already emerged as a prosperous state. The remains of any building or structure of archaeological interest pertaining to the earlier period are yet to come to notice.[2] According to a Meitei tradition,[3] the first systematic attempt to improve the house structures in Manipur was made in the time of Nongda Lairen Pakhangba (33-154 AD), the first crowned king of the Ningthouja dynasty. It is said that Laisna, the consort queen of Nongda Lairen Pakhangba, introduced the architecture of hut made of weeds and reeds of thatch, when Poirei (the land of Manipur) had not known the art of architecture in any form. From this version of the tradition it can be presumed that there were only thatched huts in the valley during the time of Pakhangba (c. first-second century AD) and even the king lived in a thatched hut. From other records[4] it is also evident that the hut, which Nongda Lairen Pakhangba lived in, was of three chambered rectangular type. Some of the *Puyas*[5] recorded the existence of temples much earlier in the BC, but the archaeological findings do not support this theory.[6] In ancient Manipur, the temples and buildings were constructed with perishable materials like bamboo, wood and thatch, which did not last long. So, there is virtually no structural remain in Manipur till the sixteenth century AD (i.e., King Khagemba's period) other than a section of the mud wall of the Kangla fort.[7] According to *Cheitharol Kumbaba*, Khagemba introduced the brick masonry works in Manipur by using the Chinese masons.[8] However, the archaeological sites and the artifacts of the pre-colonial period can be broadly grouped into three; namely, (a) seats of authority, (b) temples, and (c) works of public utility.

(a) Seats of Authority

Kangla, the original seat of the Ningthouja chiefs, became the capital of the Meitei Kingdom after the establishment of the kingdom under the leadership of the Ningthoujas. It is an important archaeological site in Manipur. The coronation of the first Meitei king, Nongda Lairen Pakhangba, took place in Kangla which continued to be the capital of the kingdom throughout the Meitei rule, although the palace was shifted to other places for brief periods from time to time due to wars and foreign invasions and other exigencies. The early kings excavated water channels around the complex, maintained the site as a sacred place, and developed the complex itself as a large fort within which all the requirements for the residence of the royal family, administration of the kingdom and security system were available. However, the remains of the masonry development of the palace complex are found only since the time of King Khagemba (1597-1652 AD). The royal palace, the site of coronation of Pakhangba, some sacred sites of worship, the temples, and the brick-wall fortresses are the chief areas of historical attractions within the complex. A careful study of the urbanization processes in the region is expected to reveal that the modern city of Imphal had developed around the infrastructure of Kangla, although some of the heritage structures of the old city were destroyed by the disastrous earthquakes of 1869 and 1897 and during the imperial wars in the medieval as well as the colonial periods. King Khagemba constructed the brick wall around the complex by using the Chinese masons and his son, Khunjaoba, extended the walls covering the main gate and raised the arches. In 1873, Maharaja Chandrakirti constructed a fort to serve as a masonry artery for storing the equipments and war materials. However, the original Kangla Fort, consisting of the royal residence, citadel and the fortress, is located in the heart of the modern Imphal city, between Imphal and Nambul rivers. This old Kangla was originally surrounded by the mud walls on three sides, and on the fourth or the western side the Imphal river formed its boundary. The brick-built citadel of 29 ft. height was constructed in 1611 AD by King Khagemba. There are sacred sites of ancient shrines and monuments inside the fortress. The statue of Bir Tikendrajit and the temple of Brindabanchandra in the south-western section and the temple of Sri Govindaji and the *Beithob*, durbar hall and the graveyard in the south-eastern section of the old complex are modern additions. A section of the old mud wall is still preserved as a relic of the past. The *Thangapat* (moat, popularly known as Kangla Moat), surrounding the capital complex to protect it from the invaders, was dug during the reigns of Maharaja Garibniwaz (1709-48 AD) and Maharaja Chaurjit Singh (1803-13 AD). Maharaja Chandrakirti re-excavated the moat (90 ft. width) around the capital. The two-storied coronation hall (*Uttra*) was also constructed during the time of King Khagemba. The Dragon statue (the mythical beast of the Meiteis) was installed in front of the old palace during the time of Garibniwaz, possibly after it was brought from Burma as a war trophy. The Govindaji temple complex at Kangla, consisting of the temple and the *Beithob*, owes its origin to the reign of Maharaja Bhagyachandra who constructed a temple for Sri Govindaji in the newly constructed Langthabal palace in Imphal. The Govindaji temple at Kangla was constructed during the time of Maharaja Nara Singh in 1846 AD with bricks and teak wood. It is an imposing building with a separate veranda in the front, exterior walls decorated with elaborate floral designs, and the interior of the shrine consisting of the sanctum hall. The temple was damaged by the earthquake of 1869, but it was rebuilt by Maharaja Chandrakirti in 1876 AD. Maharaja Chandrakirti also constructed the *Beithob* in 1885 AD and dedicated the same to the Govindaji temple. A stone inscription, dated 1895 AD, in the palace compound of the time of Maharaja Marjit Singh describes the construction of the outer wall of the palace of bricks (9 cft. in height).[9]

Another important archaeological site is Sekta, 18 kms away from Imphal city, in the Imphal district, on the Imphal-Ukhrul road, which, according to some local chronicles, was associated with the early rulers of Manipur and was once inhabited by the Chakpas.[10] The excavation and exploration in the site in 1980 revealed that the site might have been a sprawling habitation with at least six demarcated burial areas about five centuries ago, although the habitational area has been completely disturbed by plough and cultivations. Seven layers with urn burials in all the layers were encountered. These are secondary burials and inside the largest urn the fragments of human bones, skull fragments, teeth, pieces of long bones along with other funerary goods have been found. Each burial has at least 6 to 7 pots, mostly jars, lids, globular vases of red ware, with a small black vase at the centre. The pots are hand made and each group of pots is so placed that they do not overlap with another group. The human skulls have been found inside the large pots in layers IV and V. The skulls have copper mask covering the face. The antiquities recovered from the jars that contain bones include the terracotta paste, semi-precious stone-blades, copper-rings, bangles, bracelets, bell-metal miniature pots and iron implements. The iron objects are mostly arrow-heads, spear-heads, scythes, knives, draggers, etc. In one of the middle level burials a bell-metal relic casket of Buddhist origin has also been recovered. The tops of the jars containing bones and antiques are covered either with an inverted lid or by placing another globular jar upside down inside the bigger jar. The central base is generally black ware. The hand made pots have a variety of mat, cord, pinched or stamped sunray and fish-bone designs. In case of three skulls recovered from within the urns the teeth were found to have been removed. One was the skull of a child and another of a middle aged man. The latter has cut marks inflicted by a sharp instrument on the right parietal region. All the skulls were placed in pots facing south-west. The layer II offered a copper coin of Maharaja Garibniwaz. The exploration in Pidonu hill, in the neighbourhood of Sekta, also revealed a habitational site from which a pot decorated with incised marks and three other potsherds were recovered. A life size stone statue of a snake-hood in sandstone was also noticed in the site. In village

Pungdongbam, next to Sekta, the owner of a house while digging in the courtyard for extension of the house accidentally came across burial spots in the north-east and south-west alignments. Two big burials, which were thereafter excavated, revealed the associated finds of skeletons, beads, iron objects, smoking pipes of terracotta, etc. In fact, there were six mounds in the region. The exploration in one case recovered a human skull decorated with head-gear made of fine gold foils along with a horse with hood. A skull with similar horse made of silver was earlier discovered in a part of the Imphal city while excavating for a school building. Some of the antiques recovered from the Sekta region in various explorations and excavations are preserved in the Manipur State Museum and the Manipur University Museum.[11]

As stated already, the Ningthouja (Meitei) kings temporarily shifted their headquarters from place to place due to political exigencies. The six other clan-principalities had their own headquarters in different places, which might also have changed sites due to wars and invasions before the consolidation of the Meitei rule. Of them, the Moirang principality maintained its independence, or at least autonomy, for a longer period, despite the mounting pressure from the Ningthoujas. Those sites are yet to be explored or excavated. The archaeological explorations and excavations in the places mentioned in the chronicles and other sources as the seats of authority of the principalities and chiefdoms might some day enable the detailing of those early political centres enriching the history of state formation in Manipur.

(b) Temples

The shrines and temples are scattered in Manipur (particularly in the Meitei inhabited valley region) and these institutions are invariably rooted in the religion of the people. On the basis of these historical sites as well as the corroborative literary evidence, the religious history of Manipur can broadly be divided under two phases, i.e., the religion in (i) the Traditional Meitei Society and (ii) the Hindu Meitei Society. In other words, the chronological division may be between the Pre-Hindu and the Hinduised periods. On the other hand, it is evident that the Meiteis continued to practice the rites and rituals and to follow the belief system and philosophy of traditional Meitei religion even after the Hinduisation (more precisely, Vaisnavisation). The worship of Sanamahi and the ancestor worship never lost their importance in the way of life of the Meiteis. However, an assessment of the role of religion in social and economic life of the people from the first century AD would reveal that during the Pre-Hindu period the traditional religion of the Meiteis played an important role in socio-political and economic growth of Manipur leading to the consolidation of different communities, although any archaeological record of that period to explain the process of change is virtually non-existent. During that period the people in Manipur did not worship idols and, therefore, the concept of shrines or temples or the religious functionary was different from that of the Hindus. No wonder, the archaeological sources, inscriptions or other written records, like *Puyas* (chronicles), pertaining to the Pre-Hindu period hardly reveal any evidence about the existence of temples. The abodes of *Umanglais* (the village gods) were always in existence, but to know about them only the literary works, myths and legends and sacred places are the sources.[12]

It is difficult to decide precisely the date of beginning of the Hindu period in the history of Manipur. It seems that Hinduism and the Brahmins penetrated slowly and gradually into the kingdom over a long period of time. A copper-plate inscription of the time of King Khongtekcha (8th century AD) declared him as the worshiper of Lord Shiva. It mentions a host of temples and places of worship all over Manipur and as many as 363 gods and goddesses which included Siva, Devi, Hari, Viswakarma and Ganesha of the Hindu pantheon.[13] King Kyamba (1467-1508 AD) is said to have received a statue of Lord Vishnu from the kingdom of Pong and thereafter he constructed a temple in Bishenpur, installed the statue in that temple and entrusted the day-to-day worship of the deity to a Brahmin. The construction of the brick-temple at Bishenpur, which may still be seen in good condition, is attributed to Kyamba.[14] King Khagemba (1597-1652 AD) is said to have constructed a temple of Nongshaba (the Sun God) in 1633 AD and installed a statue of Vishnu in a temple during the royal boat race.[15] This fact suggests, beyond doubt, the prevalence of the dual worship of traditional Meitei and Hindu deities in the kingdom. However, King Charairongba (1697-1709 A.D.) was the first Meitei king to be formally initiated to Hinduism. By then the number of immigrant Brahmins in Manipur had also considerably increased. The scholarly Brahmins were employed by the king in important positions and they began to exercise influence in the affairs of the court. In April 1704, Charairongba was formally initiated to Vaisnavism by a Brahmin, named Krishnacharya, who originated from Puri. Charairongba was also the first Meitei king who adopted a Hindu name, Pitambar Singh. Charairongba was, therefore, the first Meitei king who had a Hindu name. He constructed a number of temples for the Meitei deities like Panthoibi, Sanamahi, and others, and installed bronze statues of Panthoibi and Sanamahi in the respective temples. He also constructed temples for Hindu deities like Lord Krishna, Visnu, Kalika, etc.. The construction of the Krishna temple at Brahmapur, Imphal, is also attributed to him.[16] His son and successor, Garibniwaz (1709-48 AD) was initiated to Nimandi Vaisnavite sect in 1717 AD by Guru Gopaldas. This was followed by the arrival of Shantadas Mahanta Bairagi from Sylhet, under whose influence there was a mass initiation of the Meiteis to Vaisnavism. Garibniwaz declared Vaisnavism as the state religion of the Meitei Kingdom in 1730 AD. This was followed by the construction of many other Hindu temples, signaling the beginning of organized religion in Manipur.[17] The tradition of constructing temples was carried farther by Maharaja Bhagyachandra (1749-98), who was initiated to the Gauriya (Bengal) school of Vaisnavism. The famous Govindaji temple was constructed in the premises of the Langthabal palace during his time. As desired by the king, four images of Lord Krishna, namely, Govindaji, Vijaygovinda, Advaita and Gopinath, were made of the timber of a jackfruit tree and installed in four different temples.[18]

As a matter of fact, the construction of temples began during the reign of Kyamba and there was a striking increase in the number of temples since the time of Garibniwaz. The temples in Manipur were built under the initiative of the kings, members of the royal family or officials as well as by the wealthy merchants and landlords. Some of those temples have survived the stretches and strains of time and circumstances. The temples built through royal donations are located at royal palaces and administrative headquarters, such as Vishnu temple at Bishenpur, Govindaji temple at Kangla, Govindaji temple at the present royal palace (Konung), while some temples are at palaces of the royal families, such as Radharaman temple at Purana Rajbari (Konung Mamang), Bijoy Govinda temple at Sagolband (Imphal), etc. Like other temples in India, smaller accessories of temples, such as subsidiary images, bells with post, lamps, oil, etc. are these days generally obtained through individual donations. The big temples, like the present Shri Govindaji temple, are looked after by the Temple Board of the State. The Ramji Prabhu temple, located at Wangkhei Ningthempukhri Mapal, is indeed a landmark of the Ramaṇḍi cult in Manipur. The merchants and traders generously donate for the maintenance of the temples. There are also temples in the rural areas, such as Radharaman temple,

Abdeitya temple at Lamangdong (Bishnupur), Shri Govindaji temple at Kaina, which have evolved into complex institutions related not only to religious life but also to fiscal, social and cultural requirements of the people of the localities. As in other parts of India, the temples in Manipur are marked not only for the installations of idols or sculptures in the sanctums of the temples but also for the decorations and designs on the temple walls. The immigrant Brahmins served as the priests (*pujari*) for the gods and goddesses in the temples, but they have been assimilated in the local community in course of time. Historically, the Brahmanical or Hindu cults came to Manipur at a time when the indigenous religious practices suffered the symptoms of decay and fractures. The new cults were then beginning to emerge and the older traditions were also revived, allowing scope for new approaches to the faiths and rituals.[19]

(c) Works of Public Utility

The works of public utility of the Meitei kings are remembered through traditions, folk memories and legends as well as the structural remains scattered all over Manipur. The *Puyas* and other literary sources credit the period of reigns of the immediate successors of King Pakhangba (33-154 AD) with several technological inventions and works of public utility, particularly the digging of river-channels to flash out the stranded water which had submerged the Manipur valley from the days of the yore. The technology was used for repeatedly dredging the lakes and rivers, changing the courses of the rivers, and the constructions of dykes and embankments to protect the settlements from floods and for irrigating the agricultural fields which resulted in land reclamations and boosting of the agriculture and crafts. All these enabled the economy of the kingdom to flourish and generate surplus. Pakhangba was succeeded by his son Khuyoi Tompok (154-264 A.D.). During period of Khuyoi Tompok the use of metal was first introduced with an advanced technology. His coronation at Kangla, the ancient palace, was attended by the chiefs of different clan-principalities, such as Luwang, Khuman and Moirang. The king maintained good relations with the chiefs of different ethnic groups as a policy towards consolidating the superior status of the Ningthouja dynasty on a permanent basis. The peaceful situation in the kingdom offered favourable conditions for inventions and innovations towards enhanced productivity and economic growth. Several technological developments took place during the time of Khuyoi Tompok. The king was personally associated with a number of inventions. It is said that he invented the drum, made of wood and animal skin, which came to be used during wars, dance, music and other social and religious occasions. The bronze smelting and bell-metal casting began in his time. The bell-metal gong, *Senbung* was manufactured during his reign. The development of weaving, textile designs, dyeing in colours, silk rearing, boat making, exploration of minerals are also attributed to the reign of Khuyoi Tompok.[20] The reign of the next king, Taothingmang (264-364 AD), son and successor of Khuyoi Tompok, is memorable for water management and development of agriculture. The draining of the marshes and dredging the streams and rivers, and the reclamation of land for agriculture by draining the lakes and marshes, including the great Loktak, are splendid works of public utility introduced during this period.[21] The works of water management and reclamation of cultivable and habitable land continued during the reigns of the later kings. The sites of dykes and embankments, public granaries, markets, roads and bridges of the time of the Meitei kings are still scattered all over Manipur.

Conclusion

The archaeology is undoubtedly an important key for studying the state formation processes and the emergence of the early states. In case of Manipur, the archaeology needs to be fully explored for an understanding of the stages of evolution of the Meitei Kingdom. The seats of political authority are always important archaeological sites. The remnants of the tools, equipments and pottery and the works of art and architecture are the specimens of economy, technology and culture in various stages of development and socio-economic changes. The temples, in particular, needs to be studied specially as these were the nucleus of urbanization in the ancient world. Grahame Clarke, while writing about Southern Mesopotamia, stated that such level of social development could have been realized only by the civilized societies, *i.e.* societies with political as distinct from merely familial or social institutions, the institutions which ensured the functions of the individuals of increasing specialized roles.[22] Similarly, Gordon Childe observed that the temples played a key role in the formative phase of the Sumerian civilization. They were central to the development of political institutions and helped to shape economic activities. The major function of a temple was to organize irrigation. It is evident by the discovery of huge mud-brick built temple at Eridu.[23] In the context of ancient India, Romila Thapar observed that the temple was an institution of the Puranic sect which also played a civic role. The priests had a big role in controlling the agricultural products, urban corporations and also had a close association with administrative and commercial organizations.[24] In ancient Manipur, the role of temple might not have been so effective as in other parts of the subcontinent but it certainly promoted urbanization in the region. It had a crucial role in the consolidation and unification of small principalities. The Ningthouja dynasty, which was the ruling dynasty of the Meitei Kingdom, had its capital at Kangla which was also a sacred place to all the Meiteis and it was from Kangla that the Ningthoujas integrated all the clans and the clan-principalities of the Meiteis into one kingdom.

Finally, the extant archaeological remains and the artifacts scattered in Manipur, though not very plentiful in extent, are indeed fundamentally relevant to the state formation processes in early and medieval Manipur. The seats of authority, the royal seclusion, the differentiated social status, the majestic symbols are the edifices of social stratification that hastened the rise and sustenance of public authority. Similarly, the temples, shrines, the priestly orders and the universalisation of culture are among the indicators of common ideology of the state, while the stray artifacts are the evidence of material culture attributed to the wealth of the state, and the agriculture, art and crafts, hereditary professional specializations of the social groups, clans and lineages, taxes and tributes constitute the instruments of surplus generation which is so fundamental to the formation of the early states. The archaeological research is thus an invariant component of the state formation studies in social sciences to which Manipur could not be an exception.

NOTES & REFERENCES

1. J.B. Bhattacharjee, "Economic Dimension of Meitei State Formation" in F. A. Qadri (ed.), *Society and Economy in North-East India*, Volume 2, Regency Publications, New Delhi, 2006, pp. 58-76.
2. This has been ascertained by the author while writing L. Kunjeswori Devi, *Archaeology in Manipur*, Rajesh Book Depot, Delhi, 2003.
3. O. Bhogeswor Singh, *Ningthourol Lambuba,* Imphal, 1967; *Sangton,* an unpublished manuscript in the custody of B. K. Shany, Imphal.
4. Nongmaithem Manaoyaima (ed), *Tutenglon,* Kakching, 2000, pp. 30-31. The manuscript of *Tutenglon* is in the custody of B. K. Shany, Manipur State Archaeology, etc.
5. *ibid.*
6. L. Kunjeswwori Devi, *Archaeology in Manipur*, Rajesh Book Depot, Delhi, 2003.
7. M. Shantirani Devi, "The Relics of Kangla (OldPalace)",

Proceedings of North East India History Association, XIIth Session, Jagiroad, 1991, pp. 124-28.

8. L. Ibongohal Singh & N. Khelchandra Singh (ed.), *Cheitharol Kumbaba*, Manipuri Sahitya Parishad, Imphal, 1967, pp 32, 38 (hereinafter, *Cheitharol Kumbaba*).
9. *Cheitharol Kumbaba*, pp. 2-4, 7-8, 20-21, 28, 71-72, 83-86, 172, 192, 209; M. Shantirani Devi, "The Relics of Kangla (Old Palace)", *Proceedings of North East India History Association*, *op.cit.*, pp. 124-28; For more details, see L. Kunjeswori Devi, *Archaeology in Manipur*, *op.cit.*
10. Gangmumei Kabui, *History of Manipur*, vol. I, National Publishing House, New Delhi, 1991, p. 124.
11. L. Kunjeswori Devi, "Ancient Discoveries in Sekta, a Village in Manipur", *Proceedings of North East India History Association*, XIIth Session, Jagiroad, 1991, pp. 120-23; For more details, see L. Kunjeswori Devi, *Archaeology in Manipur*, *op.cit.*
12. T.C. Hudson, *The Meitheis*, (First published London, 1911) Reprint Low Price Publications, Delhi, 1989, pp. 37-49.
13. Gangmumei Kabui, *History of Manipur*, vol. I, *op.cit.*, p. 120.
14. *ibid*, pp. 200-01
15. *ibid*, pp. 222-23; T.C. Hudson, *op.cit.*, pp. 123-31.
16. *Cheitharol Kumbaba*, pp. 56-60; M. Chandra Singh (ed.), *Panthoibi Khongul*, Manipuri Sahitya Parishad, Imphal, 1972; Gangmumei Kabui, *op.cit.*, p 257.
17. *Cheitharol Kumbaba*, pp. 36-81; Gangmumei Kabui, *op.cit.*, p 251-56.
18. *Cheitharol Kumbaba*, pp. 112-35; T.C. Hudson, *op.cit.*, pp. 73-76; Gangmumei Kabui, *op.cit.*, p 274-78.
19. Mutua Museum Publication, Bulletin No.1, *Coins of Manipur*, Imphal, 1981; Bulletin No. 2, *Sculptures of Manipur*, Imphal, 1982; Bulletin No. 3, *Temple Architecture of Manipur*, Imphal, 1983; Bulletin No. 5, *Rock Carvings and Inscriptions of Manipur*, Imphal, 1985; Bulletin No. 6, *Forts and Monuments of Manipur*, Imphal, 1987.
20. Gangmumei Kabui, *op.cit.*,pp. 87-88.
21. ibid., p.97.

22. Grahame Clark, *Archaeology and Society*, Penguin Books, London, 1966 (Reprint, 1997).

23. Gordon Childe, *What Happened in History*, Penguin Books, London, 1965 (Reprint, 1995).

24. Romila Thapar, *Early India*, Panguin Books, New Delhi, 2002, pp. 357-62; For more details and explanations on the Indian situation, see Amar Farooqui, *Early Social Formations*, Manak Publication Ltd., Delhi, 2001; R. S. Gupta, *Iconography of the Hindu, Buddhist and Jains*, Bombay, 1972; Sisir Kumar, *East Indian Bronzes*, Centre for Advanced Study, Dept. of Ancient Indian History & Culture, Calcutta University, 1979; N. L. Mathur, *Sculptures of India*, New Delhi, 1976; H. D. Sankalia, *Archaeology of Gujarat*, Poona, 1941.

5

Coinage and Economy of the Meitei Kingdom

N. G. Rhodes & S. K. Bose

Located strategically in the north-eastern part of India, Manipur represents a land of immense variety of climate, landscape and inhabitants.[1] The state comprises an area of 8000 square miles, of which only one-eighth is level land forming the central valley. In the past, it should have had a flourishing trade and economy, being strategically located between India and Burma (Myanmar). Alexander Mackenzie, however, portrayed early Manipur as a land of war, marked by constant raids of the Manipur army into Burma and the Burmese into Manipur, coupled with internal feuds of the most savage and violent nature.[2] On the other hand, a careful examination of the reasons for the hostility between Burma and Manipur might reveal that the control of trade was the bone of contention between the two kingdoms. Similarly, the so-called internal feuds were due to the fact that the hills of Manipur were inhabited by freedom loving tribes of different ethnic roots and tradition, and the occasional remonstrations of the tribes by the Meitei kings became necessary for the sake of integrity of the kingdom.

Glimpses of Early Economy

Although the lines of communication in the region in early times were very difficult and hazardous, Manipur was endowed with a rich cultural heritage and it found mention in many early Sanskrit, Chinese and even Greek and Roman sources.[3] Indeed, Manipur was on an early trade route between India and China.[4] Some of the European travellers to the subcontinent had visited Manipur during those times.[5] Besides the traditional ties with Burma, the valley formed an important highway between the neighbouring countries and it ultimately succumbed to the British imperialism during latter's rule in India.[6] Manipur was, in fact, rich but underdeveloped, iron and gold being locally available. There were also many brine springs in eastern Manipur. Coarse salt was produced by boiling the spring water and used in food and as medicine. In the hills, the deposits of limestone and coal were also available. Mackenzie has confirmed that iron and gold were found in Manipur.[7]

As in other pre-colonial north-eastern kingdoms, paddy was the principal crop of Manipur. Due to the favourable climate and fertile land, the farmers in central Manipur, without much labour, could produce a huge quantity of rice.[8] According to Janakinath Basak, a nineteenth century trader from Kolkata, who had been at Imphal on business, the production of rice was more than either Bengal or Assam. He also recorded that in earlier times the cost of six *sangbai* (bamboo basket) of paddy was only one rupee. As each of the baskets could accommodate thirty *seers* of paddy, the six baskets contained four and half *maunds* of paddy, the value of which was only one rupee. Among other pulses, vegetable and plantain crops were freely available.[9] Jiggery was made from sugarcane. As the handling of production of sugarcane was by and large restricted to the Muslim women, it may be suggested that such activity entered Manipur in the medieval period. Fruit trees provided a major cash crop, and large plantations grew mango, pineapple, jackfruit, lemon, tamarind, banana, orange, berry, *gulabjam, kamranga* and wood-apple.[10]

Besides agricultural productivity, tea grew in Manipur in wild profusion. In fact, during the early period of British rule in India, when Manipur was still an independent kingdom, the collection of tea seeds from Manipur and Burma had already begun due to the demand of such seeds in the tea gardens in Cachar. The price varied as high as between rupees seventy and eighty per *maund* (=40 seers =37 kg.) in those days.[11] This fact alone might have been sufficient to attract the British government to extend their authority over Manipur.

The available sources suggest that the Manipuris were not interested in alcohol. There was no system of royal excise duty on alcohol, *ganja* and opium.[12] Interestingly, although the use of tobacco for smoking the *hukka* was highly popular and tobacco was cultivated almost by every household, the quality tobacco was imported from Rangpur (now in Bangladesh) via Cachar in the nineteenth century and the price of such tobacco was between rupees thirty five and forty per *maund*. Incidentally, some details of the trade between Manipur and Bengal are known from the work of Janakinath Basak.[13]

The sources inform us that towards the end of the nineteenth century the land revenue system in Manipur was oriented towards labour service. The subjects were required to provide ten days' labour services for every forty days to the king, known as *lâlup*, for which no remuneration was payable. In addition, a portion of the harvested crop had to be handed over to the royal authorities.[14] It can, however, be inferred that such revenue collection system was based on an age old practice that prevailed from a period before monetisation.

The Meitei kings collected certain taxes, such as taxes on birth, death and marriage. The contributions, known as *mâgan*, were also collected for various festivals. The taxes were so elaborate that it was levied even if a cow died. The rate of tax on the sale of a Manipuri horse was as high as one *mohur* which was equivalent to twenty two rupees. As the use of *mohur* was a late introduction in Manipur, it can be assumed that such a system of payment of taxes in cash was probably introduced only after 1758 AD, during the reign of Gaura Simha, when the *mohur* was struck for the first time. Incidentally, specimens of such gold *mohurs* can be seen in the British Museum coin cabinet, London.[15] The imports and exports were also subject to taxation. However, the commodities like cattle and rice, and even 'women', were exempted from taxation.[16] We are not sure whether the 'women' was related to female slaves or bringing female labourers from outside the kingdom.

During the British period, the royal exchequer enjoyed some income from the colonial connections. For instance, Rs.700/- per month was paid by the British administration for the maintenance of *Dâk* (postal) service between Kohima, Silchar and Tamu. The Kabo valley (Kabaw) or Tamu, within Manipur dominion, was handed over to the British East India Company in 1834 against an annual payment of Rs. 6,000/-. Amongst other sources, the records indicate that water tax was realised to the tune of about Rs. 7,000/- annually. In all probability, such taxes were collected on the movement of boats. Sale of elephant tusks and the forest produces, like wax and rubber, also contributed to the income of the king. The house tax, between Re.1/- and Rs.2/-, was realised from the Naga and Kuki subjects in the kingdom.[17]

The Meitei kings sometimes earned monetary gains in the form of charges or compensations for extending support to the British rulers in latter's military campaigns and operations in the areas bordering Manipur. They facilitated the British expeditions to the Lushai (Mizo) hills and extended material support during wars with the Burmese by supplying the hard-working Naga labourers. Fifty percent of the salary payable to those labours was credited to the king's treasury. Despite the occasional bitterness due to high-handedness of the British officials, it appears that there was a considerable flow of money from the British treasury to the royal exchequer, which increased the pace of circulation of medium of exchange or high value coins in Manipur from the eighteenth century onwards.[18]

The Meitei kings exercised control over the markets and collected taxes and duties of various sorts. This is confirmed by the location of the main *kaithen* or market place, which was close to the western gate of the *kanung* or *pât* (Royal palace). The location of the main market in the kingdom probably indicates that the sales and purchases were mainly concentrated in and around the seat of authority of the rulers, though the markets were traditionally managed in Manipur by the women who were also mainly involved in sales and purchases in the market places. There were, of course, many *hâts* (market places, especially in villages) at various places, which worked during the day time. However, the main market in front of the palace opened in the evening and continued for few hours.[19]

It seems that in earlier times the Manipuris had developed a unique counting system in which they used knotted rope, cane or bamboo sticks as calculators to facilitate counting. They were also able to count the fractions, probably fractions like ½, ⅓, ¼, etc. to units, tens and in multiples thereof. Interestingly, unlike in Mughal India or in the rest of the sub-continent, the counting in Manipur was accurately maintained by using the decimal system.[20] In this context it may not be wrong to observe that the development of an indigenous system of counting is perhaps an indication of the growth of a market economy and the monetization processes, which might have begun in Manipur towards the end of the medieval period and was facilitated by the local coinage, particularly of the smaller denominations.

Beginning of Meitei Coinage

It is indeed a fact that the early history of Manipur is not yet fully explored. The dearth of reliable source materials for that period is always problematic for the scholars. Much of the information available in the chronicles has no corroborative support. However, from the seventeenth century onwards the records of some of the major political events and the numismatic data do provide such evidence. The analyses of the available records do testify that the coins of the Meitei kings constitute some of the most reliable contemporary documents, although the beginning of the numismatic history of Manipur is still debatable.

At the end of the nineteenth century, T. C. Hudson was shown a bell-metal coin which was said to have been issued by the mythical king Pakhangba (33-154 AD).[21] Apparently, this coin was a very thin disc, about 3.5 inches in diameter, with no marks on it. N. K. Singh says that coins, known as *Taret maji Naiba* were used in ancient times to worship gods, but these early accounts of coins have been doubted by K. Sobita Devi as well as L. Kunjeswori Devi, because of the lack of any evidence behind the attribution other than tradition.[22] The most important ruler of the seventeenth century AD was King Khagemba alias Mayangamba (c.1597-1652 AD). He was one of the great kings of Manipur and has been regarded as the champion of socio-cultural revival.[23] He arranged for the transcription of oral information into *Puyas* (local chronicles). The greatest achievement during his period was apparently the defeat of a Chinese invading army. According to Hudson, a Chinese army under general Moyadana had entered Manipur around 1630 AD with an intention to invade the kingdom. But the Chinese general was killed in the battle and the prisoners of war were settled within Manipur at a place called Khagempalli. Historians differ with regard to the name of the then Meitei ruler as well as the exact period of the war.[24] The chronicle *Vijoy Pânchâli* informs us that the war took place around 1564 AD, but the pottery items found after excavation at the village site where the prisoners were settled apparently show that those belonged to the seventeenth century AD.[25] However, since '*Khagi*' means China and '*Yanba*' stands for "to kill", it is more probable that King Khagemba defeated the Chinese and assumed this name.[26] Kunjeswori Devi suggested that Khagemba, after winning the war, assumed the title *Mayang Ngamba* i.e. the conqueror of *Mayang* or the outsider.[27] According to her, the bell metal coins bearing the legend '*Ma*' in archaic Manipuri script were struck by Khagemba alias *Mayang Ngamba*. Such coins were apparently circular and they measured one cm. in diameter. If such be the case, Khagemba can be credited with the introduction of coinage in Manipur. The Chinese connection and the settlement of Chinese prisoners in Manipur suggest that the technical knowledge might have come from the war prisoners themselves. However, although some bell-metal *sel* coins are known with the letter '*Ma*' in *Nâgari* script, these are datable only to the nineteenth century. Moreover, no such coins with archaic Manipuri or Meitei script have yet been identified. Therefore, the suggestion that Khagemba struck some coins cannot yet be accepted as a proven fact.

Paikhomba (1666-1697 AD)

The next known ruler is Paikhomba. No artefacts are yet known of this ruler, except a drawing of a bell metal coin that has been attributed to this period. However, it is known that trade and commerce of the kingdom flourished at this time, especially with the neighbouring kingdoms. The drawing of this coin was published by N. Khelchandra Singh[28] in his book entitled *Manipuri Language : Status and*

Importance (Imphal, 1975). The coin apparently bears '*Pa*' in archaic Manipuri script and can tentatively be identified with Paikhomba. This is, according to Singh, apparently the last time that coins were struck routinely bearing the archaic Manipuri script.[29] It should be noted that neither of the authors of this paper has ever seen or handled such a coin. Hence, further information must be awaited before it can be confidently accepted that Paikhomba issued any significant coinage. The subsequent rulers of Manipur, who struck coins mostly on bell metal flans, used either the *Devanâgri* or Bengali scripts.

Charairongba (1697-1709 AD)

One coin in *Devanâgri* script has been attributed to King Charairongba, though otherwise such script does not seem to have received royal patronage during that period.[30] This type of bell metal coins, of which specimens are preserved in the State Museum, Mutua Museum and also at Kakching in Manipur and in private collections, are round in shape and just over 1cm. in diameter. The coin bears the legend '*Śri Kṛṣṇa*' and the attribution has been suggested because the name of the *Guru* (Preceptor) of Charairongba was Shrikrishnacharya. However, in the absence of any corroborative evidence, the attribution of the coin to Charairongba may be seen as speculative, and there may be other interpretations of the above letters. In particular, we believe that the circumstances in which such coins have been found do suggest a late eighteenth century issuing date, rather than a date around 1700 AD.

Unlike the neighbouring countries, the use of bell metal alloy was possibly a conscious attempt in Manipur to produce a low value coin for the use of the common people.[31] This was certainly appropriate in view of the low cost of consumer items available in the markets in Manipur for the day-to-day use. Except for the use of cowries, such low value coins were rarely produced in Northeast India. Presumably, the bell metal was procured from Burma (Myanmar) where it was widely used for bells, gongs and other objects.[32] R. Brown, in the nineteenth century, suggested that the metal was obtained mainly from Burma, in the form of old gongs, while some of it was also procured from the British provinces. An analysis of the metal conducted at the Calcutta Mint in 1838, gave an alloy of 73.6% copper, 23.2% tin and 3.2% zinc for the coins which were then in circulation.[33]

Garibaniwaz (1709-1748 AD)

A rare square shaped, and apparently base silver half rupee coin, is preserved at the Manipur State Museum which bears a date only as *Chaitra sudhi / Terase 2 / San 164(6?).* The size of the coin is 17 mm. x 15.5 mm. Apparently, this coin was struck by King Garibaniwaz.[34] V. Chowdhury and P. Ray published this coin. They also commented that the inscription appearing on one side of the coin in question is consistent with the traditional bell metal coins of Manipur, which are all uniface.[35]

Coin of Garibaniwaz
published by Chowdhury & Ray

P. K. Bhattacharyya suggested that the complete date of the above mentioned coin of Garibaniwaz must be *Śaka* 1646. This has been accepted by some historians and numismatists. The full date is also clearly visible on the attached illustration of a different example. Bhattacharyya, however, observed that the coin is struck from bell-metal, and not silver.[36] An identical coin is in the collection of the British Museum in London, but although it appears to be struck in a whitish metal, the metal is clearly not silver, but bell-metal. It is our strong feeling that the coin in the Manipur State Museum is actually struck in bell-metal, and not in base silver.

In this context it may be noted that as many as seventy bell metal coins of Garibaniwaz were found at Heirok and are now preserved at the Mutua Museum, Imphal. All the pieces have a diameter of about 2 cms., some are circular but others are square shaped with rounded corners, similar to the coin illustrated above. The weight ranges from 3 gms. to 5.4 gms., averaging about 3.8 gms., but more significantly, some of them have a clear legend reading [coin] "of Gariba Niwaja, king of Mekhale (Manipur) and Gomati, the queen", while others read "[in the month of] *Chaitra*, bright half, Sunday the second day, *Samvat* 164(6)" and a number of others have fragments of a similar legend. Significantly, this latter legend is identical to that on the supposedly silver coin mentioned in the last paragraph. This legend clearly shows that these coins were struck during the reign of Garibaniwaz, who is generally accepted to have reigned during the period 1709 to 1748 AD.

Garibaniwaz is perhaps the most famous king of Manipur. He became a *Vaishnava*, and was successful in wars against the Burmese. The coins of this ruler also bear an exact date. It may therefore be presumed that some event of historical importance must have taken place on the day of issuance of the coin. It is known from the historical sources that Garibaniwaz successfully fought many wars against Burma and Tripura between 1723 and 1727 AD and he was the first Manipur king to formally become a *Vaisnava*. In 1727 AD, Garibaniwaz successfully invaded Tripura and took the title of *Takhelnamba* (The Victor of Tripura).[37] He might have issued medals and coins to commemorate those major events and the assumption of titles by the king. The issuance of the coin dated 1646 *Śaka* (i.e. 1724 AD), which is under discussion, was also in all probability to commemorate the victory in the war against the Burmese and the assumption of the title of *Mahârâjâ* by King Garibaniwaz. In fact, 1724 AD happens to be a very important year in the history of Manipur under King Garibaniwaz. It is known from more than one chronicle of Manipur that Garibaniwaz, in 1724 AD, successfully invaded Burma while repulsing a Burmese force which made incursions in the eastern frontier of the Meitei kingdom across the Chindwin river. In the same year, Garibaniwaz was given the title of *Mahârâjâ* in a formal investiture ceremony. The king was also given a Hindu name, i.e. Gopal Singha, and his wife *Mahârâni* Gomati, and since then the Meitei kings came to be known as '*Manipureswar*' and '*Mekleswar*'.[38] The 1646 *Śaka* or 1724 AD was, therefore, a very significant year in the history of Manipur. The issue of the coin, besides commemorating the historical events, might have also signified the beginning of the process of Sanskritisation in Manipur. It was indeed the first example of a coin with an exact date in Northeast India. The subsequent coins of Garibaniwaz also gave the name of the queen, which is an important information not available from other sources.

The coins of Garibaniwaz are also remarkable in being uniface. However, there seem to be obverse and reverse dies, albeit used on different coins. This feature strongly indicates that the Mint Master was unable, technologically, to produce double sided coins of bell metal. He might have found it easier to strike the coins with a single die, placing the blank flan on a flat surface. Nonetheless, the reign of Garibaniwaz is an important landmark in the numismatic history of Manipur.

Gaura Simha (1756-1764 AD)

No coins are known that can definitely be attributed to Garibaniwaz's immediate successors, his sons Ajit Shah and Bharat Shah, unless the letter 'A' that is said to appear on one coin refers to Ajit Shah. The royal chronicle, *Cheitharol*

Kumbaba, mentions that Chit Shah, the son and successor of Garibaniwaz, ascended the throne in 1748 AD[39] and reigned for only four years.[40] A bell-metal coin bearing the letter '*Cha*' in *Devanâgri* on a small flan has also been attributed to the reign of Chit Shah, but it seems to us that the small flan coins were introduced only after 1800 AD, and sinçe '*Cha*' may also refer to Chaurajit Simha (1804-12 AD), and as the flan is of the same size as other nineteenth century *sel* coins, we are unable to accept this particular piece as a medium of exchange struck by Chit Shah without further corroborative evidence. Our suggestion is that the round bell-metal coins with the legend *Śrî Kṛṣṇa*, and other squarish pieces of similar fabric to the coins of Garibaniwaz, but with shorter legends, can be attributed to the second half of the eighteenth century AD.

Gaura Simha, the eldest grandson of Garibaniwaz, who ascended the throne in about 1756 AD,[41] struck some fine square silver and gold coins in that year. Apparently, he was crippled and unfit to rule on his own. So, he associated himself with his younger brother, Jaya Simha, and they are said to have ruled alternately. This is, however, not proved by the coins, which only have the name of Gaura Simha until his death in about 1764 AD.

Square gold *mohur* dated *Sambat* 1678

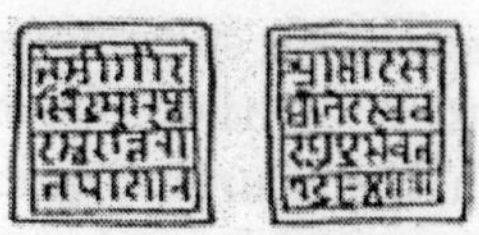

Gold *mohur* dated *Sambat* 1684

Gold quarter *mohur*

Square silver *ṭankâ* of Goura Simha dated *Sambat* 1678

In September 1762 AD, owing to the continuous threat from Burma, Jaya Simha and Gaura Simha asked for help from the British East India Company and reached an understanding with the latter regarding the British help to the king of Manipur in repulsing the Burmese attacks. In October in the same year, the emissaries of Gaura Simha arrived at Chittagong and confirmed the terms of the treaty, but they pleaded that as Manipur had been thoroughly devastated by the Burmese, their king was unable to meet the expenses of the British troops, which were stationed at Khaspur (Cachar), as demanded by the British. However, as a token of sincerity, they offered '500 *meklee* gold rupees', to be valued at twelve silver rupees each.[42] Gold coins in the name of Gaura Simha are still found. These are dated to the month of *Âsâḍa, Śaka* 1684 (1762 AD), which is also the date of the treaty. It may, therefore, well be said that the surviving specimens form part of the production for payment to the British. The only known specimens of the gold *mohur*, half *mohur* and quarter *mohur* were published by Marsden, in 1825 AD, and are preserved now in the British Museum.[43] Earlier, in *Vaisâka,* 1678 *Śaka*, a few very fine gold and silver coins were struck, presumably on the occasion of the installation of Gaura Simha as the king of Manipur.[44]

Jaya Simha (1764-1798 AD)

Jaya Simha became a fulfledged ruler of Manipur in 1764 AD, on the death of his elder brother. On three occasions he was driven out from his kingdom by the Burmese; the first was soon after his accession, and he returned in about 1768 AD, after spending his time in Cachar and Assam. He married his daughter to Rajesvara Simha, the Ahom king, and formed a valuable alliance with this most powerful kingdom in the Northeast. In 1770 AD, the Burmese again invaded and drove away Jaya Simha from Manipur. But the king was able to regain his throne fairly soon after, with the help of the Ahom king. It was perhaps on this occasion that he struck some fine gold coins, dated *Śaka* 1694. An example of this coin was published by Marsden, and is now in the British Museum.[45] It is possible that the coin was presented by the Manipur king to the ruler of Assam in recognition of the help in recovering his throne, and the same piece may have been acquired by Col. John Peter Wade or one of his officers, when they were in Assam in 1794 AD. Jaya Simha perhaps struck some square silver coins in *Śaka* 1711, but the quality of the calligraphy seems to be very poor and the reading is also very uncertain.

Square silver half *ṭankâ* of Jaya Simha

Some gold coins in the name of Jaya Simha surfaced in Kolkata in the 1970's and these were published during the last quarter of the twentieth century. However, these were probably modern forgeries.

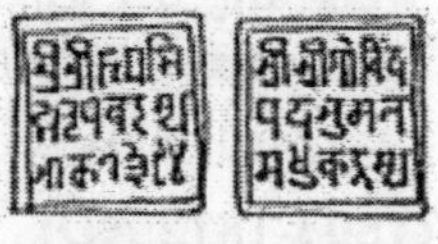

Square gold *mohur* of Jaya Simha

Jaya Simha also struck *sel* coins, made of bell-metal, on round as well as square shaped flan with rounded corners. There was some initial confusion as to whether the initial letter '*Ja*' in Bengali or in *Nâgari* on the *sel* coin (bell metal) actually represented the name of Jaya Simha.[46] However, in the Khangabok hoard, discovered at Khangabok Khunou village in Thoubal district (Manipur) in July 1984, a number of *sel* coins bearing the full name 'Jaya' were noticed. In fact, as many as 46 coins bear 'Jaya' in *Devanâgri* and one in Bengali. These pieces are comparatively large square shaped coins, slightly concave in appearance, and on an average three centimetres across.[47] Jaya Simha, despite the turbulence suffered during his reign, had spared no pains in making significant development in his kingdom, particularly in the fields of spiritual, social and economic activities. Improvement of agriculture was one of the key areas, which received his attention.[48]

Labanya Chandra (1798-1801 AD) & Madhu Chandra (1801-1804 AD)

Jaya Simha was succeeded by his eldest surviving son, Labanya Chandra, also known as Rabinchandra. Edward Gait refers to him as Harsha Chandra.[49] No genuine gold or silver coin in the name of Labanya Chandra is known. The only gold coin published in 1980 is probably a fine example of modern forgery.[50] No other coins can be definitely attributed to Labanya Chandra or his successor Madhu Chandra, except perhaps the small *sel* with letters '*La*' and '*Ma*'. If this attribution is correct, it would indicate that the change from the large flan *sels*, weighing 3.7 gms., to the smaller *sels*, weighing less than 1gm., may have taken place around the turn of the century.

Chaurajit Simha (1804-1812 AD)

Chaurajit, the fifth son of Jaya Simha, is normally

thought to have occupied the throne after defeating Madhu Chandra in 1806 AD.[51] However, as the earliest coin in his name is dated *Śaka* 1726, it is apparent that he became the king no later than 1804 or early 1805 AD. He continued the tradition of striking square silver coins and his coin dated *Śaka* 1734, the year in which he lost the throne, are the least rare of all the square silver coins of Manipur.

Square silver half *ṭankâ* of Chaurajit Simha

Chaurajit also struck rare half and quarter *ṭankâs*, as well as full *ṭankâs* in several earlier years. One gold coin, dated *Śaka* 1731, of Chaurajit was published in 1980 AD which seems to be of doubtful authenticity, as the weight of 12.5 gms. is indeed heavy for the period, and the dies are not the same as those used for silver coins, as one would expect.[52]

A few small *sels* are known with the letter '*Cha*' which also can, perhaps, be attributed to the reign of Chaurajit.

Marjit Simha (1812-1819 AD)

In 1812 AD, Chaurajit Simha's younger brother Marjit Simha sought help from the Burmese to gain the throne of Manipur, even agreeing to the vassal status. The Burmese army invaded Manipur and Chaurajit was forced to flee to Cachar. Marjit became king of Manipur. Although Marjit Simha agreed to a vassal status, he ruled almost independently and struck a few rather debased silver coins, on round and square flans. One genuine fine gold coin of Marjit Simha is known from the British Museum collection. He may have also struck *sel* coins in his reign and the *sel* bearing the letter '*Ma*' has been attributed to him. In 1819 AD, he offended the Burmese by refusing to attend the coronation ceremony of King Bagydaw to pay homage. As a result, the Burmese army invaded and expelled Marjit Simha to the neighbouring Cachar kingdom where Chaurjit Simha had already taken refuge. The Burmese occupied Manipur and devastated the kingdom for about seven years.

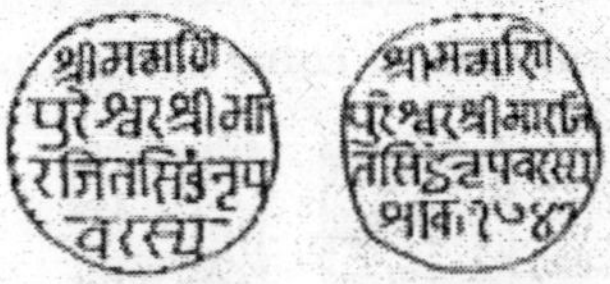

Circular Gold *mohur* of Marjit Simha

Burmese Occupation of Manipur (1819-1826 AD)

The Burmese not only invaded Manipur but also entered Assam and occupied the Ahom kingdom. When the danger to the British possessions in India became apparent, the war was declared by the British and the Burmese were driven out of Assam. Soon after, Gambhir Singh, the youngest son of Jaya Simha, took financial help as well as support in arms from the British. He then recaptured Manipur by defeating the Burmese and was ultimately recognised by the British as the king of Manipur. The British appointed a Political Agent to help the king in administering the kingdom. During the Burmese occupation, all the precious metals were said to have been carried off to Burma, perhaps accounting for the great rarity of the silver and gold coins of Manipur today.[53]

Gambhir Singh (1826-1834 AD)

Only one gold coin of Gambhir Singh has been recorded, a gold coin with the date 1043 in the lunar (*Chandrâbdah*) era.[54] The conversion of this date as equivalent to 1831-32 AD, was successfully achieved by V. Chowdhury and P. Ray, thanks to an inscription on a bell which gave the date both in the *Chandrâbdah* and in the *Śaka* era.[55]

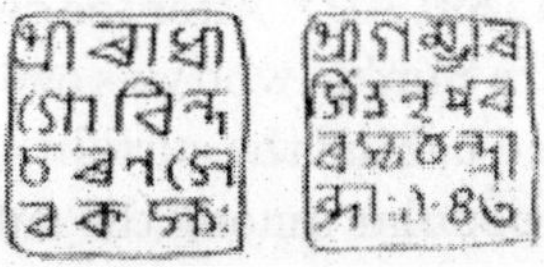

Gold *mohur* of Gambhir Singh

Chandra Kirti (1834-1843 AD & 1851–1886 AD) & Nara Simha (1844-51 AD)

Chandra Kirti became the king of Manipur in 1834 AD and, except for a spell of about seven years (1844-50 AD), he continued on the throne until his death in 1886 AD. When Chandra Kirti ascended the throne, he was only two years old. As such, Nara Simha, the great grandson of Garibaniwaz, who was the *senâpati* (commander-in-chief), became the regent of the minor Chandra Kirti. Unfortunately, Nara Simha, despite his sincerity, fell prey to a palace conspiracy and, in 1844 AD, an attempt was made to assassinate him. Nara Simha was able to escape. After the failure of the plot, Maharani Kumudini Devi and her son Chandra Kirti left Manipur and went to Cachar for political asylum. Nara Simha "suspecting the complicity of the Maharani in the attempt on his life did not hesitate to proclaim himself the *Râjâ* of Manipur".[56] In the year 1850 AD cholera broke out in Manipur in an epidemic form and as a result the king also died.

No gold or silver coins of Chandra Kirti and Nara Simha are known. A gold coin in the name of Nara Simha appeared in Kolkata in late nineteen seventies, showing Lord Krishna playing his flute. The weight of this coin, at over 13 gms., seems to be very irregular, and we have no hesitation in pronouncing the said coin as modern counterfeit. However, as suggested by R.C. Temple, Nara Simha struck some *sel* coins bearing the letter '*Ra*'. The coins are generally well worn, consistent with circulation of over forty years before being withdrawn in 1891 AD.[57] After the death of Nara Simha, his brother Debendra Simha, who was one of the conspirators but always remained behind the curtain, usurped the power. Debendra was not popular among the subjects. Meanwhile, Chandra Kirti returned to Manipur from exile. He had the support of the three sons of Nara Simha. Ultimately, Debendra fled to Cachar and his short lived reign ended after three months. No coins are known from the reign of Debendra Simha. Chandra Kirti then ascended the throne for a second time.

It is believed that some *sel* coins bearing the letter '*Ma*' were struck during the period of reign of Chandra Kirti. In a letter from the Political Agent dated 8th July, 1838, it has been stated that "no meaning is attached to the Nagri letter '*Ma*' on the coins, further than that when a Rajah comes to the throne, the Pundits assemble to fix upon a fortunate syllable to be stamped on all the *sel* made during his reign, and that, the Nagri syllable in question, has been fixed upon as the lucky one for the present rule..... the authorities would not therefore wish it to be changed".[58] Since the most common of the *Sel* coins are those with the letter *Śrî*, and as Chandra Kirti reigned for a long period, it is likely that many of the coins struck during his reign had the letter *Śrî*.

Sura Chandra (1886–1890 AD) & Kula Chandra (1890–1891 AD)

After the death of Chandra Kirti in 1886 AD, the political situation in Manipur deteriorated because of the disputes between his sons. The eldest son Sura Chandra was unfortunately a weak character, and in 1890 AD he was ousted by his brothers in a palace revolution. Kula Chandra was made the king, but although the people generally approved of the change, the British expressed their disapproval and tried to interfere in the internal politics of the kingdom. Affairs were badly handled by the representatives of the British Indian government and culminated in several British officials being killed. A full scale military offensive was then launched in order to restore the British supremacy in the kingdom. As a result of the British victory in the war, Kula Chandra was deported to the Andaman Islands and his most capable brother Tikendrajit was executed. In September, 1891, Chura Chandra, an obscure descendant of Nara Simha, was made the king, and the administration passed into the British hands. Soon after that, the *sels* were withdrawn from circulation, British India copper coins were forced on the population, and the Manipur mint was closed permanently.[59]

We have been able to examine some of the *sel* coins of Sura Chandra and Kula Chandra, which are still found in various collections. The *sel* coins of Sura Chandra depict the letter '*La*' in *Devanâgri*, while Kula Chandra struck *sel* coins with the Bengali letter '*Ku*'.

Uniqueness of *Sel* coins

The *Sel* coins of Manipur were a unique coinage in Northeast India. It provided a currency for the common people, which were widely used for the day-to-day purchases in the markets and other monetary transactions, in contrast to the silver and gold coins, which were used mainly for ceremonial purposes and for large scale transactions. Most interestingly, besides the Manipur mint, at least on one occasion, the *sels* were also struck in the Calcutta mint, but although the total number of the pieces struck in the Calcutta mint was 50,378 in number, none are known today. The production was stopped possibly because of the high cost, compared with the low value of the coin, which ranged from c250 to c470 to the rupee, depending on supply and demand.[60]

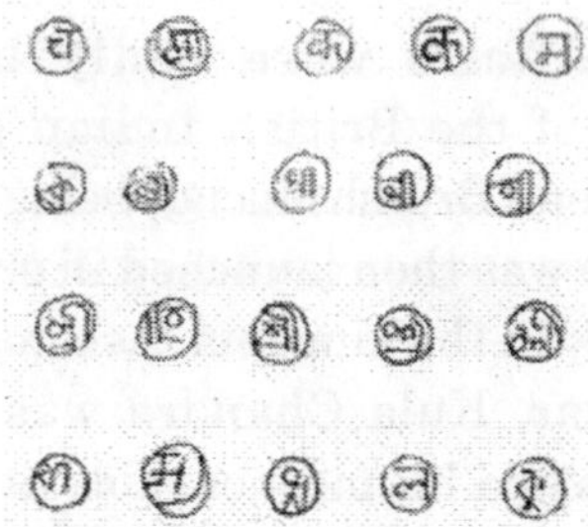

***Sel* coins of Manipur (Line drawings)**

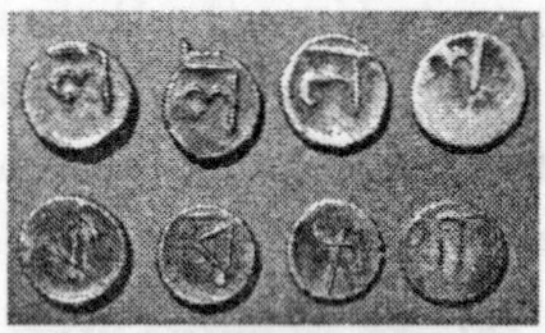

***Sel* coins of Manipur**

Modern forged coins of Jaya Simha and Nara Simha

Modern forged coins of Jaya Simha

Coin of Harsha Chandra – A modern forgery

Unlike a normal piece, the weight of this coin is 13.9 gms., and it is likely to be a modern forgery

Conclusion

As can be seen from the above, the coinage of Manipur exhibits many features which are not present in the coins of the neighbouring kingdoms, perhaps reflecting the strong independent tendencies of the Meitei people. Unlike Manipur, no neighbouring kingdom struck a small coin for use in the markets. The small bell-metal coins were struck in Manipur to fulfil the need of the common people for coins. The date of introduction of such coins was not later than 1724 AD, and this may have been even earlier. The silver and gold coins were initially square in shape, and of a heavier weight than the coins of any neighbouring state. The weight was eventually reduced to that of the Indian rupee, but the unique square shape was retained, along with the legend in *Nâgari* script, rather than the Assamese/Bengali script used by other Northeast Indian states. The rich tradition of an independent coinage in Manipur ceased to exist when the British took over the Meitei Kingdom in 1891 AD and introduced their own currency in Manipur.

NOTES & REFERENCES

1. T. C. Hudson, *The Meitheis*, (London, 1908) Reprint Low Price Publications, Delhi, 1989, p.1.
2. Alexander Mackenzie, *History of the Relations of the Government with the Hill Tribes on the North- East Frontier of Bengal*, Bengal Government Press, Calcutta, 1884, p.149.

3. N. N. Acharya, "New Light on the Sources of History of Manipur and Adjoining Areas", in S. N. Pandey (ed.), *Sources of the History of Manipur and Adjoining Areas,* National Publishing House, New Delhi, 1985, pp. 19-28.
4. N. G. Rhodes, *The Coinage of North-East India*, Kent, 1994, p. 177; R. B. Pemberton, *Report on the Eastern Frontier of British India*, (Calcutta, 1835) Reprint DHAS, Gauhati, 1966, pp. 37-38.
5. *ibid.*
6. Alexander Mackenzie, *op. cit.*, p.149.
7. *ibid.*
8. S. K. Bose, "'Intriguing Manipur' : The Views of a 19th Century Trader", *Proceedings of North East India History Association*, XXVIIth Session, Aizwal, 2006, p. 210.
9. *ibid.*
10. Janakinath Basak, *Manipur Prohelika* (in Bengali, henceforth to be referred to as *Prohelika*), Kolkata, 1891, p. 18.
11. *ibid.*
12. *ibid.* pp.9-10.
13. *ibid.* p.208.
14. *ibid.* pp. 103 & 115.
15. N. G. Rhodes, *op. cit.*, p. 194.
16. *Prohelika*, p. 23
    # Kabo valley/Kabaw valley
17. *ibid.*, p. 23-24.
18. *ibid.*, p. 13.
19. *ibid.*, p. 22.
20. *ibid.*, p. 14.
21. T. C. Hudson, *op. cit.*, p.36
22. K. Sobita Devi, "Numismatics: A source of Manipuri History", in S. N. Pandey (ed.), *Sources of the History of Manipur and Adjoining Areas, op.cit.*, pp.51-67.
23. L. Kunjeswori Devi, *Archaeology in Manipur*, Rajesh Book Depot, Delhi, p.44.
24. Jyotirmoy Roy, *History of Manipur*, (Firma K. L. Mukhopadhyay, Calcutta, 1958) Reprint 1999, p. 39.

25. *ibid.*, p. 8.
26. *ibid.*
27. L. Kunjeswori Devi, *op. cit.*, p. 44.
28. N. G. Rhodes, *op. cit.*, p. 192.
29. P. Gunindro Singh, *Manipuri Numismatics*, Imphal, 1983, p. 24.
30. L. Kunjeswori Devi, *op. cit.*, p. 45.
31. *Ibid.*, p. 44.
32. N. G. Rhodes, *op. cit.*, p. 180.
33. R. Brown, *Statistical Account of Manipur*, (London, 1874) Reprint Sankaran Prakashak, Delhi, 1975, p. 89.
34. F. Pridmore, "The East India Company's bell metal coinage for Manipur, 1838", *Seaby's Coin and Medal Bulletin,* No. 652, London, 1972 (No.12), p. 480.
35. V. Chowdhury & Parimal Ray, "The Coinage of Manipur", in J. P. Singh & Nishar Ahmed (ed.), *Coinage And Economy of North Eastern States of India,* Varanasi, 1980, p.103.
36. P.K. Bhattacharyya, "An Interesting Coin of Manipur", *Journal of the Numismatic Society of India (JNSI),* Vol. XXXIX, Varanasi, 1977, pp. 182-85.
37. Gangmumei Kabui, *History of Manipur*, vol. I, National Publishing House, Delhi, 1991, pp. 246, 256. Kabui cited *Cheitharol Kumbaba, Ningthourol Lumbaba, Takhel Ngamba, Sanamahi Laikan*, etc. as his sources of information.
38. R. Sarma, *Political History of Tripura*, Calcutta, 1986, p.124.
39. L. Ibungohal Singh & N. Khelchandra Singh (ed.), *Cheitharol Kumbaba,* Manipuri Sahitya Parishad, Imphal, 1967, p. 106.
40. L.Kunjeswori Devi, *op. cit.*, p.46.
41. Most authors stated that Gaura Simha ascended the throne in 1758 AD, but the coins dated *Śaka* 1678 (1756 AD) are contrary to those contentions.
42. Jyotirmoy Roy, *op. cit.*, p. 57.
43. W. Marsden, *Oriental Coins*, London 1825, Part II, pp. 801-3 & Pl. LIII.
44. Interestingly, these first gold and silver coins of Manipur, which are in the British Museum collection, all weigh about 12.5gms, whereas those struck in later years are of normal

rupee weight of c11.6 gms. The significance of this high weight standard is not yet understood.

45. W. Marsden, *op.cit.*
46 S.K. Bose, "Sel Coinage of Manipur and the Coins of Jaya Singh", *Coin - 2007,* Kolkata, 2007, p. 48.
47. Mutua Bahadur & P. Gunindro Singh, *Khangabok Coins Hoarding* (Hoard), Imphal, 1985, pp. 8-12.
48. Jyotirmoy Roy, *op. cit.* pp. 68-69
49. Edward Gait, *A History of Assam*, 3rd edition, Thacker Sprink & Co., Calcutta, 1963, p. 324
50. Some of those coins were first published by Rhodes in "The Coinage of Manipur", *Coinage And Economy of North-East India*, Hythe,1980, pp.103-11.
51. J. & S. Parratt, *Queen Empress Vs Tikendrajeet, Prince of Manipur*, New Delhi, 1992.
52. V. Chowdhury & P. Ray, *op.cit.* p. 105, Pl. VII (2).
53 N. G. Rhodes, *op. cit.* p. 185
54. S. P. Basu, "A Rare Gold Coin of Manipur", *JNSI*, Vol. XXVII, pt. 1, Varanasi, 1965, pp. 110-11 & plate X.
55. V. Chowdhury & P. Ray, *op. cit.*, nos. 12 and 18.
56. Jyotirmoy Roy, *op. cit.*, p. 97
57. R. C. Temple, *Indian Antiquary*, 1898 AD.
58. F. Pridmore, "The East India Company's bell metal coinage for Manipur, 1838", *op.cit.*, pp. 477-78.
59. N. G. Rhodes, *op. cit.*, p. 191.
60. F. Pridmore, *op.cit.*

6

Technology, Occupational Distribution and Settlement Pattern in Early Manipur

S. Amal Singh

To understand the pre-colonial society and economy of Manipur one has to rely upon two types of historical source materials, viz. (i) the traditional historical literature, and (ii) the colonial historical writings. The traditional historical literature of Manipur focused on the indigenous concept of history which is expressed by the Meitei word *Puwari* (meaning, story of the forefathers). The *Meitei Puwari* consists of the legends, religious accounts, genealogies and the dynastic accounts of the clan chieftains. The local chronicles (*Puyas*) - with or without chronology - has been a very important source of history. The second type is a large body of colonial historical writings which included the reports, accounts and memoirs of the British colonial writers and officials who were deputed to collect information or assigned the duty of maintaining political relations or posted in Manipur to assist in local administration as well as to maintain the official records of the day-to-day governance. As observed by Gangmumei Kamei (Kabui), a well known historian of

Manipur, the colonial historiography in Manipur started with R. B. Pamberton's *Report on the Eastern Frontier of British India* (1835) which devoted a large section on Manipur's history, geography, economy and ethnography.[1]

Technology

The local chronicles and literary texts recorded the accounts of the discovery of paddy, practice of shifting cultivation, development of bronze and iron technology for making *daos*, axes and hoes for agricultural and allied purposes. Agriculture has been the main occupation of the people and the backbone of economy in Manipur right from the early period. Before developing the knowledge of wet rice cultivation, the people in Manipur practiced shifting cultivation on the hill slopes or dry land forest areas. The main implements were axes and *daos* for felling trees and clearing jungles and small iron hoe for digging the soil. The royal chronicle - *Cheitharol Kumbaba* - refers to several irrigation works by dredging the rivers and making canals to drain out stranded water from the low-lying marshy areas of the central Imphal valley, which were undertaken at the initiative of the early Meitei kings and continued by their successors. Another chronicle, *Naothingkhong Phambal Kaba* refers to the system of shifting cultivation being practiced by the Shelloi Langmai tribe of Nongmaiching hill and adoption of wet rice cultivation by the valley dwellers (Meiteis). Similarly, the *Loiyumba Shilyen*[*] and the *Mashin*[+] refer to the rates of revenue prescribed for the agricultural fields by the state to be paid by the peasants. This definitely implies the prevalence of wet rice cultivation in the valley of Manipur. The pre-historic and archaeological findings are very also helpful in approximately reconstructing the features of early agricultural practices. For instance, the excavation at Napachik site[2] points to the prevalence of agriculture which indicates that a settled life and economy was in place in the Manipur valley. However, we do not find a definite mention of the use of iron plough pulled by bullock in the early literature of Manipur. In this regard some scholars have pointed out that in the early period the people of Manipur grew rice and vegetables by digging the soil menially. The extensive farming was, therefore, non-existent in the early periods. It is as late as in the sixteenth-seventeenth century AD that the Manipuri farmers were found growing paddy, pulses and vegetables on a much bigger scale by using plough drawn by a pair of bullocks. This was a distinct improvement in the agricultural technology in Manipur. Further, in Manipur the plough is called *laangol* - a word derived from the Sanskrit *Laangola*, which was in all probability introduced in Manipur by the immigrants from other parts of eastern India who were gradually assimilated in the local society as Manipuris.[3] These immigrants, especially the Muslim peasants from the neighbouring Barak-Surma valley, are said to have introduced the improved agricultural technology, including transplantation of paddy seedlings, thereby putting an end to the age old practice of broadcasting or *Punghul*. However, as recorded in the manuscript *Maputhiba*, some scholars assumed that the tool *laangol* was already in use in Manipur and it was made of wood by taking the design of the bill of a bird (Crane). This particular bird is traditionally known as *Wainu* in Manipur. It is further argued that because of the development of knowledge in metallurgy, especially iron, and the prevalence of regular trade between Manipur and other states of India and the neighbouring countries of Southeast Asia (particularly Burma), there is a possibility that the technique has been modified to suit the local conditions. This technology is believed to have started from the time of the Meitei king Naothingkhong in the eighth century AD.[4]

To understand the role of technology in economic change in early Manipur it may be useful to examine extensively the agricultural practices before and after the advent of the immigrants in Manipur, because it goes without saying that the technology is closely related to the science of engineering and it deals with the tools and techniques for carrying out the recurrent activity, while the technologist is the specialist who carries out the scheme of action for the purpose of accomplishing a specific function in a specialized way. With the improvement in agricultural technology the social life in Manipur became more stable, housing became more comfortable and the habitation more settled. Weaving, pottery, basketry and other activities became institutionalized and attained considerable significance in the life of the people. Moreover, the advanced skills required in these pursuits led to micro occupational specializations. The occupations in almost all cases became hereditary. The role played by the Meitei kings in this context was significant. By virtue of his authoritative position and as representative of the agricultural community, the control over distribution of land was vested in the king who was theoretically the owner of all land - cultivated or waste - along with all natural resources. This position enabled the king to ensure the self-contained and self-reliant growth of the localities or villages while allotting land to the settlers.

Occupational Distribution

In early Manipur, the settled human life began with the birth of the villages, and in every village some professional workmen were settled by the chiefs or headmen who looked after the needs of the people and supervised the division of labour. As a result, every village included the households of such artisans and craftsmen whose services were necessary for the self-contained life of the village community. These hereditary workmen grew either from within the ranks of the indigenous ethnic folds or by an indigenization of the immigrant communities. The evolutionary view of development generally suggests that a civilization or the structure of tradition (which consists of both cultural and social structures) grows in two stages; first, through orthogenetic or indigenous evolution and second, through heterogametic encounters or contacts with other cultures or civilizations. The fusion of the two processes produces a new one (in a system of cooperation) which is a categorical social process. The Meitei social formation also seems to have passed through these processes, since the families of artisans or workmen like the blacksmiths, goldsmiths, potters, basket-makers and other craftsmen are found in each village. The presence of these artisans within every large village might have been considered necessary to enable the villagers to get all their requirements within the village. The artisans thus contributed to the autonomous growth of the self-sufficient and self- contained villages. The weaving was almost a household activity for a Manipuri family, but there were families for whom weaving was also the means of livelihood.[5]

Blacksmiths

A sub-clan or lineage, known as *Thangjam* or professional blacksmith, hereditarily worked in iron. They manufactured various types of *daos*, small knives, furnaces, tongs, etc. which were essential equipments or implements for daily use of the individual families and their occupations. The *Thangjams* maintained their livelihood through this activity. A particular place in the market area of the village, called *Thangjam Potpham*, was assigned to them by the chief or the king considering their importance in the community life of the village. No other sub-clan could encroach upon this place once it was allocated to them in the market areas. The *Thangjams* had to pay some tax or rent for this place, in cash or kind, either to the chief or to the state authorities, through the tax collectors for the markets.[6]

Goldsmiths

The goldsmiths, who played an important role in the Meitei society, were also settled by the chiefs in their respective areas. This profession was hereditary to certain sub-clans, such as *Konsam, Kangabam* and *Keisham*.[7] Only those sub-clans could carry on the profession in the areas allocated to them. They lived in clusters and in some areas they had villages exclusive to themselves. It was a thriving profession as the Manipuris were generally fond of ornaments. The gold ornaments included *Kiyang Likphang, Heikru Pareng, Sandrembi, Heibi Mapan, Marei, Ngangoi Pareng, Kongdum Pareng, Koichik Pareng*, etc., while the rings were of different varieties, namely, *Khoi Mahum, Lairen Makhoi, Parei Khudop* and *Charo Khudop*. The members of the royal family used some special ornaments, which the commoners were not allowed. The *Takopi Sana* (thinning of gold) and *Sana Phuhing* (purification of the gold) methods were used by the above sub-clans for making ornaments for the *Ningthou* (king) only. The possibility of some of the goldsmith families originally coming from outside Manipur cannot be altogether ruled out, since it is a well known fact that the people coming from outside Manipur in the early times were also absorbed into the social fold of the Meiteis at the behest of the chiefs. Many of those settlers were craftsmen who were skilled in making ornaments and other works. However, it is generally believed that the outside influence could not have significantly changed the designs and patterns of the ornaments as the people migh. have already developed taste for certain designs and patterns as indigenous and they always favoured the indigenous ones. Nonetheless, the designs brought by the immigrant artisans and craftsmen with them might have been adjusted with the local designs to produce new designs. The process of change might have been slow as the customs and traditions, besides the royal restrictions, played very important role in the manufacture and use of ornaments.[8]

Pottery

The explorations and excavations of the pre-historic and archeological sites in the Manipur valley have brought to light the specimens of earthen jars and pots in almost all the sites. The earthen pot – *ghata* – has an important place in various rites and rituals in the Manipuri society. In the early historical period, pottery was made by a particular ethnic group in Manipur, namely, the *Chakpas*. They are also believed to be the first users of pottery. The tradition suggests that the first pottery was made by a Chakpa by imitating the shape of a flower plant - *Nura Kondonglei*, and the first *Chakpa* who made that pottery was named Chakpa Oinam.[9] Oinam is also the name of a village which is famous for its pottery in Manipur. The Oinam pottery is commonly used even these days all over Manipur. The Chakpa area is endowed with the sources of clay that is suitable for very good quality pottery. This may explain why some of the Chakpa villages specialized in pottery. In fact, the pottery-making in Manipur is said to be very old and it is believed to have been in existence since the beginning of the *Chak* era (an equivalent word of the Sanskrit *Yug*). The oldest variety of the earthen vessels is called *Chak-Phu*, because it was evolved through different stages during the course of the *Chak* era. The chiefs encouraged pottery making as it was a very useful craft for the society and it played an important role in the social, economic, cultural and religious life of the Manipuris. This is true for the people both in the hills and the plains of Manipur. The myths and beliefs related to pottery are many. For instance, the *Ishaiphu*, or the earthen vessel for storing water, represents the divinity of the Mother Earth, while the water contained inside the vessel symbolizes the essential component of life itself. The belief is that if the water in the vessel dries, there shall be misfortune and ailment in the family. Water is an important element connected with many rituals and everywhere it is associated with '*ghata*', which are pots and containers of the 'life giving force'.[10]

Salt Manufacturing

Salt has been locally manufactured in Manipur since time

immemorial. The Loi and the Chakpa communities specialized, or perhaps were forced to specialize, in the activity of manufacturing salt from the several salt wells spread over in the valley and the hills of Manipur. The activity was exclusive to these communities. The salt manufacturing was their singular contribution to meet the requirement of the people and to the economy of the state. In the past nearly the entire volume of salt consumed by the people of Manipur was obtained from the salt wells situated in the valley. Small quantities were occasionally imported in times of scarcity from Burma, Cachar and Assam. The Lois and the Chakpas specialized in the salt manufacturing for two reasons: firstly, the salt wells were located in the foothill region which was inhabited by these communities, and secondly, the foothill region was not enough suitable for agriculture and, therefore, under compelling circumstances the people had to look for alternative economic activity, like salt manufacturing and pottery making, for their survival. The principal salt wells were situated at the foot of the hills to the northeast of the valley, at Ningel, Chandrakhong, Sikhong, Waikhong, etc. The people in the villages surrounding these salt wells were engaged in salt manufacturing. The Meitei kings encouraged salt industry by constructing roads connecting the villages which manufactured salt. Under the law of the land, all the salt wells belonged to the king and these were worked for his benefit. The people employed in the enterprise were remunerated by allowing them to retain the larger portion of the manufactured quantity for themselves. The king was entitled to 30% of the quantity manufactured, and the remaining 70% was divided among the workmen and their families. The amount of salt manufactured varied from season to season. Salt was manufactured mainly in the cold weather, when the brine water used to be at its strongest. The method of production was simply by evaporation and the product used to be clean and free from foul smell. According to some sources, which are dated to the beginning of the colonial period in the history of Manipur towards the end of the nineteenth century, about 150 *maunds* of salt were locally manufactured in Manipur every month. This approximately amounted to about (150 x 12) 1,800 *maunds* in a year. This quantity of locally manufactured salt was found to be sufficient to meet the requirement of the people in the kingdom before the British colonization. However, as the population of Manipur was increasing fast under colonial conditions in the later part of the nineteenth century, the locally manufactured salt was found to be insufficient to meet the total demand. The commodity was then imported from Burma, Cachar and Assam.[11]

Bamboo Crafts

The Meitei texts like *Panthoibi Khonghul, Porieton Khungthokpa, Thanga Chinggoirol, Yumsharo', Ningthourol Lambuba* do mention about the uses of bamboos and canes and their products. The *Pena* singers in the bardic tradition of Manipur sing in praise of the use of bamboos and canes. In fact, bamboos formed part and parcel of the social and economic life of the inhabitants of Manipur since early times, while basketry or basket making became an integral part of the life of the people over the period of time. The tribes in the hill areas and the dwellers of the valley alike used bamboos and canes to meet many of their day to day requirements. The *Ningthourol Lambuba* mentions the use of a basket, called *Pai*, by the Meiteis. These baskets were hung on the shoulders to carry light commodities. It appears that from about the seventeenth century the use of *Pai* became minimal in the valley. While the Meiteis started using bags made of cloth, the people in the hills continued to use *Pai*. The chiefs in the tribal areas encouraged basketry as a means of livelihood. The technology of basket was also improved upon over the time by treating the materials with smoke so that the longevity or durability of the products could be enhanced. There were also changes in the shapes and designs of the baskets when the baskets became less conical and four legs or stands came to be added to support the base of the containers. The loops and other projections acting as hand-hold or handle were also introduced. These improvisations possibly suggest that life in Manipur was becoming more settled and the storage facility was becoming important in the changing lifestyle of the people. To meet the growing needs of the society the baskets were also emerging in different forms, shapes and sizes. The Meiteis gradually discarded the conical baskets, but the tribal people in the hills and the Andro and Phayeng people in the plains continued the use of those baskets and the craftsmen gradually improved upon them to suit the taste and requirement of the people.[12]

The basketry continued to be a very useful craft among the Meiteis even in the modern times as it is evident from the popularity of different types of baskets. As a matter of fact, bamboo was an integral part of a villager's life in Manipur as it was associated with everyday life of the rural people as well as the ritual practices. Apart from the fact that bamboo was the most important construction material for the houses to live in and the delicious recipes could be made of bamboo shoots, the belief system and the customary rites related the bamboo plants to the life of the people from birth to death. The Meiteis considered the bamboo nodes just like the human beings to the extent that they also sleep in the nights as the humans do.[13] Good or bad fortune comes to the people with the uses of particular types of bamboos in the same way the good or bad people do influence the lives of others. The flowering of bamboos was considered to be an omen of bad times, and it is believed that if a youth plants a bamboo seedling his life span will be curtailed. The beliefs about the evil impact of bamboo flowering are almost similar throughout Manipur, except for the village of Leimaram where the villagers believe that the flowering of bamboo brings good fortune to the people if the appropriate rituals are performed. On certain ritual occasions the age old customs regulated the use of bamboos. One such notable custom is the use of *Paya* (fine bamboo splits) by the womenfolk as waist belt when they go to attend a funeral. It is believed that the evil spirits are kept at bay by this practice. A festival called *Sharoi Khangba,* involving the bamboo plants, is celebrated on the first Saturday of the *Lamta* month (March-April) every year so that no evil spirit can cast spell on the community.[14]

The indigenous techniques or methods of basket-making were closely guarded by different ethnic groups from being pirated by others. In the past, a craftsman of a particular ethnic group used to manufacture only those items which were required for his people. It was an accepted but unannounced social code that was strictly followed. The craftsmen also customarily kept to their respective ethnic crafts and did not imitatc the methods of other ethnic groups. It is generally claimed that the Meitei technique of applying *Khe* oil to baskets for strengthening them and for making them water-proof was not known to the tribal craftsmen in Manipur for a long time. It was used only by the Meitei craftsmen. *Pheeruk, Yendai, Chengbon, Chengjamuk, Sangbai, Likhai Luk, Sairuk, Lokmai* are some of the popular baskets used by the Meiteis. They have a peculiar weave for making *Pheeruk* in which separate weaves are done for the inner surface and the outer surface respectively. For the outer weave, the dyed bamboo splits are used to give it a more decorative look. *Yendai* was used for cleaning vegetables before cooking. *Chengjamuk* was used for washing rice and *Sangbai* for measuring the quantity of paddy at the time of barter or measuring the total produce. *Likhai Luk* was commonly used for measuring the quantity of rice, *Sairuk* for keeping the rolled threads (*Langchak*) and other items of weaving and for keeping small utensils to be carried to the market for sale, *Lukmai* were common container baskets for every Meitei household in rural and urban areas, and. *Chengjamuk* for washing the rice meant for cooking. *Tumbas* were used for carrying rice-beer or water. *Shamuk* (a small container basket), which was used for rituals in death, could be weaved only on a particular day. A basket similar to *Ngarubak* in the form of the *Lubak* basket was used by the Meiteis to contain the image and the spirit of *Sanamahi* (the deity). This basket itself symbolized the presence of *Sanamahi*. The Meitei women of Kwaktha village in Chandel district even now use conical baskets. These are primarily used for carrying things like the firewood, field implements, grains, vegetables or even water in bamboo containers. *Tabus* are big baskets for keeping clothes, utensils, etc. in the hill areas of Manipur. The tribal people of Manipur even these days offer close-weave conical baskets as part of the dowry or gift when a daughter in the family is married. Among the Andros a basket called *Chapot* is presented as dowry when a girl is married. It normally contains the clothes presented to her by the parents and then it is taken to the bridegroom's place by the women who accompany the bride to her new home. The *Heijin Kharai* signifies the bride-price. It is made on the day of the marriage. Normally, it is not sold in the market. It reflects an established social custom which has been ritualized.[15]

Amidst such social beliefs the utility of bamboo got extended to cover almost every aspect of human activity, including the games and sports. *Kangjei* or polo-sticks were made from bamboo stems and *Kangdrum* or polo-balls were made from bamboo roots. Similarly, umbrellas, headgears, armlets, wristlets, shields and weapons of war like the bows and arrows and spear handles were made from different types of bamboos. Musical instruments and religious totems like the *Shattara* were also made from the bamboos. These *Shattaras* were erected to appease and honour the *Umanglais*.

The Maring people erect *Yaakiyo* totem to announce to the people and the ancestors of the particular families that the ceremony is being performed. On the tip of these totems, the replicas of birds and animals were hung.

Basket played a very important role in every family of the Manipuri society, while the use of bamboo for varying activities was possibly a great unifying factor in early Manipur. It gave meaning to many of the social, economic and religious beliefs of the people in the valley and the hills of Manipur. It gave rise to occupational groups as it gradually became a specialized vocation. It gained quality and aesthetic values as well. It was also commonly used in the rites and rituals of every *salai* (clan). It is used even today. Besides bamboo, canes were also used in the households for making utility-items. Cane objects were extensively used in the past, and the furniture exclusively made of *cane* was used by the chiefs. The multiplicity of weaving patterns made basketry a complex and tedious but a graceful art. In course of time, bamboo and cane crafts were commercialized.

Sericulture and Weaving

Weaving has always been considered a noble profession in Manipur. Every family seems to have nurtured it since the earliest times, although the handlooms are supposed to have been introduced later on. The development was through stages. The reeling of thread was possibly the first stage, weaving of clothes the second, and introduction of loom thereafter. Thread is said to have been first introduced by the Khaba king Taram Khoinucha's wife Panthoibi,[16] who was a trail-blazer in thread making. It is believed that Panthoibi had learnt it from a spider who was reeling its thread to catch the insects. Thus, the reeling of thread in the form of cocoon started in Manipur. During the time of the first Ningthouja king, Nongda Lairen Pakhangba, a particular thread known as *Moitang Lang* was introduced.

The place where this thread was first reeled is still known as Moitang Pok.[17] The quality of the thread was fine. However, this thread could not be used in making clothes for common use because of its fine quality, as the commoners were not allowed to use such fine clothes. Therefore, a general variety of three or four-fold thread was prepared for cloth-making during the same period. The method of using the folded thread was known as *Taret Khonphang Thok,* and the folded thread was called *Kanda Kithi Lang*. It is a traditional belief in Manipur that Panthoibi introduced such a thread and Pakhangba encouraged the method of preparing the thread as well as weaving as an art and a profession throughout the territory. Pakhangba always insisted on the handling of threads in a proper way and he designed the *Pang Iyung,* later on called *Panyong,* which is identified today as a traditional loom in Manipur. It is indeed a typical shuttle which weaves cloth.[18]

The tradition of weaving and textile in Manipur is thus as old as the reign of the founder of the Ningthouja dynasty, King Nongda Lairen Pakhangba. Some improvisations were carried out during the reigns of some of the later rulers. For example, during the period of Khuyoi Tompok (154-264 AD) the designed cloth, *Lairen Huikok Mayek,* was first introduced by a person named Khoriyan Phisaba.[19] The *Khwang Iyang,*[20] a fishing net, was introduced during the reign of Yoimongba Taothingmang (264-364 AD). During the reign of King Naophangba (428-580 AD) a design was developed which is said to have been adopted from the patterns on the ventral side of Pakhangba, the serpent god worshipped by ethnic Meities. The person who first introduced this design was named Ako.[21] Before making the design, he is said to have performed a traditional ritual. The king was very pleased to see the design on the cloth and rewarded the designer. During the time of King Yanglou Keiphaba (969 AD) the knitting of *Khoi* pattern (*khoi lonba*) on the border of *Phanek* was first introduced.[22]

With the passage of time various designs were introduced by the weavers and dyers. The introduction of new designs and models from time to time helped in the development of the world view of the Meiteis and ideological understanding of the Meitei way of life and practices. The role of the chiefs was singular and dynamic in the development of weaving and textile in Manipur. However, the quality, the designs and the patterns of the clothes reflected the fact of stratification in the society. These were different for the king, members of the royal family, high officials, aristocracy and the commoners.

Textiles, Costumes and Colours

The Meiteis in early times used natural herbs, plants and bark of trees for making different colours. The kings encouraged natural colours and ascribed them to different ethnic communities. This might have been meant for segregating or identifying different communities on the basis of colours. There were also different clothes for different communities from the seventh century AD onwards. For example, the *Khament Chatpa* is a typically designed cloth which is stamped. The stamp is made of wood engraved by skilled carpenters and the colour is extracted from an indigenous herb called *Khumoo*. This is known as *Khumoo Unam* till today. This colour is akin to the chest of a python. This typical cloth could be used only by those members of the nobility whom the king had selected. In the past, the persons who used these clothes were respected by the people. Thus, the method of stamping the border of clothes was introduced. Another aristocratic cloth is *Lamthang Khullat*. It was derived from the design and colour of the dragon head. This cloth was prepared from the fine silk available in the Chin hills and the Imphal valley. This cloth was used exclusively by the descendants of the king. The others were never allowed to use this cloth. Similarly, *Phiran Namba*, which was designed after the head of the serpent or the dragon-king

Pakhangba, could be used only by the kings as turbans. However, a cloth called *Ningkham Sanajen*, which was designed after the side of the body of Pakhangba, was awarded by the king to the nobles only. The *Ningthou-Phee-Saijonba* was a shirt particularly used by the king and his high ranking military officers. The shirt was loose and a long one. The cloth was made from silk. This design was after the features of Pakhangba and it could not be used by the commoners. The famous women garment *Hija Mayek* was introduced during the period of King Yanglou Keiphaba in the tenth century AD. The typical design for this garment was by a carpenter who, while making a canoe for an ensuing royal canoe race, was impressed by the beautiful natural texture of the wood. He showed it to the King and the Queen who were charmed by the beauty of the texture. The queen asked him to knit that typical design. This design, an imitation of the wood texture, embroidered as the borders of women's garments became popular as *Hija Mayek*.[23]

The assignment of specific social and economic functions to the clans or sub-clans or individual families during the reign of King Loiyamba (1094-1122 AD)[24] was a very important and historic step towards social and economic development of the Meitei Kingdom. By a royal edict or charter issued in 1110 AD, popularly known as *Loiyamba Shinyen*, King Loiyamba had assigned social and economic functions to specific families or lineages or sub-clans. This measure of the king had ensured division of labour in the society and facilitated professional specializations. It was also a boost to the development of textile in Manipur. In the meantime, Manipur had already made a great stride in hand-knitted clothes which were stamped with various deigns and were known under different names, like i) *Ningthou Phee ii) Sharong Phee iii) Kabui Shingnanglan, iv) Shingkhai Phee, v) Laiyengpuram Phee, vi) Pharoi Phee, vii) Layeng Purum Phee, viii) Pumthil Phanek, ix) Khunungnum Phee, x) Phimu*

Lanphi, xi) Phingang Langmu Phee, xii) Thangli.[25] The weaving was, therefore, an old craft in Manipur that was going on for a long time. It was almost a household vocation for many families. What King Loiyamba actually did was formalizing the occupation for those who were doing it satisfactorily. Loiyamba perhaps assigned the occupation to them so that in course of time it would become hereditary and the artisans would become so by birth and would practice the art from the childhood. His edict divided the traditional weavers into two categories, *viz.*, weavers and dyers. The families were identified separately for weaving and dying. Under Loiyamba's dispensation, the weaving of different varieties of clothes was assigned to the different sub-clans according to their skill and aptitude.[26] The names of the varieties of clothes and the incumbent sub-clans can be seen in Table I.

Table I

Weaving of Clothes assigned to Sub-Clans by King Loiyamba

Sl. No.	*Name of the Cloth*	*Name of Sub-Clan*
1	*Tonkap Phanek*	*Chakpa Thiyam*
2	*Phiren (Ngabong)*	*Chakpram*
3	*Langdom Phee*	*Kongbajam*
4	*Yarong Phee (Moirang Phee)*,Pakhangbagi Marong Marong,*Longba Yengduna Saba Phee*	*Thongabam*
5	*Sharong Phee*	*Laikhuram*
6	*Leirum and Londham*	*Shanjibam*
7	*Phuroi Phee*	*Abujam*
8	*Shengthan Phee*	*Thoidingjam*

(Contd...)

Sl. No.	*Name of the Cloth*	*Name of Sub-Clan*
9	*Laying*	*Thongbam*
10	*Purum Phee*	*Kongbam*
11	*Pumthil Phanek (Punemakhi Makok)*	*Thingbam*
12	*Khunung Kakhum Phee(Ngabong Pungkhri Konba)*	*Okthujam*
13	*Chungbam Phimu*	*Khoishnam*
14	*Lanphi Phimu*	*Khoishanam*
15	*Phingang*	*Chungkham*
16	*Langsu Phee*	*Wangbijam*
17	*Thangli*	*Thangjam Sabam*
18	*Ningthou Phe*	*Nongthonbam* and 35 other sub-clans
19	*Phee Lonba*	*Ahongsangbam*

Source : Kh. Ibungoyaima, *Manipurgi Pisha Lonsa Amasung Hourakpham*, Imphal , 1997, p. 8.

The dress and colour codes introduced by the Meitei kings from time to time had to be strictly maintained by the weavers and the dyers. The methods of dying were well developed and for each variety of clothes specific dyes were used. The following are some of the indigenous plants, herbs, barks, creepers and seeds which were generally used in the past for making dyes of different shades and this traditional art of dying is still maintained in Manipur:

Kumna : *Kumna* is a plant from which black, blue (*Staabi lanthas flaciedifolius*) and green colours were extracted.

Ureirom : Red, orange and golden colours were extracted from the *Ureirom* (*bika orellana*) seeds.

Kuhi	:	*Kuhi* (*castamopsispp*) offered brown and fawn colours.
Kusum Lei	:	*Kusum Lei* (*curathamus Texetoruis*) for Pinik and Rhodium.
Unapu	:	A plant for yellow colour.
Yaingang	:	Offered redish and yellow colours.
Chingsu Mana	:	A source of black colour.
Cha (lac)	:	Dark red was extracted.
Khuhi and Moyum	:	Maroon colour was extracted from the bark of *Sahi Kuhi* (*castamopsispp*) and *Moyum* trees.

An important colour-yielding plant of Manipur is *Kum* (*Strabilanthes-flacudifoluis*) from the leaves of which the dye called *Kum Kumbang* is prepared. The techniques of producing colours had already been developed in the pre-colonial period. A big earthen jar used to be filled with the *Kum* leaves and water. After three to four days, it would be stirred thoroughly by using a hard stick. The *Kumbang* was thus formed. Another material called *Kumsunu* used to be made from the outer cover of the oyster after getting it burnt. The use of *Kumsunu* as a dyeing material was originally practiced by the Lois. This material was used to stimulate the colour. The blue colour (*higop machu*) required an earthen jar with flat mouth in which the ash-water of straw was poured with *Kumsunu* and stirred by a hard stick. It would be kept as such for the whole night and the next day the threads were immersed into the jar. The threads were then dried and again dipped into the same jar to get a clean blue colour. The colour of the thread became black (*amuba*) when the thread was dipped into the liquid of *Kumhi* and again dipped into the liquid of *Kuhi*. The black colour became permanent when the thread was dipped into the liquid of *Kuhi* leaves and teak leaves frequently. This colour was popularly known as *Meitei Kum*. For the green colour (*asangba)* the thread was first dipped into the turmeric liquid. After keeping for a night and the next day it was again dipped into the liquid of *Kum* and thus fine green colour was obtained. The red colour (*angangba*) was obtained from the juice of *Heibung* fruits and dust of *cha* (lac) after putting those together for two or three days. It was then dipped into the boiled liquid of *Ureirom* (*vela orellana*) and *Kairang*. The thread was coloured golden orange (*suna phigi machu*) by mixing the liquid of the seed of *Ureirom* mixed with the straw ash water, and then the thread was dipped into and boiled. For yellow colour (*napu*) the thread was dipped into the liquid of turmeric and then boiled in the liquid of *Unapu*. The thread was coloured maroon (*uchi anganba*) by frequently dipping into the crushed and boiled liquid of *Moijum* leaves. For brown colour (*uchi amuba*) *Kuhi* and turmeric liquids were mixed, then the thread was dipped into it and finally, it was dipped into the liquid of *Kumhi*. The thread was coloured pink (*lei machu*) by preserving it in the ash water of dry *Khuchumpere* (*acanthoraic*) for three days and then dipping in the same jar frequently. These methods of colour making and colouring the threads for weaving clothes is going on in Manipur for a very long time.

The Meitei sub-clans or lineages (*Yumnam*) specialized in the preparation of dyeing colours that were produced from *Kum* (*stratilanthes flaciedifolious*). For example, the *Sapam* and *Ahantham* sub-clans made *angangba* (red), *napu* (yellow), *uchi angangba* (maroon), *uchi amuba* (brown) and other dye-colours. The officials in the plains and the chiefs in the hills supervised the reeling of silk from the cocoon. The Kukis and the Chakpas were excellent weavers of silk. The *Kabo Nupi* or Shan women practiced rearing and reeling of silk from cocoons. They were well known for this work. The silk made by them was of fine quality and more durable. The silk worms were groomed on *Uyung* and *Nongnangkori* leaves. The Loi villages such as Leimaram, Khurkhul, Phayeng, Kameng and Thongjao were well known for silk products. The Meitei women also made and wore various silk clothes. The women of hill societies were also familiar with reeling and weaving. They used to weave clothes by way of wrapping around their waist. They grew cotton plants for reeling threads and weaving their own clothes. If the cotton grown was in excess of own requirement, they sold the raw-cotton to others. Silk and wool were also known to the hill people. They made clothes with elegant designs. The design and colour combination revealed their social and ethnic compositions. The social and political life was also reflected in the colours and designs. The designs were according to the ethnic traditions. One tribe would not imitate the design of another. Cotton was the main staple for weaving clothes.

The reeling, weaving and knitting was the domain of the womenfolk in Manipur. Under the kings of Manipur the *Lallup* system required every male between 16 and 60 years of age to serve the state for ten days out of every forty days in the army, in agricultural field, clearing the river bed, making roads and highways, digging ponds, etc. as would be assigned to them by the officials on behalf of the king. Besides, they had also to do the agricultural and other works for their own families. Therefore, the household work, including the reeling and weaving, were left for the women. As a matter of fact, the weaving is a common hobby to all the women of Manipur, both in hills and plains. Beginning from the planting of seeds, nursing the plants and cropping to the reeling and dyeing of thread and weaving, it was traditionally the job of the women and they took pride in the work. The proficiency in weaving was considered an important qualification for the brides. A traditional social institution, called *Shinaipham Kaba*, played an important role in inducing the young girls to weaving. This institution required the young girls to meet each other before going to bed every night. The venue would be one of the houses in the locality by rotation. In that gathering they not only practiced reeling and weaving but also learnt from the elder women the moral lessons and social usages to be maintained after marriage. The chiefs patronized the institution in early times and non-participation by young girls was punishable.[27] Evidently, the tradition of handing down the knowledge of weaving and textile, like other customary practices, from generation to generation was institutionalized in Meitei society and this explains how the indigenous knowledge survived the stresses and strains of modernity.

Settlement Pattern

Archaeological reports indicate that the settlements grew rapidly in the Manipur valley after water was gradually drained out from the marshes in early times. The lands were reclaimed for agriculture and habitation. The material remains suggest that the Chakpa settlements were the earliest and this fact is corroborated by the extant chronicles. The structural remains at Kangla do not yield any major structure for the earlier periods with the exception of the citadel area which is revered by the people of Manipur even today. The shrines, channels, brick-platforms indicate the existence of a seat of power. This Kangla area seems to have witnessed remarkable human activities, especially during the rule of King Khagemba, when the Imphal river was made to pass through Kangla and several other channels were also dug up.[28] After Pakhangba's death the place was already converted into a shrine, although it remained a seat of political authority. The habitations in the valley shifted from time to time, but Kangla remained the epicenter of the political and social life in Manipur throughout the historical period. In early times a large number of tribal groups seem to have intermingled to define an area of habitation which is identified as 'Manipur' today. Thus, from sociological point of view, the conglomeration of a large number of ethnic groups led to the emergence of an indigenous or autochthonous cultural tradition, which provided a strong base for future acculturation. The kings played the major roles in the settlement of the various ethnic groups in different areas in the valley. This is clearly borne out by the legends, the notions of the people about their past, the local chronicles and the writings of the British officials and authors. For instance, the manuscript *Kangla Houba* informs that for the construction of the palace in Kangla the wooden pillars were brought by the chiefs of different ethnic communities from their respective localities, including the hills. Each tribe or community prepared a special or unique type of wooden pillar. It is stated that the main pillar of Kangla was made from the wood of *Haiyukhok* tree which is found in the Koubru hills. The pillar opposite to the main pillar was made from the wood of *Chingthang Upan* available in the Chingkhei hills. The wood for the pillar next to the main pillar was brought from Wangbren hills. The wood for its opposite pillar was made of *Tumitla* tree brought from Pishum hills. The next pillar was made from the wood of *Taimeran* tree brought from Langing Ching and the next one, opposite to this pillar, was made of the wood brought from Chingthang. *Ukhoten* was the name of another pillar brought from Heibok hills. *Sanayumbi,* another pillar, was brought from Thanging hills. The four pillars for the four directions were provided by the four *panas*, namely, *Ahallup*, *Naharup, Khabam* and *Laipham*. Later on, these *panas* were renamed as *Leikais-Khwai, Yaiskul, Khurai* and *Wangkhei* respectively. *Kangla*, which was the name of a beam, was brought from Khebuching. *Khangen*, another beam, was collected from Langol hills. *Ura-Umdang* (*Kanchi*), which was a typical bamboo, was collected from Thanga Karam. *Charot* was obtained from Langmaijing hills for thatch roofing. *Paya* (bamboo ribon) was obtained from Wabagai. The chiefs of the various *Leikais* (localities) were made responsible for the collection of different kinds of wood and other building materials.[29]

It may be conjectured that the arrangement for construction of the Kangla palace from woods and other construction materials brought from different places was an attempt to integrate and consolidate the influence of the kings over the people living in different parts of the valley as well as in the hills. The contributions to the construction of the royal palace might have symbolized the allegiance of the ethnic groups within the territory to the Meitei king as the supreme authority in the land. The settlement pattern in the various divisions of the state was singular in the sense that the particular ethnic groups lived in the particular localities. On the other hand, Kangla was the capital of all divisions and all the communities. Therefore, all the ethnic communities should share their wealth with the state with a sense of fealty. This concept worked very well in keeping the ethnic and cultural groups in the kingdom together. Kangla thus developed as a common heritage of all the groups in a polyglot structure. However, it was integration at the apex plane, whereas at the societal level the kingdom was multi-ethnic and multi-cultural. The coming together of the large number of ethnic communities under one umbrella called the 'Meitei' led to the generation of integrative forces which impelled the people of smaller social groups to spontaneously merge and coalesce with the dominant one. In the meantime, the formation of the Meitei society comprising of seven clans had already made it a 'model' for all other groups within the territory that later on spontaneously came to be identified as Manipuris. It is difficult to observe to what extent the pan-Indian Brahmanical model of integration had influenced the social processes in Manipur at the early points of time, but it is evident that some importance was given to the number 'seven' as in the mainland of the Indian subcontinent, like the emergence and growth of communities into seven groups or seven folds and the significance of the concepts like *Saptarishi, Sapta-matrika, Sapta Sindhu, Saptapadi, Saptanga, Saptakula, Saptadvara*, etc. It is possible that these ideas had filtered down to the groups living in the distant frontiers like Manipur as well and thus a tradition grew in which the innumerable tribes or ethnic groups living in the Manipur valley slowly and gradually came together to form a larger society of the seven constituents. Although the number of ethnic groups in the Manipur valley was initially more than seven, all the identities were re-grouped into seven *salais* or principal clans and the number of clans has remained to be only 'seven' till these days. The historical evidence clearly indicate the existence of various ethnic groups and lineages in the valley, namely, Angom, Luwang, Ningthouja, Khaba, Nganba, Leisangthem, Chenglei, Haorok Konthoug, Manting Mara, Lokha, Haokha, Chakpa, Huirem, Khunjan, Moirang, Thanga, Kambong, Urok, Usai, Haokha, Loukha, etc. But when the *salai* or clan identity emerged the number became limited to seven, namely, Ningthouja (Mangang), Angom, Luwang, Khaba-Nganba, Sarang Leishangthem,[#] Khuman and Moirang. The development in the valley probably impacted the communities in the hills of Manipur. Thus, the presence of seven is noticed even in case of the hill people, as given in Table II.

It is generally believed all over Manipur that all the clans of different ethnic communities originated from seven male progenitors and the same number of women progenitors. The genetic mapping of all the indigenous people of Manipur may establish the truth or otherwise of this belief system. However, from the functional point of view this myth played wonder in bringing about the homogeneity among the people living in Manipur towards the formation of the larger Manipuri society. The Meiteis maintained their dominance over other groups politically, but at the social level all the ethnic groups maintained their own identities. The geographical

Table II

Seven Tribes and Seven Branches or Clans

Tribe	*1*	*2*	*3*	*4*	*5*	*6*	*7*
Tang-khul	Khudang	Khopudang	Sithu-dang	Chou-dang	King-dang	Duidang	Sada-ng
Maring	Sampen	Raj	Dalla	Ding-thoi	Ching-dur	Thanga-nga	Thoi-tak
Kabui	Kammei	Gangmei	Long-mei	Maring-mei	Golmei	Phaomei	Palmei
Moyon	Nungru	Bungouhei	Sirbum	Ruin	Chiru	Segong	Song-sher
Mon-shang	Langrom	Cham	Turip	Nangaran	Nungchin	Hungam	Khartur
Anal	Nurchal	Pasen	Masem	Chanting	Runval	Hrangung	Yasha
Koireng	Miple	Leison	Sonthu	Yeite	Tumtin	Walbe	Tonti

Source: W. Ibohal Singh, *The History of Manipur*, Imphal, 1986, p. 609.

distribution of the settlements enabled the preservation of the ethnic identity.

Organization of Settlements

The settlements in the Maniur valley grew around the homestead or *Ingkhol* which was originally occupied or assigned to a family. A family lived in a house (*Yum / Yumjao*) built in an *Ingkhol*. A number of houses made a *Kollup*. When the son begot a child, a new house was built inside the *Ingkhol* of the parents. This meant the birth of a new family. Likewise, a new house was built for each of the other sons whenever the need arose. This continuous process accommodated the growth and expansion of the original families as well as the settlers. A number of *Kollups* made a *Leikai* which was formed when different *Kollups* emerged in the same locality. A road, called *Leirak Konshang*, connected all the *Konthong* (gates) of the houses. Thus the *Leikais* were formed along the *Leirak Konshang*. At the next stage, a number of *Leikais* made a *Khul* or village and a number of *Khuls* or villages made an area called *Pana* which was developed as an administrative district when the Meitei state came into existence. A number of *Panas* thereafter made a segmentary state with considerable local autonomy and a small bureaucracy for its governance. The Meitei kings played a great role in the formation of different types of villages and determining their structure in different areas and thereby established a hierarchic relationship between the different types of villages within different *Panas*. In terms of spatial location of different categories of villages the Manipur valley may be divided into three major zones, namely, the northern fertile plains, the marshy low land and the peripheral foothill zones, depending on both physical and social ecology. The villagers within a zone enjoyed equal status, and the different zones were knitted together in a hierarchical order. However, in terms of the fertility of soil, productivity and professional practicability of the inhabitants the status of the zones substantially differed from each other.

Immigrations and Settlements

The immigrations and settlements in the Manipur valley over a long period of time led to the emergence of the larger Meitei society through a process of assimilation and absorption of the immigrants into the Meitei social fold. The original Meitei society, at least since the time of Pakhangba, had seven clans (*salai*), each of which consisted of a large number of sub-clans (*sagei/yumnak*). The *Sagei Salairol*, an early Meitei text, provides a list of about four hundred and thirty two (432) *sageis* (*yumnaks*) for the traditional seven *salais*.[30] Those are listed in Table III.

Table III

Number of *Yumanks* in Seven Traditional *Salais*

Salai	*Yumnaks*
Ningthouja	116
Angom	47
Chenglei	31
Luwang	57
Khuman	101
Moirang	64
Nganba	16
Total	**432**

Source : *Sagai Salairol*, Manipur State Kala Academy (MSKA), Imphal, 1994.

The number of original *yumnaks* or household lineages in the Meitei society was, therefore, only around 432. The number increased over the years as more people immigrated from the east and west of Manipur and settled in the Manipur valley. The Meitei society accommodated and absorbed these new-comers or immigrants into its own fold. They were admitted to the Meitei society either by creating new *Yumnaks* or by admitting them into the already existing original

Yumnaks. The migration from the east was mostly from Kabo valley (Shan states) and China. The migrants from the west were larger in number. They included the Bishnupriyas, Brahmins and the Muslims. The majority of them were from the adjoining territories of Manipur, viz. *Basa* (Cachar), *Lairikyengbam*, *Takhel* (Tripura), *Tekhao* (Assam), etc. The Bishnupriyas (locally known as *Mayang Kalisa*), were first settled at Mayang Yumpham (now known as Mayang Imphal). Later on, they spread due to various areas in the valley, such as Khangabok, Ningthoukhong, Heirok, etc.[31]

The local sources testify the existence of regular routes which connected Imphal with Chasad in Burma, Silchar in Barak valley and Kohima in Naga hills. Manipur was indeed the gateway for the Southeast Asian people to the Indian mainland. These routes facilitated immigrations from all directions and the settlement of the immigrants in Manipur.[32] When Poireiton came to Manipur (possibly from the east) with a large number of his followers, each of the followers was assigned specific duties. They brought with them food items, household and weaving materials and different types of paddy and vegetable seeds. The weavers, blacksmiths and various other craftsmen were included in their ranks.[33] On his way to Manipur Poireiton had given names to a number of places which are now said to be identifiable in the Kabo (Kabaw) valley, e.g., *Thengya, Kiyang, Chagourok, Okthakland, Tangsa, Tomphang, Haiku, Tongsa, Mukusa, Mangsa, Tingkat Sakhuthok, Munoi, Hairou, Sungsang, Koktong, Chupli, Bosa, Maru, Pansa, Haimu, Loutangkhul, Sarel Tekhaorei, Thiongba, Maram, Agam*, etc.[34] These place names were given for certain reasons. For instance, in case of *Thengya* he tried to drive away the evil spirit for which the place was supposedly notorious. '*Kiyang*' is the corrupted form of '*Thengya*'. While passing through the hills and plains, Poireiton interacted with the local people in various places. The people of Kabo presented him with a roll of plantain leaf. That place is called *Tongsa*, as the plantain leaf was known as *Tong*. It is believed that a number of cultural traits and food materials which are still extant in the Manipuri society were gathered by Poireiton on his way. Some scholars maintain that Poireiton and his followers were subsequently absorbed in the Meitei clans.[35]

The *Nongpok Haram*, a local chronicle, mentions that large number of people immigrated to Manipur from Yunan, Burma (Myanmar) and the Shan states.[36] There was also blood relationship between Shan king Chaopha Khikhompa and the Meitei king Kiyamba of the fifteenth century AD, and the foundation stone for the Koumudo Pegoda temple was laid by a Manipuri Brahmin, named Swamy Chibananda.[37] Sir Johnstone mentioned that the Chinese captives taught the art of brick making to the Manipuris, although they had initially been made captives by the Meitei king Khagemba who had defeated their king Chaopha Hongdei in 1520 AD. They were settled at a place called Suisha Kameng in Imphal.[38] However, like all other immigrant groups in the Manipur valley those Chinese settlers also seem to have been assimilated in the Meitei society.

Most of the migrated groups of Shans are recorded in Meitei genealogies. For example, in the genealogy of the *Chengsubam*, a sub-clan or *sagei*, it is mentioned that *"Chengsubam di Kengsen Leibaktagine"*(i.e. the *Chengsubam* sub-clan came from the land of Kengsen). The word *Kengsen* means a place of that name in the erstwhile Shan state.[39] Moreover, the people from the east, including the Shans, who settled in different parts of Manipur during the reigns of the early Meitei kings are mentioned as *Nongpok Haram*. These migrations took place since the time of King Naothingkhong (663-763 AD). All those who migrated were assimilated in various Meitei *Yumnaks*. Some of the immigrants came with their wives, while others were allowed to marry local girls.[40]

Similarly, the people who migrated from the west (*Nongchup Haram*) were also integrated in the Meitei society through the same process of assimilation and absorption. It is stated that people started coming to Manipur from the west, like Cachar, Tripura and Assam, since the reign of King Thawanthaba (1195-1230 AD). The Meitei society accommodated them either by enlisting them in one of the original *Yumnaks/Sageis* (lineages) or by introducing new ones. A large number of families came along the entourage of Chengurembi, a princess from the west (Bengal), who was married to Kwakpa Thawanthaba (14th century AD). These people were also adjusted in the society when new *salai* names were given to them. The Brahmins, who are now known as *Meitei Bamon*, maintained their identity. However, they were also given the *Yumnaks*, e.g. *Kakchingtabam, Laipubam, Phurailatpam*, etc. No compact area or *Piba* was given to the Brahmins. Their *sagei* (surname) are quite different from those of the other groups. It is also said that some *Yumnaks* were given to them on the basis of their ancestral home, or the place of first settlement in Manipur, or their occupation. The descendants of a Brahmin whose original surname or title was *Bachaspati* belong to the *Bachaspatimayum*. The Brahmin who settled first at the place named *Kakching* got the name of his lineage from that place (viz. *Kakchingtabam*). The descendants of Laipubam, who arrived in Manipur during the reign of King Charairongba (1697-1709 AD) with a statue of Lord Jagannath, got the lineage name *Phurailatpam*. However, the Brahmins were allowed to retain their respective *Gotras*. There are lineages like *Luwang-In-ba, Ningthouja-In-ba*, etc. which can be interpreted to suggest that the migrated person might have resided in the locality of a particular clan, like Luwang, Ningthouja, etc. The Brahmins came to Manipur mostly from Gauda in Bengal, but there were some who came from Orissa, Gujarat and Nepal. In fact, only one from Nepal is mentioned in the *Bamon Khunthoklon*. They came with their families and the idols of the deities, e.g. Lord Krishna. Of them, the sub-clan *Kongrailatpam* settled at Singjamei, *Labuktongbam* at Yumnam Leikai, *Gurumayum* at Brahmapur, *Harimayum* at Imphal Bazar, *Brajamayum* at Thangmeiband, etc. They played a very important role of nucleating in the Meitei society as they became indispensable in every *Leikai* (locality) as priests and preceptors and they gave a boost to the process of social consolidation and state formation in Manipur.[41]

Since of the reign of Garibniwaj, the sons and grandsons of some of the kings married hill tribal and *Mayang* (outsiders) girls. The hill tribes and *Mayangs* were then allowed to serve the deities of the kings and occupy important positions in the state according to their skill. A large number of hill people descended to the plains and got absorbed in different clans and sub clans of the Meiteis in early times. The *Keikoi*, a manuscript, contains some instances. The *Soibam* sub-clan, which settled in Phoijing Chingmei, belonged to the Maring tribe. Similarly, the *Moirangthem* of Langsombi belonged to Kabui Haochong tribe, the *Kollom* and *Akangjam* of Takyel and the *Karam* and *Arambam* of Sagolband belonged to Achep tribe, the *Haobism* of Yurenjam and Thounoujam belonged to Haokei tribe, the *Waribam, Konjengbam,* and *Thoudam* of Khurai belonged to Nongchup tribe, the *Akoijam* of *Thoubal* belonged to Maring tribe, the *Konsam* of Khurai belonged to Kabow tribe, the *Yanglem* of Samurou belonged to the Maring tribe, the *Leitanthem* and *Mangsatabam* of Thoubal belonged to Tangkhul tribe, the *Thongam, Chanam* and *Khogjam* of Thiyam belonged to Chingshang tribe.[42]

The Pangans or the Muslims, who originally migrated from Bengal, were picked up as captives and surrendered soldiers when the Meitei king Khagemba (1597-1652 AD) defeated the kings of Cachar, Tripura and adjoining areas. They mainly came from the districts of Sylhet and Cachar. Basically they are divided into three categories - *Sheikhs, Pathans* and *Syeds*. They were also given the sub-clan status with new surnames, e.g. *Iphams, Urup Mayum, Phumdrei Mayum, Mayang Mayum Anouba, Keinou Mayum, Khulakpam, Khutheibam*, etc. The immigration of the most of these Muslims dates back to 1606 AD. The king asked them to settle down in different localities beyond the Lilong area. Professionally, the Muslims had four principal divisions, viz. soldiers, gardeners, turners and potters, but all of them were zealous agriculturists and they introduced in Manipur the technique of transplanting paddy. The *Nongsamei Puya*, an important manuscript, informs that the most important contribution of the Muslims to Manipur were in transplanting paddy, carrying of *Dolai* (palanquin), growing *Hidak Thakpa* (tobacco), paper making and reinforcing the Meitei army as specialist soldiers and officers. There are instances that the Muslims fought side by side with the Meiteis against the Burmese.[43] There were also stray migrants from the west who contributed to local economy. For instance, one person, named Kandan, who was detained as a trespasser during the reign of Khagemba (1597-1652 AD) had brought with him a machine for crushing sugarcane. Similarly, a grass-cutter, named Deikha Subhak, and a professional burglar named, Lakhi Narayan, were caught for offences by the officials. After serving punishment, they were allowed to remain in Manipur and they became Meiteis in the same process as other immigrants and settlers. The technology and skill that they possessed and shared with others in their adopted home had a lasting impact on the Meitei economy.[44]

It is a common sentiment in Manipur that the immigrants–whether from east or west – immensely contributed to the development of Manipur and that the Meitei culture has been enriched by the traditions and practices that the immigrants brought with them. The immigrants as well as their culture became unidentifiable in course of time as they were completely assimilated in the local milieu. The geographical location of Manipur at the meeting point of two great cultures, namely, Pan-Indian and Southeast Asian, enabled Manipur to enrich itself by receiving peoples, ideas and goods from both ends. The pleasant climate and rich vegetation, fertile land with plenty of lakes, the small size of the local population in the neighbourhood of the hill tribes in early times and the abundant availability of fallow land were inviting to the immigrants who were fascinated by the salubrious climate of the valley and the captive hospitality of the people to happily identify themselves with the land and local culture of Manipur and, in course of time, they spontaneously influenced the formation of a larger Meitei society in the valley through commingling and acculturation.

NOTES & REFERENCES

1. Gangmumei Kamei, *Philosophy of History and Historiography of Manipur*, Manipur University Research Club, Manipur University, Imphal, 1997, p. 21.

**Loiyumba Shilyen/Loiyamba Shinyen*

+*Mashin/Mashil*

2. Napachik is a small hillock which is located at Wangu village in Bishnupur district of Manipur. For details see O. Kumar Singh, *Stone Age Archaeology of Manipur*, Imphal, 1997, p. 66.
3. R. K. Jhalajit, *History of Manipur from 1508-1709*, Imphal, 1999, p.71.
4. B. Kullachandra Sharma & Badr-ud-din (ed), *Meitei Pangal Hourakpham*, Imphal, 1991, p.146. The author is also thankful to Padmashree N. Khelchandra Singh, a renowned Manipuri scholar and historian of Manipur, for the relevant information.
5. For details of the discussion in this section, see Amal Sanasam, "Sociology of Settlement Pattern in Manipur Valley", *The Insight*, Vol. I, No.I, January-June 2006, pp. 71-90. *Sagei Salairol*, Manipur State Kala Academy (MSKA), Imphal, 1994, p. 42.
7. *ibid*, p.35.
8. Mutua Museum, *Jewelleries of Manipur*, Imphal, 1988, pp. 15, 174; L. Ibungohal Singh & N. Khelchandra Singh (ed),

Cheitharol Kumbaba, Manipuri Sahitya Parishad, Imphal, 1967.

9. L. Kunjeswori Devi, "Ancient Discoveries in Sekta, a Village in Manipur", *Proceedings of North East India History Association*, XIIth session, Jagiroad, 1991, pp. 120-23; Ng. Kulachandra (ed.), *Chakpa Khunda Khunthok,* Imphal, 1993, p. 5. The *Chakpa Khunda Khunthok,* which is an old *Puya,* says that the Chakpa people were the earliest settlers in Manipur. The *Cheithrol Kumbaba* and all other historical texts also recorded the Chakpas as one of the pre-Meitei inhabitants of the Manipur valley. They were included among the Lois when the Loi, Chakpa and all other pre-Meitei autochthones of the valley identified themselves as Loi in the wake of the Meitei consolidation. The Chakpas are now the inhabitants of the Loi area as part of the Loi community in Manipur, but they are also scattered all over Northeast India. This Chakpa-Loi group of people has been manufacturing pottery and salt for the whole of Manipur since earliest times as the sources of clay and saline brines are located in the foothill region inhabited by those communities. They are the expert potters and salt-manufacturers.
10. Tribal Museum & Research Centre, *Workshop on Indigenous Pottery of Manipur*, Imphal, December 13-19, 1999, sponsored by Ministry of Human Resource Development, Department of Culture, Govt. of India.
11. R. Brown, *Statistical Account of Manipur*, (London, 1874) Reprint Sanskaran Prakashak, Delhi, 1975, pp. 64-69; T. C. Hudson, *The Meitheis*, (London,1911) Reprint, B. R. Publishing House, Delhi, 1981, pp 33-36.
12. Ancient people all over the world were using bamboo as a material for different kinds of products - baskets for storage, houses, palanquins, shields, amulets, etc. The uses of bamboo were many and its applications were varied.
13. Mutua Bahadur , *Cane & Bamboo Crafts of Manipur*, Imphal, 1994, pp. 9, 11.
14. *ibid*, p.13.
15. *ibid*, p. 72.
16. According to *Ningthoukol Seireng* (an old Meitei manuscript), Panthoibi prepared the costumes of the Gods and Goddesses of Manipur for the occasion of *Lai Haraoba* (annual dance festival of Manipur).

17. Kh. Ibungoyaima, *Manipurgi Pisha Lonsa Amasung Hourakpham,* Imphal , 1997, pp. 1-3.
18. *ibid*, p. 1.
19. N. Khelchandra Singh (ed), *Chada Lahui,* Imphal, 1966, p. 1.
20. Kh. Ibungoyaima, *opcit*, p. 2.
21. O. Bhogeshwor Singh (ed.), *Ningthourol Lambuba,* Imphal, 1967, pp. 11-12.
22. L. Ibungohal Singh & N. Khelchandra Singh (ed.), *op.cit*, p.8. Also see K. Sobita Devi, *Traditional Dress of the Meiteis,* Imphal, 1998, p.5.
23. Kh. Ibungoyaima, *op.cit*, p.6.
24. L. Ibungohal Singh & N. Khelchandra Singh, *op.cit*, p.9.
25. K. Sobita Devi, *op.cit*, p. 9.
26. Kh. Ibungoyaima, *op.cit*, p. 8.
27. *ibid*; N. Khelchandra Singh, *Manipuri to Manipuri & English Dictionary*, Imphal, 1964, p.95. The information for the section on Textiles, Costumes and Colours were also collected by the author during field work among the traditional weavers and dyers.

28 L.Ibungohal Singh & N. Khelchandra Singh (ed.), *op.cit*, p. 38.

29. N. Khelchandra Singh, *Ariba Manipuri Shahityagi Itihas,* 3rd edition, Imphal, 2004. P. 69.

\# Sarang Leishangthem/Chenglei

30. MSKA, *op.cit*, p.p. 28-43.
31. *Nongpok Haram* (manuscript) preserved in Archival Library, Uripok Ningthoukhongjam Leikai, Imphal.
32. N. Khelchandra Singh, *op.cit*, pp. 3-4.
33. M. Chandra Singh (ed.), *Poireiton Khunthok,* Imphal, 1995, pp. 8 –9.
34. *ibid*, pp. 24-32.
35. *Luwanglon Khongun* (manuscript) in custody of Ch. Hemchandra Singh of Uripok Naoremthong, Imphal.
36. *Sorarel Machana Khungumba* (manuscript) preserved in Archival Library, Uripok Ningthoukhongjam Leikai, Imphal.
37. D.G. E Hall, *History of Southeast Asia,* London, 1968, pp. 384-385.

38. James Johnstone, *My Experience in Manipur and Naga Hills*, London, 1896, p. 80.

39. *Chengsubam Shageigi Puya* (manuscript) in custody of Ch. Hemchandra Singh of Uripok Naoremthong, Imphal.

40. Atombapu Sharma, *Manipuri Itihas*, Imphal, 1942, pp. 303-306.

41. *Chingurembi Naoun* (manuscript) in custody of Ch. Hemchandra Singh of Uripok Naoremthong, Imphal.

42. *Keikoi* (manuscript) preserved in Archival Library, Uripok Ningthoukhongjam Leikai, Imphal.

43. *Nongsame* (manuscript) in custody of B. Kullachandra Sharma of Bamon Leikai, Imphal.

44. These facts were gathered by the author during field study in various places in Manipur.

7

Indigenous Weaving Technology of Manipur

L. Basanti Devi

The ancient kingdom of Manipur was a country encircled by nine blue hill ranges and the centre of the kingdom was ornamented by the enchantingly green valley with its sparkling lakes and glittering rivers. The hills were inhabited by the fascinating tribes belonging to the Naga, Kuki and other allied extractions, while the central valley was inhabited by the Meiteis, the Manipuri Muslims, the Mayangs and the Lois. Manipur is endowed with rich cultural traditions and a glorious civilization. The written history of Manipur dates back from the time of Nongda Lairen Pakhangba, the first historical king of Manipur, who is said to have ascended the throne in 33 AD. It passed under British colonial rule following the Anglo-Manipur War of 1891 AD.[1]

Amongst its many splendoured human achievements, Manipur is known to be a land of handicrafts since early times. Though metal technology might not have been highly developed in Manipur, the state could claim a proud heritage in handloom. It was particularly in the field of weaving and related arts like dyeing, printing and embroidery that

Manipur excelled amongst all her neighbours. The history of weaving in Manipur dated back to the times immemorial and it is associated with the mythical accounts of the creation of the universe. The *Leinunglon*,[2] an unpublished Meitei *Puya*, mentions that the supreme god *Asheeba* created *lang* (thread) from the cobwebs which were produced out of himself. The supreme goddess *Leimarel* then started the art of weaving with it and the art was then transmitted to the humankind as one of the basic necessities of life. During the *Lai-Haraoba* dances performed by the priestess and her followers one could see the depiction of the cultivation of land and the sowing of the cotton seeds, plucking the cotton ginning, carding the spinning, weaving of cloths, cutting it and, finally, dedicating the same to gods and goddess for the prosperity and well being of the people and the land. This particular dance is called *Phisha Jagoi* (dance of weaving).[3] It is also stated that the goddess *Panthoibi* first learnt the art of weaving by imitating the pattern of a spider's web.[4]

Originally, the raw materials used for weaving were cotton and silk yarn. The woolen yarn, however, was not known in ancient days. In *Leinunglon*, it is also mentioned that *Tamitmu*, one of the seven primeval celestial ancestresses of the Meiteis, produced cotton for manufacturing cloths. For this act of first production of cotton, *Tamitmu* is known till these days as the goddess of cotton in the Manipuri society. Another source of information is *Lashing Meihoubarol* which recorded that *Ema Leimarel* (Mother Goddess/Supreme Goddess) produced cotton yarn by pulling out fibres from the cotton ball and by rolling the fibres on the thigh with the palm of her right hand while her left hand pulled the cotton ball away, thereby twisting the cotton fibre-strands into twisted yarns.[5] In both plains and hills of Manipur, cotton was widely grown. There were three types of cotton available and used in Manipur. These are (i) white cotton, (ii) reddish cotton and (iii) tree cotton.[6] In later periods, cotton began to be imported into Manipur from other states as the demand for the raw-material increased due to population growth and commercialization of the products. Now-a-days, most of the cotton cultivated lands have been turned into agricultural lands for cultivation of paddy.

The silk industry also developed in Manipur from very early times. The variety of mulberry silk worm, known as *Leimatil* (queen's worm) in Manipur, was discovered by Nongmainu Ahongbi, the Queen of King Khuyoi Tompok, from the graveyard of her deceased daughter. The village, where silk worm rearing was first done professionally, is still known as Leimaram. Sir George Watt, an authority on the history of silk industry, was of the opinion that silk industry originated in Manipur. He further added that Manipur was the home of the silk worm, and that the real mulberry silk insects originated in Manipur and it went from there to China.[7] T. C. Hudson also observed that "Manipur was the real home of silk worm, the real mulberry silk insects originated in Manipur."[8] The *Pakhangba Phambal*, an old Manipuri text, recorded that at the time of the coronation of King Nongda Lairen Pakhangba, who ruled in 33 AD as the first historical king of Manipur, his queen Laisna wore silk cloths called *kabrang** *Kanak* and *kabrang khaon*.[9] This tradition of wearing silken robes by the queens at the time of coronation ceremonies continued throughout the monarchial history of Manipur. The silk cloths were also produced for offering to the deities.[10]

In early times, the weaving was a compulsory occupation for the womenfolk in the Manipuri society. There is a reserved room, called *Ningolka* (daughter's room), in the traditional Meitei houses. The unmarried girls of the locality, with their items of weaving like spinning wheel and thread (*Tareng* and *Lang*), used to assemble in that room and perform the work of spinning till late night and engaged themselves in a sort of competition for bringing out the best product. This tradition was known as *Shinaipham Kaba* (going to work). This was done on a rotational basis, from one house to another. The *Shinaipham* is a social institution for women for building their domestic careers. If a woman occasionally misbehaved or used some unsocial etiquette, she would be given the bad name of one who did not attend the *Shinaipham*.[11] The importance of weaving in the life of a Manipuri woman can be observed from several ritual practices. Thus, at the time of the marriage of a girl the different items of weaving, such as *Khwang Iyong* (loin loom), *Pang Iyong* (throw shuttle), etc., were some of the essential items of dowry. In case of the Meiteis who were settled in Cachar, a woman would stand in front of the bride with a *Tareng* (spinning wheel) when she goes to her husband's house to remind her of the compulsory duty of the women. In the Kwatha village of Manipur, when a baby girl is born, on the day of the *Ipan Thaba* ceremony (*swasti puja* performed on the sixth day of the birth of a baby) a *Phisha tem* is worshipped.[12] This *Phisha tem* is a sword-like wooden instrument which is used in the loin loom.

The process of making quality yarns from cotton includes different stages, such as ginning, carding, rolling, spinning, winding, etc. The process has been developed by the artisans themselves over the generations through practices and without any textual guidance or importation of ideas. It is indeed a fine example of indigenous knowledge developed in the land of Manipur, which have been improved upon and continuously refined over the ages to suit the expanding requirements and changing taste of the users. The age old methods and practices of the weaving community have been continuing in Manipur till these days without interventions and hindrances.[13]

Ginning

The ginning is done by a wooden machine, called *Kaplreng*. By this process the seeds are removed from the cotton and then dried in the Sun.

Carding

The dried cotton is put inside a basket, called *Lashing Kappon*. An instrument known as *Huitri* made of bamboo is used for straightening the fibre of the cotton. The loosen cotton fibres are straightened by this method.

Rolling

The straightened cotton is taken out and spread on a wooden flat stool. Then a stick called *Long-gom*, measuring about a palm's length, is placed in the centre of the stool with the hand pressing on it. The cotton is thus rolled and then the stick is removed. This is called *Moithap thaba* (rolling the cotton).

Spinning

The spinning is conducted with the help of a tool, called *Tareng*. This is done by the right hand against the thigh. A small piece of stick is attached and the rolled cotton is inserted to the stick which is then held high with the right hand. Letting the spindle to hung below, the cotton is spun with the right hand against the thigh. This is said to be the traditional way of spinning in Manipur. However, *Tareng* (spinning wheel) and *Tarengy* or spindle seems to have been developed in the later periods for spinning the thread.

Winding

The winding is done by making the thread to hang so that it can be transferred to the *Langchak* (bobbin). In working out this process, the tools called *Tawot* and *Tamang* are used.

In case of the Mulbery silk, the Meitei women reel the Mulbery silk thread from the mulberry cocoons. In the process of reeling the silk thread different types of indigenously developed tools and instruments are used, namely, *Yakabi* (split bamboo), *Chegap* (long bamboo), *utong* (smooth bamboo), and *Tamang* (twisting implement). The work of reeling is called *Khere Chingba*.

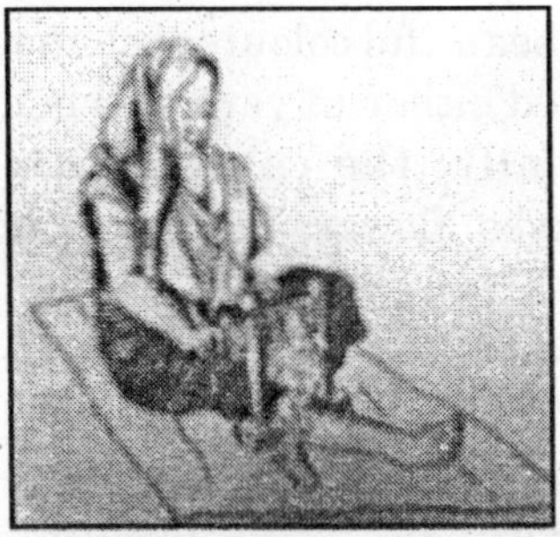

1. Indigenous Process of Ginning

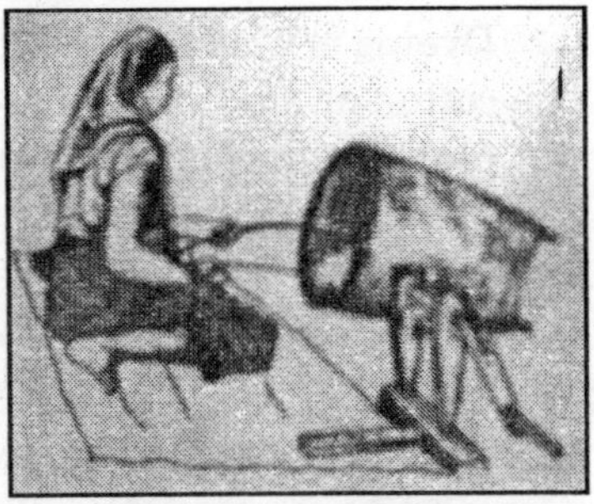

2. Carding in traditional way

3. Cotton Rolling

4. Cotton spinning in traditional way

5. Silk twisting

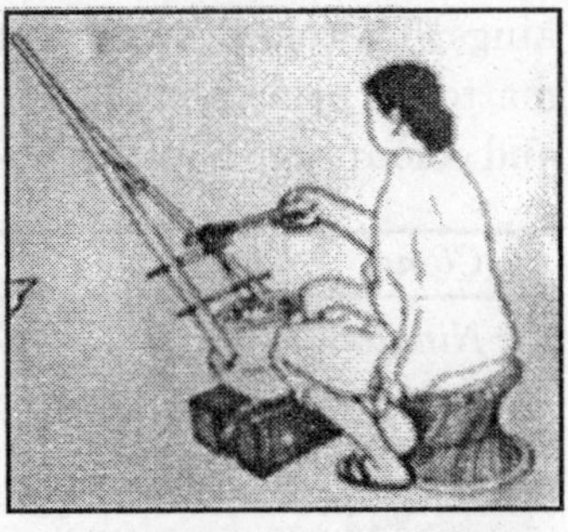

6. Traditional mulbery reeling by using *Khere*

Source : Mutua Bahadur, *Traditional Textiles of Manipur*, Imphal, 1997.

Dyeing is used for producing beautiful colours of cloths. The cotton or silk threads are dyed either in yarn or when the cloth is woven. Traditionally, the colours were manufactured from the plant leaves, flowers and barks of trees, namely,[14]

Khuchum Pere	-	*Acanthaceae* (Bot)
Kairang	-	*symplocos Racemosa* (Bot), a mordant
Kum	-	*strabilathes – Flaciedifolius*
Ureirom	-	*Bixa Orellana* (Latin)
Kushum Lei	-	*Carathamus Jinetorian* (Bot)
Kuhi	-	*Castamopsis PP* (Bot)
Yaingang	-	Turmaric

The popular colours prepared in the traditional way are blue, black, yellow, reddish black, brown, fawn, rhodium, etc. The use of chemical dye began in Manipur only around 1905. However, the indigenous method of preparing colours has not yet lost its popularity. In fact, the colours signify the traditional seven clans (*Salai*) of the Meiteis and the four *Pana* or administrative divisions of Manipur under the Meitei kings. Therefore, the traditional colours are preferred as a matter of pride and identity of people. The clans, divisions and colours are as follows :–[15]

Clans		*Colours*
Ningthouja	-	Red
Angom	-	White
Luwang	-	Blue
Khuman	-	Black
Moirang	-	Yellow with red strips
Khaba-nganba	-	Green
Sarang Leishangthem	-	Brown

Pana		*Colour*
Laipham Pana	-	Red
Khabam Pana	-	Green
Ahallup Pana	-	White
Naharup Pana	-	Yellow

The sources suggest that in the early times Manipur was self-sufficient in the essential materials for weaving and colouring. These materials were available through the initiative of the kings from different parts of the hills and the valley of Manipur. As for instances, *Khuhi* was available from Andro, silk from Sekmai, cotton from Tangkhul village, *Huitri* from Chothe village, *Kumna* from Maring village, etc.[16] The sources also inform that there were three types of looms in early Manipur, namely, loin loom (*kwang-Iyong*), throw-shuttle (*Pang-Iyong*) and the fly shuttle (*Pangandem*). The existence of loin loom can be dated before the Christian era as Panthoibi is said to have first began to weave by loin loom.[17] The loin loom weaving was confined to the womenfolk in Manipur, both in hills and plains. It was in all probability an indigenously invented mechanism.[18] The *Pang-Iyong* (throw shuttle-loom) became more popular in the modern period with improvisations in the throw shuttle and better production was facilitated by modernization of the loom. It enabled the weaving of cloth of greater length and breadth with different designs. The throw shuttle loom in its present form was introduced in Manipur after 1920 by a carpenter named Ch. Yaimabi Singh from the village called Moirangkhom.[19]

According to the customary code of dress culture the traditional and habitual dresses of the Meiteis can be divided into the following categories :[20]

a) King's costume
b) Queen's costume
c) Ordinary dress
d) Visiting dress
e) War dress
f) Occasional dress
g) Religions dress

Besides the above mentioned dresses or cloths, several other types of cloths were also prevalent. Those included the dress called *Manaphi* (i.e. cloth for reward). The *Manaphi* used to be awarded to the person who did a heroic deed for the king or for the state. Although the art of weaving was generally confined to the womenfolk, these special varieties of cloths were woven by the menfolk. The use of the silk cloths was customarily reserved for the aristocracy and the royal family. The commoners normally wore only cotton cloths. Different designs were used in weaving, namely, *Namthang Khulak, Kamen Chatpa, Sarongphi, Ningkham Shamjin, Hija Mayek.*[21]

It is historically accepted that the art of weaving had developed in Manipur alongside the establishment of the royal weaving institutions. The names of the royal head weavers, such as Laikokshu of the time of King Khui Tompok (154-264 AD), Ako in the reign of Naophnagba (428-516 AD) and Roso in the reign of Loiyumba (1074-1112 AD), are mentioned in the sources.[22] The reign of Loiyumba is particularly remarkable for the development of textile culture in Manipur. The *Loiyumba Shinyen* (*Shinyen* = distribution of labour), the royal edict of Manipur, clearly shows the development of textile industries in Manipur. King Loiyumba+ divided the weavers and dyers in the separate categories with their appropriate surnames or family names. The assignment of the weaving of cloths of specific varieties to the particular surnames (sub-clans) had already been in practice in the earlier days. The royal dispensation of Loiyumba had only formalized the assignments for the posterity. However, the historic *Shinyen* of the king projected the possibility of a well organized economy of the state. It also seems that the agrarian economy of the Meitei state was supplemented by the growing handicraft and handloom industries.[23] The large variety of the cloths and the dresses, the weaving of which was formally assigned to the equally large number of families,[24] is an indication of the social and political stability and economic prosperity of the state.

Surnames	*Types of cloths (phi)*
Thingucham	*Mungphi*
Ningthoujam	*Chinphi*
Lairellakpam	*Laiphi*
Kaswam	*Wana katang phi*
Chakpa Thiyam	*Laiphi Tonkap*
Chakpa Lampam	*Phiren*
Kongpacham	*Langtomphi*
Thongkabam	*Yarongphi*
Khumallabam	*Chamiphi*
Haokhom	*Tongkap phi*
Laikhuram	*Sarongphi*
Salchiram	*Leirumphi*
Wahengbam	*Doleikup phi*
Kabacham	*Doloi Thanaba phi*
Apucham	*Pheiroiphi*
Haodeijam	*Heikoiphi*
Thodingjam	*Singkhalphi*
Thongpam	*Laiyek phi*
Kongbam	*Purum phi*
Chingakhanpam	*Phakangphi*
Thoudam	*Taraophi*
Thinpam	*Pumthit Phi*
Taibangcham	*Phimu yekpa phi*
Yumlempam	*Nongphi*
Wokthiyambam	*Khunung Musum phi*
Khoirisumbam	*Khunung Chumkhan phi*
Yumnak Shangbam	*Chingkhong phi*
Khoisnam	*Phimu Lanphi*
Singkhangbam	*Khunung Mathang phi*
Chingkhamwapam	*Korou phi Phingang*
Wangpacham	*Shangmu Langmu phi*
Thangkangshapam	*Thangli Sakara*
Ahongshangpam	*Khutsutri Khongli lonlo* (embroidery)

The last mentioned surname or lineage (*yumnaks*), namely, *Ahongshangpam,* as it is apparent from the above, was specifically allotted the work of embroidery, besides, weaving the specialized type of cloth, *Khutsutri Khongli lonlo.* It brings home the fact that, like weaving, the embroidery had also become popular in Manipur as early as in the twelfth century AD when the royal edict, called *Loiyumba Shinyen,* was actually issued. The embroidery in Manipur must also have been based on indigenously developed knowledge of the techniques and equipments. However, like weaving and embroidery, King Loiyumba's dispensation distributed the task of dyeing to different surnames or families.[25]

Surnames	*Colour of the yarn to be dyed*
Akangkham	*Leirel Khoipaklei* (light pink)
Chingkhwampam	*Chingshang Muyumlei* (maroon)
Yiroibam	*Ureirom Makong Meiri* (saffron, dark flam red)
Khumalthenpam	*Higok Nanou lei* (light blue)
Khumukcham	*Kumlang Kumpal lei* (black)
Yipushangbam	*Chingya Napu Lei, Taoching lei* (grey, yellow, green, deep maroon)
Washiyampam	*Wana katang Namba sanglen Yaichu lei* (greenish red shade, produced by mixing green and red)

The institutionalization of the craft is also borne out by the fact that the textiles of Manipur were associated with the social and ritualistic purposes from the very remote times. It played a significant role in the economic life of the people. The surplus productions of the families were put on sale, which gave a fillip to the market economy. The duty from trade and commerce was also one of the important sources of income for the state. The products were exported from Manipur on a large scale to the neighbouring areas, especially to Cachar.[26]

The export items included *Mussoom phi*, Mosquito curtain, *Saloon Phanek*, *Hekok Phanek*, *Lai Phanek*, *Ormit Khess*, bed sheet, *Murning phi*, *Chader thin*, *Khoomnung phurit* or coat. The state prohibited export of certain articles, because those either represented status symbols or had ritual values or were intended for presentation to persons for the services rendered to the state. They included *Khamenchatpa* (coloured silk *dhoti*), *Lamthang Khullak* (loced *puggree*), *Ningthou phi* (king's shirt-like garment) and *Lai Chappa* (coloured shirt).[27]

Resume

The available source materials and the living traditions suggest that the weaving technology in Manipur has been an indigenous one. Panthoibi, to whom the origin of weaving is attributed, was a historical personality in Manipur and because of her pioneering contribution to weaving, which became an integral part of the way of life of the people, she was elevated to the status of a divine deity in the belief system of the people. The Spinning, weaving and dyeing were fairly developed in Manipur since time immemorial. It played an important role in the social and economic life of the people of Manipur throughout the ages. The traditional skill of weaving was not only a status symbol for the womenfolk but also an inseparable aspect of the way of life of the indigenous people of Manipur. Later on, the handloom industry further developed with the introduction of fly shuttle and weaving machines. It is one of the largest and the most important cottage industry of the state even today. Both loin loom and handloom have continued side by side till now.

NOTES & REFERENCES

1. For details see Jyotirmoy Roy, *History of Manipur*, Firma K. L. Mukhopadhyay, Calcutta, 1958; Gangmumei Kabui, *History of Manipur*, vol. I, National Publishing House, Delhi, 1991.

2. *Leinunglon*, a Meitei *Puya* (chronicle), manuscript in custody of the family of Late N. Chandrasing, Pandit Khongman, Imphal.
3. M. Chandrasing, *Lai-Haraoba and Ras*, Imphal, 1963, p.64.
4. Kh. Iboyaima, *Manipurgi Phisha Lonsha amasung Hourakpham*, Imphal, 1997, p.1.
5. *Lashing Meihoubarol*, a Meitei *Puya*, manuscript in custody of the family of Late K. Dhono Singh, Keishampat, Imphal.
6. Mutua Bahadur, *Traditional Textile of Manipur*, Imphal, 1997, p.22.
7. P.C. Chaudhury, *History of the Civilization of the People of Assam*, DHAS, Gauhati, 1959, p.353.
8. T.C. Hudson, *The Meitheis*, (London,1908) Reprint Low Price Publications, Delhi, 1989, p. 87.

* *kabrang* = silk.

9. Kh. Yaima, *Pakhangba Phambal*, Imphal, 1967; Kh. Iboyaima, *Manipurgi Phisha Lonsha Amasung Hourakpham*, Imphal, 1997, p.1.
10. K. Sobita Devi, *Traditional Dress of Manipur*, Imphal, 1998, p.3.
11. Irom Mangi, *Yelhoungei Manipurda phi shabagi Lam*, Imphal, 2002, p.70; Kh. Iboyaima, *op.cit.*, Imphal, 1997, pp.1-3.
12. K. Dhono, *Meitei Puya Wari Machang*, Imphal, 1974, p.3; Irom Mangi, *op.cit.*, pp.70-71.
13. The process has been observed by the author during her field work in different areas in Manipur.
14. Information gathered from the knowledgeable people during field work.
15. Information gathered from the knowledgeable people during field work.
16. Irom Mangi, *op.cit.*, p. 63.
17. L. Kunjeswori Devi, "History of Traditional Textile Industry in Manipur", Paper presented at international seminar on Traditional Art in Asia held at Bangkok in February 2010.
18. Mutua Bahadur, *op.cit.*, p. 11.
19. Kh. Iboyaima, *op.cit.*, p. 17.
20. Mutua Bahadur, *Meitei Phizet Leiteng*, Imphal, 1997, p.4.

21. *Ningthou Phishaba*, a Meitei *Puya*, manuscript in custody of N. Khelchandra Singh, Imphal.
22. *Loiyumba Shinyen*, a Meitei *Puya*, manuscript in custody of N. Khelchandra Singh, Imphal. Also see Kh. Chandrashekhar Singh (ed.), *Loiyamba Shinyen*, All Manipur Umanglai Haraoba Committee, Uripok Naoremthong, 1982.

+ Loiyamba

23. *ibid.*
24. *ibid.*
25. *ibid.*
26. L. Ibungohal Singh & N. Khelchandra Singh (ed.), *Cheitharol Kumbaba*, Manipuri Sahitya Parishad, Imphal, 1967.
27. N. Ibobi, *Manipur Administration*, Imphal, 1976, p.159. For further details see L. Basanti Devi, 'A Study of Political History of Manipur from Pakhangba to Khagemba, 33 A.D to 1652 AD.' An unpublished Ph. D. thesis, Manipur University, 1988.

8

Interpreting Slavery in the Meitei State

M. Jitendra Singh

Whether or not 'slavery' existed in some form in the Meitei (Meetei) kingdom or 'early state' in pre-colonial Manipur seems to be a plausible area of academic discourse of the social scientists.[1] Before attempting at any theorization, it may be academically more sound an approach to empirically look into the system of labour mobilization, or the labour service, locally called *Lallup*, that had been historically functioning in Manipur, in light of the definition of 'slavery' given in the *International Encyclopedia of Social Sciences*, which had based its formulation on a generalized perception that in early and simple societies the procurement of slaves depended above all on warfare.[2] In this context, it has to be clearly understood that in pre-colonial Manipur the Meitei kings had ensured the continuous flow of labour service to the king and the state through the *Lallup* system, which was an institutionalized practice and under which all the male commoners (citizens) between the age of 16 and 60 were required to render to the state the compulsory labour service for ten out of every forty days.[3] The *Lallup* system was, therefore, an institutionalized or a legalized practice, which was formally enforced by the state and legalized the issue of a royal edict (*Loiyamba Shinyen*). But this was not the only method of extracting labour service in pre-colonial Manipur. There were several other operational methods by which the rulers and the powerful elites extracted labour service in early Manipur, and of these, the 'warfare' seems to have been the earliest and the most widespread in the sense that it covered all the inhabitants in the territory as well as in its vicinity or neighbourhood which could be targeted for raids and wars, whereas the *Lallup* system covered only the subjects within the Meitei kingdom. Moreover, the *Lallup* system could be introduced by the Meitei kings only after the kingdom had been already established.

The historical records, on the other hand, show that the frequent wars and raids among the Meitei clan-principalities, *viz.*, Mangang (Ningthouja), Luwang, Khuman, Khaba-Aganba, Angom, Chenglei, Moirang, etc., in the valley, and in the adjoining villages in the hills, might be for the extension of the sphere of influence or suzerainty of the chiefs of the principalities over the bordering hill tribal villages, in early times had resulted in the enslavement of the people by the rulers of the clan-principalities. The inter-clanish wars and conflicts were more endemic before the emergence of the clan-principalities when the number of the clans and the ethnic groups in the valley was much more than seven and those were re-grouped into seven principal clans (*salai*) to include within the fold of one clan several other minor clans as sub-clans (*sagei*). Those seven clans with their delimited territories had eventually emerged into clan- principalities or chiefdoms. The Ningthouja chiefs, who proved to be the ablest of all the chiefs of the clans in the later centuries, captured the defeated persons in raids or wars and made them settle in various parts of the valley as 'slaves' of the chiefs. The chiefs of other clans also followed the same method, possibly, to increase the population of the respective principalities and to expand the catchments for the extraction of labour services. The process continued even after the establishment of the kingship under the leadership of the Ningthouja chiefs.[4]

The inter-clanish raids and warfare at the local levels, or outside those connected with the rise of the Meitei state, also often resulted in the enslavement of the war captives. The children captured from the hills were often sold as 'slaves'.[5] Among the Nagas, occasionally, the captives in the raids and battles were made 'slaves' by the captors, although more frequently they were killed for their heads.[6] The number of slaves, or even slave families, might have gone on increasing over the years due to those methods of enslavement. However, the increase in the number of slaves in the later years was surely a result, and not a cause, of the wars and raids. There would be no justification in assuming that they waged wars against each other because they needed slave labour, although the wars and raids seem to have been the initial factor for the rise and growth of slavery in Manipur.

Besides the wars and raids, the economic backwardness of the masses in the region was another important factor for the process of enslavement of th poor, distressed and the marginalized sections of the society in pre-colonial Manipur. In times of general scarcity or individual distress, the poor people sold themselves or their children either temporarily or permanently, for food,[7] for funeral expenses,[8] or for bride price which was prevalent among the Nagas.[9] The hill people, sometimes, sold themselves, but they were sold more frequently by their relatives.[10] We could not come across a single document which gives the names of the sellers and buyers, but it is evident from the report of R. Brown, a British Political Agent in Manipur, that the documents were made when the sale was finalized.[11] It is also evident from other sources that indebtedness often impelled the poor people to serve their creditors as slaves in conformity with the customary practice regarding debt which required that when a sum of money had been borrowed and not retuned within a year, the sum due would become double the amount borrowed.[12] As this was the law of the land, the person in debt continued to be a slave as long as he confessed his inability to repay and agreed to serve the creditor in lieu of the interest on the original debt, or until such time that the debt could be actually repaid.[13] As for example, W. McCulloch, another Political Agent, cited the case of one Asalba who worked for the creditor in lieu of the interest on the money paid to him.[14] In such cases, when the claim of the creditor was not settled and no satisfactory arrangement was made for repayment of the original debt, the family of the debtor also used to be seized and sold.[15] However, a person may serve the creditor as a slave but there would be nothing towards remission of the original amount of money paid to him on credit, because the labour service to the creditor was only against the interest on the original amount of debt, and not against the amount of debt. In other words, the inability to repay the debt would result in perpetual indebtedness and this would occasion the family of the debtor to be seized and sold for the original debt. Sometimes, as among the Kabuis, the persons voluntarily accepted slavery to pay off a debt.[16] Therefore, poverty and indebtedness also seem to have caused slavery in Manipur.

The slavery could also be a punishment for criminal offences. There are some instances that the criminals were made slaves to recover the losses suffered by the innocent victims of the crimes. In case of theft, when the culprit was caught but the stolen goods were not recovered in full, the thief and his family might be seized and sold, unless all the stolen goods were recovered.[17] In adultery cases, when the claims for damage could not be realized, the same punishment as in case of theft would be the result.[18]

The global experience of those who have worked on slavery shows that in any society the actual number of the slaves can hardly be known.[19] However, in case of Manipur, though the number of slaves owned by the private individuals or state officials is not known, there are some records of the number of slaves owned by some of the Meitei kings. The number of slaves of those kings varied from 1,200 to 1,500. These slaves were classified into three categories, namely, (i) *Ayokpa,* (ii) *Tengkul,* and (iii) *Kei.* The *Ayokpas* were allowed to cultivate one *pari* of land each (about two and half acres) and they were required to render '*Lallup*' services. This *Lallup* was an important social institution which played a vital economic role in the Meitei Kingdom. The word '*Lal*' literally means war and '*Lup*' means organization (*Lal* + *Lup* = *Lallup*). Thus the literal meaning of *Lallup* should be the 'organization for war'. Since there was no regular or standing army in the Meitei state in early times, it was the duty of every able-bodied man, who was between the age of 16 and 60, to serve the chief or state as '*Lalmei*' or soldier for ten days out of every forty days. In peace times, the same '*Lalmei*' was engaged in public works. After the organization of the 'Manipur Levy' by Maharaja Gambhir Singh (1826-1834 AD) the *Lallup* became a purely civil organization. Some of the British administrators described the *Lallup* as a system of 'forced labour' on the ground that those who worked in the *Lallup* system were not paid any salary. However, though all the members of the '*Lallup*' had to work for the state without any salary, they were given a plot of agricultural land measuring 2½ acres each for their maintenance in lieu of salary or remuneration. Therefore, the *Lallup* service may be regarded as a tax paid for the land in the form of labour to the king or state. For the *Tengkul* slaves, the chief duty was the gardening. They sometimes collected stones and made vessels of that material for the king. The *Keis,* who numbered about 200 families, cultivated land for the king and pounded rice for the royal household.[20] As T. C. Hudson wrote, "This work of the Keis is not confined to the supply of rice, but they may be said to embrace any work or the supply of any article the Raja chooses."[21] Besides, they also had to do their '*Lallup*' works. During that time, they were mainly employed in making brooms and baskets for use in the king's stables.[22] The other *Keis* were divided into '*Hedakphalba*' and '*Poysangba*'. The '*Hidakphanba*' attended to king's *hooka* and the *Poysangba* spread the cloth for sitting on.[25] The later also took care of the king's property.[23] In the hills, the system of working for the village chiefs by the common villagers closely resembled to that which existed in the valley for the *Keis*, but there it was much less onerous in its nature than in the valley.[24] As in almost all the Asiatic societies before the nineteenth century, in pre-colonial Manipur also the agriculture was of far greater importance than industry. The importance of slaves as primary producers must have mainly concerned agriculture. Therefore, it may be presumed that the wealthy farmers also owned slaves and those slaves were chiefly employed in cultivation. As regards the slaves owned by the individuals, it is indicated by the relevant sources that they were employed mainly in cultivation.[25] These facts lead us to conclude that the slavery was connected with the idea of the compulsory labour and the basis of it was the economic benefit for the ruling and the socially powerful elites.

The careful reading of the available historical data, however, reveals that the slaves in Manipur were on the whole well treated by their masters. They lived in the same house with their masters, ate same food with them, and were like the members of the same family.[26] The slaves did not hesitate to run away when they were ill-treated. The running away of a slave would be socially interpreted as the result of inhuman attitude of the master and, therefore, the possibility was carefully avoided by the slave owners.[27] The slaves in the hills were, perhaps, not so well treated as in the plains, but there were some checks on the ill-treatment of the slaves in the hills also. If the slaves were not satisfied with the conditions, they ran to some other house where the slaves were better treated. The new master made it a point to pay the price of the slave to the previous master, though it may not be in full in all cases.[28] This practice would have had a certain softening influence upon the institution of slavery, since the running away implies some limitation of the absolute power and control of the master over the slaves and provided a mechanism through which the plight could be accepted as legitimate without directly challenging the absoluteness of an owner's power over his slave property. It may also be noted that the slave could not become free simply by running away, because he must find a new master in place of the one who had treated him cruelly and the new master should agree to pay off the dues to the previous master as per customary norms and practices. It was for sometime a practice that when there was a change of the ruler the slaves of those who held offices under the previous ruler were seized and divided among the new ruler and his officials. All these might have caused some hardships to the slaves. Maharaja Chandrakriti, therefore, did not allow the slaves of the preceding regime to be divided among his officers and those slaves were made to work for him alone.[29] This might be an indication that the slaves owned by the kings had considerable freedom or were at least more comfortable than under the individual officers.

The geographical features of Manipur also might have presented a check on the masters' severity towards their slaves as the hills provided the easy recluses to some of the absconding slaves. The slaves in the valley often absconded to the hills, where they concealed themselves in the hill villages. But as they were vulnerable to be apprehended in the hills as well, they usually preferred migrating permanently to the British territory, like the neighbouring Cachar area, where they were at once free.[30] However, this should be seen as the effect of dissatisfaction among the slaves against isolated instances of cruelty or ill-treatment of the slaves by some of the individual masters. It cannot be interpreted as a conscious social opposition to the institution of slavery. There are, of course, some instances of community sentiments against the enslavement of the members of the community by others. Among the Luhupas (Tangkhuls), the idea of slavery was hateful to such a degree that on the occasion of their inability to release their children from the slavery of the Ningthouja kings, they sometimes came down to the plains from the hills, slew the captives and carried off their heads. Since then there had not been any attempt to enslave any Luhupa.[31] However, there is no reason to believe that the reaction of the Luhupas to the institution of slavery or the running away of the slaves caused the abolition of slavery.

The abolition of slavery in Manipur in the colonial period was mainly due to the opposition of the British officers to the persistence of the age old practice. It is indeed a well known fact that the slavery of any form was against the liberal and enlightened progamme of the British administration in the Indian sub-continent. This attitude of the colonial administrators towards slavery did have a significant and consequential impact on the future of the institution in Manipur. Sir James Johnstone, the British Political Agent in Manipur (1877-86), had made a strong remonstrance to the Durbar against the slavery, which, in his opinion, was prevalent in Manipur.[32] The Chief Commissioner of Assam had also initiated a proposal for the abolition of slavery in Manipur before the death of Maharaja Chandrakirti (1850-85) and he repeated the same proposal when Surachandra (1886-90), the son of Chandrakirti, came to the throne in 1886.[33] As a result of all these efforts, an opinion was already formed in the British official circle that the slavery must come to an end in Manipur as elsewhere in British India, Finally, the slavery was formally abolished in Manipur on 29th April,

1892 with the setting up of the 'Native Rule' by the British after the Anglo-Manipuri War of 1891.[34] However, what was actually abolished was only the form of slavery that was prevalent in Manipur for a long period of time.

To conclude, it may not be wrong to observe that the type of slavery in the Meitei state in Manipur was a local variety of slavery which was distinctly different from the classical type that prevailed in the western countries. The slavery has been defined in the classical Roman law as an institution whereby someone is subject to the dominium cf another contrary to his nature.[35] In this view, it shall perhaps be too harsh to name the mild form of the institution as it was found in Manipur as 'slavery'.[36] The slavery in Manipur should also not be confused with the types that worked in Brazil, West Indies, Turkey or Arabia.[37] As observed by the colonial administrators themselves,[38] the slavery of a local variety only seems to have been functioning in the pre-colonial Meitei state.

NOTES & REFERENCES

1. J.B. Bhattacharjee, *State and Wealth: The Early States in Northeast India*, DVS Publishers, Guwahati, 2010, pp. 154-57.
2. *International Encyclopedia of the Social Sciences*, Vol. 13, London/New York, 1972, p.309.
3. For details see M. Jitendra Singh, "Slavery in Pre-British Manipur: A Historical Survey", *Proceedings of North East India History Association*, Vth Session, Aizawl, 1985, pp. 79-84.
4. Nandalal Sharma, *Meitrabak*, Imphal, 1960, p. 25.
5. R. Brown, *Statistical Account of Manipur*, (London, 1874) Reprint Sanskaran Prakashak, Delhi, 1975, p. 42.
6. *ibid*, p. 46.
7. M. Ibungohal Singh & N. Khelchandra Singh (ed.), *Cheitharol Kumbaba*, Manipuri Sahitya Parishad, Imphal, 1967, p. 64.

8. James Johnstone, *My Experience in Manipur and Naga Hills*, (London, 1896) Reprinted B. R. Publishing House, Delhi, 1971, p. 118. Johnstone wrote, "Once a little girl named Nowbee came to me. Her mother sold her to pay her father's funeral expenses".
9. *ibid.* Johnstone again wrote, "For instance a Naga (a very common case), marries a girl of another Naga village, thereby incurring a debt of forty rupees to the father, that being the price of Naga bride. The man not being able to pay, his father-in-law says, 'Sell yourself and pay me'. This is done .....".
10. W. McCulloch, *An Account of the Valley of Munneepore*, (Calcutta, 1859), Reprint Gian Publishing House, Delhi, 1980, p. 24.
11. *ibid.*, p. 30. McCulloch wrote, ".... When a slave is sold, a party other than the seller himself binds as security for the owner to refund the money given in the event of the slave's death within a time agreed on ....".
12. T. C. Hudson, *The Meitheis*, (London, 1911) Reprint, Low Price Publications, Delhi, 1989, p.89.
13. R. Brown, *op.cit.*, p. 91.
14. W. McCulloch, *op.cit.*,p. 24.
15. R. Brown, *op.cit.*
16. *ibid.*, p. 52.
17. *ibid.*, p. 91.
18. *ibid.*
19. *Encyclopedia of the Social Science, op.cit*, p. 14.
20. T.C. Hudson, *op.cit.*, p.64.
21. *ibid.*
22. R. Brown, *op.cit*, p. 14.
23. T.C. Hudson, *op.cit.*, p. 64.
24. *ibid.*, p. 65.
25. *ibid.*
26. R. Brown, *op.cit.*, p. 14.
27. *ibid.*, p. 13.
28. T.C. Hudson, *op.cit.*, p. 64.
29. R. Brown, *op.cit.*, p. 15.

30. *ibid.*, p. 52.
31. W. McCulloch, *op.cit.*, p. 24.
32. R. Brown, *op.cit.*, p. 32.
33. W. McCulloch, *op.cit.*, p. 25; R. Brown, *op.cit.*, p. 31.
34. For details see M. Jitendra Singh, *op.cit.*
35. Quoted in L. Chandramani, *Manipur Itihas*, Imphal, 1970, p.200.
36. W. McCulloch, *op.cit.*, pp. 25, 92.
37. *International Encyclopedia of the Social Sciences*, Vol.13, 1972, London, p. 307.
38. R. Brown, *op.cit.*, p. 91; James Johnstone, *op.cit.*, p. 119.

9

Outlining Pre-Colonial Economy of Manipur

K. Ruhinikumar Sharma & O. Ranjit Singh

The British colonization of Manipur in the nineteenth century was closely followed by the colonial restructurization of economy and colonially sponsored social formation, as it happened in the rest of the Indian subcontinent.[1] To understand the changes which impacted the society in Manipur most, it is necessary to reconstruct the economic practices that were prevalent in the Meitei Kingdom on the eve of the British occupation, i.e., the eighteenth and early nineteenth century AD, since the economic factor is considered to be the primary determinant of the social formations.[2] The economic systems and practices that the new rule targeted to change were those which existed at the point of time of the colonization. However, those systems and practices, as extant in the eighteenth-nineteenth century, were essentially rooted in the past and had evolved over the ages since the earliest times of the social and state formations. This has to be particularly true in case of Manipur which had passed through the rule of the one single dynasty, i.e. the Ningthouja dynasty, which is said to have ruled in Manipur since the foundation of the Meitei Kingdom in *circa* first century AD till the British colonization in the nineteenth century.[3] Therefore, in this paper an attempt is made to reconstruct the economy of pre-colonial Manipur and its role in social formation, first, by profiling the main features of the economic practices as they existed during the eighteenth and nineteenth century, tracing the roots of those practices in early history of Manipur, and then, attempting to figure out the changes and continuities in the growth and the level of development the economy of Manipur had reached during the eighteenth century.

Features of Economy

The reliable information on important aspects of the economy of early Manipur is not adequately available, although the archaeological and literary sources are helpful in tentatively reconstructing the basic features of economy. The archaeological finds in the prehistoric caves at Khangkhui, Tharon and Napachik indicate the use of neolithic and bone tools.[4] These findings point to the existence of a hunting and food gathering economy in the region at some point of time. The excavation at Napachik site further reveals the prevalence of agricultural practices and settled life in the Manipur valley.[5] The prevalence of settled cultivation and its accompanying tools and technology are considered as important keys for the archaeologists and historians to understand the economy of the local communities. The Manipuri chronicles and other literary texts recorded the discovery of indigenous variety of paddy, invention of agriculture, practice of shifting cultivation, development of bronze and iron technology and the making of *daos*, axes and hoes for agricultural and allied purposes.[6] The traditions and myths, as recaptured in different literary texts, do clearly suggest that the ancient Meiteis were the shifting cultivators. Before developing the knowledge of wet rice agriculture, they carried out the shifting cultivation on the hill slopes or dry land forest areas. The northern and eastern parts of Imphal valley, which were thickly forested dry lands, provided the ideal environment for the development of this type of agriculture. The agricultural implements adopted were axes and *daos* for felling down trees and clearing the jungles and the small iron hoes for digging up the soil. There is evidence of the existence of the neolithic celts,[7] suggesting the possibility of those being used in the primitive agricultural practices long before the introduction of iron hoes. The references are available to the discovery of an indigenous variety of paddy, called *Morshi Thangyi*, in Manipur in the proto-historic period.[8] The first literary reference to paddy cultivation in the plains is also found in an early text, *Poireiton Khunthokpa*.[9] But there is no reference to employing plough or animal-driven plough in the pre-Pakhangba literature. It is probable that agriculture was further improved during the time of Poireiton, a contemporary of Nongda Lairen Pakhangba, since the references are made to the use of iron and domesticated animals, like the cattle.[10] The chronicles refer to several irrigation works and dredging the rivers and making canals to drain out the stranded water from the low lying marshy areas of the central Imphal valley.[11] The *Naothingkhong Phambal Kaba*, a very important literary source, refers to the system of shifting cultivation being practiced by the Shelloi Langmei tribe of Nongmaiching hill and the adoption of wet rice cultivation by the valley dwelling Meiteis.[12] The *Loiyumba Shilyen*,[*] the royal edict of king Loiyumba (1074-1122 AD),[13] and *Mashil*, an archaic text,[14] refer to the rates of revenue imposed on the agricultural fields by the state. These facts definitely attribute to the prevalence of wet rice cultivation in the valley region of Manipur.

There is no definite mention of the use of iron plough pulled by bullock in the earlier literary works. There are, of course, some myths which mention that the tigers were yoked by serpents and back of stork was used as plough by the gods. Because of the development in the knowledge of metallurgy, specially iron, and the existence of regular trade between Manipur and the neighbouring countries, specially Ava and the Tripuri, Kachari and Ahom states, there is a possibility that plough might have been used during the time of King Naothingkhong (8th century AD). However, it must be clearly stated that the agriculture in Manipur was greatly improved during the reign of King Khagemba (1597-1652 AD). The Muslim peasants, who migrated to Manipur from Bengal during the reign of Khagemba, had introduced improved agricultural technology, including the transplantation of paddy seedling, thereby putting an end to the age-old practice of broadcasting.[15] The *Nongshamei Puya*, another very important medieval chronicle, not only refers to the contribution made by the Muslim peasants to the development of agriculture in Manipur but it also specifically mentions the practice of wet rice cultivation and the use of plough drawn by bullocks by these peasants.[16] It is also evident from the literary sources that the contacts with the neighbouring countries facilitated the introduction of improved varieties of paddy in Manipur. The surplus production was made possible by the wet rice cultivation and the surplus from the production could be collected by the state. The state acted as the facilitating agent for agricultural activities by taking up the works like dredging of the rivers and draining away of the water deposits from the swampy areas and marshes. The royal chronicle refers to innumerable instances of the state undertaking the work of creating bunds and dykes to check inundation.[17]

The successful role played by the Meitei kings, who actually emerged from the ranks of the tribal chiefs, in the organization and development of wet rice cultivation had stabilized and strengthened the institution of kingship. The king was supposed to be the representative of the agricultural community and the control over the distribution of land was vested in him. He was the theoretical owner of all land, whether cultivated or waste, along with all natural resources. The scarcity of labour was a serious problem, particularly because the wet rice cultivation was basically labour intensive. However, the Meitei kings could solve this problem considerably by requiring the peasants to render labour service (*Lallup*) to the state. The possession of wet rice lands by the peasants was subject to their rendering periodic labour service to the state. In return of the labour service, a peasant, who was known as *Lalloi*,[18] was allowed the use of one *pari* (2.5 acre) of land subject to the payment of regular taxes in kind. The rate of tax levied per *pari* varied from two to twelve pots or baskets of paddy. Normally, a *pari* of land annually produced around 150 pots or baskets. Except for certain cases, the wet rice land, known as *Lou*, was considered to be the property of the state and, theoretically, was neither hereditary nor transferable. On the other hand, the homestead (*Ingkhol*) lands were free from taxes.[19]

We do not come across much information about the land tenure system or the land-holding pattern, rates of revenue or rent for different categories of land, the extent of cultivation in the valley, etc., which are indeed very important for analytical study of the economy in a historical time frame. However, the colonial writers and officials in the nineteenth century have left behind some useful information on the subject in the form of official reports, accounts and memoirs.[20] The land areas of the valley were generally divided into two categories, viz, *Ingkhol* (homestead land) and *Lou* (cultivable/agricultural land). The *Ingkhols* were spread over the villages. The *Lou* or agricultural lands available in the valley were classified as – (i) *Taonaro* or *Tounarou* (land under tenants), (ii) *Sarkari* or *Ningthoulou* (King's own land), (iii) *Phumlo* (*Phamlou*), (iv) *Siphailou* (land of the *sepoys*), (v) *Manaro* (*Manalou*), (vi) *Lugun-lou* (Brahmins), (vii) *Royal family*, (viii) *Maharani*, (ix) Temple (*Lairou*), etc.[21] Of these, only

Tounarou, Raja's own *Lou* and *Phumlou* were taxed which varied from two to sixty baskets of paddy per *pari* and the remaining were tax free lands. About one-fifth of the total cultivated area was covered under *Tounarou.* The rate of revenue per *pari* in the *Tounarou* was fixed at six *Chengkoks* of rice (three *maunds* approximately), which was paid in kind and sometimes in cash and calculated on the price of rice at the time.[22] The *Tounarou* holdings were of two types – (i) holding through purchase and (ii) holding through clearing of jungles on receiving permission. Those who possessed *Tounarou* through the later mode were exempted from payment of tax for one year. Except in case of default in payment of tax, the king would not evict the land holders without paying proper compensation. The land holders could either use the land on hereditary basis or dispose off the lands falling under *Tounarou* category. The king's own lands (*Sarkari*) were cultivated either by the slaves or by the free men on retal basis, but the rent were quite high as compared with other tenures. Each slave was given one *pari* of land along with plough, cattle and other implements and he had to pay sixty baskets of paddy as rent to the king. In case of the land being let to free men, they were required to pay twenty-four baskets of paddy. However, unlike the slaves, the free men were not provided with plough, cattle and other implements. Another category of land, which was held by officers and nobles in lieu of their salary, was called *Phamlou.* These lands were cultivated either by the slaves of the officials and nobles or by the free men. The rent payable by the cultivating slaves or free men was twenty-four baskets of paddy per *pari* and the incumbent officers or nobles in turn paid the revenue of two baskets of paddy per *pari* to the state. The timely payment of revenue was strictly enforced even in case of the officials and nobles. The failure of payment of revenue on time resulted in the confiscation of the *Phamlou* and its allotment to others.[23]

More than one-third of the cultivable area in the Manipur valley was under *Siphai-lou* (*Sepoy*'s land) category which was given to the *sepoys* and officers of the king's army. The *sepoys* who were in the service of the state were not paid in cash, and in lieu of salary or remuneration, they were given lands. The size of such land holdings varied according to the ranks of the holders. Incidentally, the ranks or designations of the officers and men in the army were rechristened in the British Indian style ever since Manipur became a protected state and the colonial records mentioned those designations. However, the senior officers like the *Major*, who headed number of companies, was allotted one *pari* of land against each company, calculated on the basis of the number of companies under his supervision. The *Poila* got six *pari*, a *Subedar* got four *pari*, a *Jamandar* got three *pari*, while a *Siphai* got one and a quarter of a *pari*. These allotments were revenue free. In case a *Sepoy* or officer died in harness and left behind a male heir, his family was given half a *pari* and the remaining land reverted to the state. If the son of the diseased *sepoy* joined the king's army after attaining majority (adulthood), he was given the same amount of land to which a *Sepoy* of his rank was entitled. The *Sepoy* who possessed surplus land could sublet it with the usual rent of twenty-four baskets of paddy per *pari*.[24]

The kings also granted lands to their favourites and other individuals who performed or rendered valuable services to the state. This type of land grant was called *Manalou* and was granted only for the life time of the grantee. If his heirs desired to continue the possession of these lands they had to pay revenue at the usual rate of twenty-four baskets of paddy per *pari*. Otherwise, the land used to be reverted to the king. The Meitei kings also granted land to the Brahmins. All the Brahmins in the state on taking the sacred thread (*Lugun*) were entitled to receive one *pari* of land each from the king.

When the Brahmin died, his widow was allowed to possess half of it to maintain herself and her children, and the rest was reverted to the king. The land received by the grantees under this system could not be disposed off or sold to any other person. The Brahmin lands were usually known as *Lugun-lou*. The practice of giving land to the Brahmins became widespread after the Meitei kings were converted into Hinduism in the eighteenth century. Another interesting feature of the land tenure system in Manipur was the assignment of lands to the Hindu temples and sylvan deities. The lands assigned under these categories were revenue free and never reverted to the king. For example, 'Govindaji', an important deity of the royal family, was assigned one hundred *pari* of land and these were cultivated by the *Keis* (slaves) of the temple who lived in the villages of Charangpat, Thinunggei and Uyan. Lands belonging to the members of the royal family, including the *Maharani*, and those lands whose ownership descended from father to son in the royal household, were exempted from the payment of revenue. However, the size of each such holding was fixed. Those who were in possession of land more than the fixed ceilings were liable to pay revenue for the excess land in the usual rate. Lands were also granted to individuals who rendered distinguished or meritorious services to the state during wars and such land grants were known as *Pangal-lou* (land acquired through merit and strength). These land grants were inheritable and revenue free. Besides land revenue, the Meitei kings used to exact royalties for the sale of timber, bamboo and other forest products from Jiri and thus maintained their rights over them which formed part of the state revenue. The access to the common or community lands, such as the forests, grazing grounds and fisheries, were open to all subjects in the state. To regulate the collection of revenue, two officers - *Phourungba* and *Lourungba* - were appointed by the king.[25]

The systematization of the *Lallup* service by King Loiyumba+ in the early part of the twelfth century AD had drawn the kingdom towards a more stable and organized polity. Literally, *Lallup* means 'war organization' (*lal* = war, *lup* = organization). Though originally started as a military service, it was gradually extended to non-military or economic activities of the state. The rudimentary form of evolution of this organization, outside the war purposes, was noticed during the reign of Taothingmang (264-364 AD?), when he had utilized the labour service of his subjects in dredging the Imphal river. In course of time, *Lallup* covered all state works, both military and civil. King Loiyumba's introduction of six administrative units, called *Lup*, strengthened the working system of the *Lallup* service. Though looked upon by the colonial writers as forced labour, the development of the *Lallup* system was the manifestation of the emergence of feudalism in the social, administrative and economic structure of the Meitei kingdom. The backward nature of the kingdom, which was characterized by the absence of large-scale trade and commercial activities, absence of a monetized economy and the reliance on barter system, made the system of *Lallup* system more meaningful and a necessity for the development of the country. The *Lakpa*, who supervised the *Lallup* service, enjoyed revenue free land from the state as his remuneration. Most of the hill tribes were not required to attend the *Lallup*, but in lieu of the *Lallup* service, they had to pay annual tributes to the Meitei kings, failing which punitive actions were inflicted upon them.[26]

It might be clear from the facts discussed above that the economy in pre-colonial or kingly Manipur was basically agrarian and the land was the most important factor of productivity. The Meitei kings exercised an overall control over the distribution of land. The fact that the king used to be addressed by the common people as '*Leimaba*' (meaning, owner of land) can be interpreted to regard him as the owner of the land. The control over land enhanced the fiscal power and strengthened the political authority of the successive Meitei rulers. It also enabled the kings to keep a check on any large-scale proliferation of the land holdings. The compulsory feudal service for the peasants who had taken to wet rice cultivation restrained the peasants' initiative to enlarge their holdings. The nobility were granted large agricultural lands (*phamlous*) and these lands were cultivated either by the slaves of the officials or by the free men. The rent which the nobles got from their tenants (free men) was twenty-four baskets of paddy per *pari*. On the other hand, these officers usually paid the revenue of only two baskets of paddy per *pari* to the king. However, if a noble failed to pay his share of revenue on time the *phamlou* was confiscated and allotted to others. This stringency in matter of payment of revenue significantly checked the growth of large land holdings and the concentration of land-holdings in few hands. The nobility, owing to its close links with the throne and having enjoyed the agricultural lands at the pleasure of the king, could not emerge as autonomous or powerful landlords. This explains the absence of landlordism in the Meitei kingdom.[27]

Role of State in Production

In kingly Manipur, the state played an important role in the production processes by acting as the catalytic or facilitating agent by way of organizing and supervising the agricultural proactive activities, like dredging of the rivers and canals, construction of bunds and dykes to check inundations, and the clearing of the drainages. In the population short Meitei state, the scarcity of labour could become an acute problem after the introduction of the labour intensive wet rice cultivation. However, the Meitei kings responded to this problem by evolving the highly ingenious system of labour mobilization through the *Lallup* system in the beginning of the twelfth century AD. This was made more systematic by the successive Meitei kings through inductions and modifications and it transformed the whole nature of the economic activity by bringing it under direct control of the state. The introduction of this feudal service and the improvements made upon it over the generations converted the loosely organized militias into a centralized militia pool with a regular gradation of the incumbents. An officer, known as *Lallup Chingba*, was appointed to oversee the functioning of this system. Some of the colonial writers termed the *Lallup* service as a system of 'forced labour'.[28] However, one of them, namely, James Johnstone, once a British Resident in Manipur, observed that "the native system has much good in it, much to recommend it, and that it is in many cases the natural outgrowth of the requirements of the people."[29] Johnstone strongly argued the case of the *Lallup* system. In his words, "The system (*Lallup*) was a good one, and when not carried to excess, pressed heavily on nobody. It was especially adapted to a poor state, sparsely populated. In such a state, under ordinary circumstances, where the amount of revenue is small and the rate of wages often comparatively high, it is next door to impossible to carry out many much needed public works by payment. On the other hand, every man in India who lives by cultivation, has much spare time on his hands, and the *Lallup* system very profitably utilises this, and for the benefit of the community at large."[30] Whatever Johnstone might have to say in defence of the system, there is no doubt that the *Lallup* system legitimized the strong presence of the state in the production processes. It not only ensured the control of the state over the mobilization of labour for productive purposes but also strengthened the long arms of that public authority to intervene directly in the production process at its own will. The feudal control over the vital factor of labour further signified that the economic activity was dictated by the state's own interests and policies.

Organization of Agriculture

The growth and development of the Meitei state from a small chiefdom into a fairly large kingdom was based on the wet rice cultivation which sustained the apparatus of the state. Hence, the success of wet rice cultivation was crucial to the economy of the state. However, the wet rice economy not only required large catchments of the manpower to reclaim lands, to clear the swamps and marshes and to level the soil, but also a system of efficient water control to irrigate the agricultural fields. In the Meitei case, the seasonal rainfall was abundant and the state was largely successful in providing the basic infrastructural facilities for the extension of wet rice cultivation. Through its control over the supply of labour, the state actually played a dominant role in land reclamation. In respect of irrigation or water supply, not much initiative was required on the part of the state. Although in wet rice cultivation the availability of water is considered to be most important as it is expected to provide the basic nutrients for the healthy growth of the crop, the rainfall in Manipur was abundant for the purpose. The state was required to organize only small scale irrigation facilities through the peasant community at the village level. The valley ecology was indeed immensely suitable for the wet rice cultivation which depended mainly upon the elevation of the fields and the capacity to retain moisture. For this purpose, the field was first leveled and low ridges or *Louri* were raised in a criss-cross pattern to retain water in the fields and the excess water was drained out whenever necessary. These ridges were generally not higher than one foot. The technique suited the alluvial plains of Manipur and wet rice cultivation was mostly carried out in the alluvial part of the state. Not less than nineteen varieties of paddy were grown in Manipur which are divided into early (*Anganphou)* and late crops (*Athengphou*). The early crops ripen in about three months and were ready for harvesting in September. *Sajikhong, Tumai, Kabaw Phou and Phourel Anganphou* were the favourite varieties of early crops. The great bulk of rice grown in the valley was the late varieties which ripen in about six months. This variety would be ready for reaping in the month of November. The most popular and of finest quality among them were *Phourel, Luining and Yenthik.* However, by the close of the nineteenth century a large quantity of the early variety seem to have been grown. It is possible that the peasants were more attracted towards cultivation of the early variety as it took lesser amounts of time and labour, if compared with the later variety. The successful operation of agricultural activity was, nonetheless, dependant upon the construction of river embankments. The rainfall in normal years was so abundant that the danger to cultivation sometimes arose from floods rather than the lack of water. To prevent the annual flooding of the rivers, the high embankments were constructed at the initiative of the state, besides the periodic dredging activities. These embankments also served as the bunds and high roads of the localities.[31]

It is evident from the sources that the overall impact of the introduction of wet rice cultivation resulted in increased productivity which helped to sustain the expanding state apparatus and the growing population. Though population of Manipur was greatly reduced during the Burmese occupation (1819-1826), when many of the valley dwellers left the country and took refuge in the neighbouring areas such as Cachar, Sylhet and Dhaka for safety, there were definite signs of a growing population as evidenced by the establishment of new villages in the years immediately after the expulsion of the Burmese. The population of Manipur in 1881 was 2,21,070, out of which 1,35,782 were in the valley,[32] and it increased to 2,84,465 in 1901.[33]

Industry and Manufactures

The data for reconstruction of the level of technological

development as an indicator of the quality of material culture and civilization, is indeed very scanty and scattered. The archaeological findings and the literary sources suggest that from the earliest times down the seventeenth century AD, there was a slow but steady development of technology in Manipur. As stated earlier, the prehistoric man in Manipur used both stone and bone tools. The development of pottery, which is considered as an indicator of technological development, was found to have flourished since early times. The material remains discovered in Napachik are a testimony to the work of the local potters. Other archaeological sites, such as Sekta, Khamran, Khangabok, Irengbam, Phunan, etc, also prove the antiquity of pottery in Manipur. It has been suggested that some of the potteries found at the Napachik site have affinities with the potteries of ancient northern China. The Chakpas, who were dispersed in different parts of the Manipur valley, are described as the earliest pottery makers of Manipur.[34] Some of the Chakpa villages, viz, Andro, Phayeng, Chairel, etc, are still engaged in pottery making and they produce good quality potteries which are used for cooking, preserving and storing food, both in the hills and plains areas. The Tangkhul and Paomei tribesmen also knew and practiced the art of pottery making since early times.[35] The potteries were widely used for many centuries in Manipur. However, the Muslim immigrants during the reign of Khagemba introduced improved technology of pottery making by using wheels, besides making different types of earthen vessels. The Muslim families engaged in pottery making in Manipur were given a local surname as *Phusam* (pottery making family) by the king and they were allowed to marry local women.[36]

The metallurgy seems to have been not so developed as the pottery making in early Manipur. However, there are mentions in the historical chronicles of iron, copper, bronze, silver, gold and tin. According to popular traditions King

Khuyoi Tompok is regarded as a technological innovator. During his reign, iron was discovered at Kakching, gold at Kongba Meirembi and copper at Sibong. The myth associated with a local deity, *Khamlangba* of Kakching, also gives an interesting account of the discovery of iron in that area.[37] The widespread use of bell-metal gong for religious and cultural activities leads us to suggest that bronze metallurgy was also developed in Manipur. The bell-metal is supposed to have been brought to Manipur by way of trade from Burma and Thailand. The use of iron implements (swords, spears, *daos* and other tools) in agriculture, weaponry, etc., is clearly a proof of the development of black-smithy. The accounts of Poireiton refer to the use of iron implements for the first time (1st century AD) in the history of Manipur. The account of the coronation of King Naothingkhong (264-364 AD) mentions the use of iron-made weapons and metals like tin, silver and gold. However, the introduction of guns, the gun-making and use of gun-powder in Manipur seem to be of later origin. The Meiteis perhaps learned the art of gun making from the Muslim war captives in the seventeenth century AD, during the reign of King Khagemba.[38]

The creative impulse of the people of Manipur, especially of the womenfolk, in early times was best represented in the handloom and handicraft products. Through metal technology was not so highly developed in the kingdom, Manipur can claim a proud heritage in the field of handicraft. It was in the field of weaving and related works like dyeing, printing, embroidery and appliqué art that Manipur excelled amongst all her neighbours. Queen Laishna, wife of Nongda Lairen Pakhangba, was believed to have innovated several designs of clothes based on the pattern of python, the *Phanek Phibal, Samchin*, etc., and for the borders of shawls. These designs are called *Namthang-khulak, Khamen-chatpa* and *Ningkham*, which were used by the members of the royal family and the nobility. The mulberry silk-worm, locally known as *Leimatil*, was discovered by Nongmainu Ahongbi, wife of King Khuyoi Tompok. There was a village known as Leimaram which specialized in the production of high quality silk and various handlooms, including weaving and dyeing. It might have impelled King Loiyumba to issue his famous decree known as *Loiyumba Shilyen (Loiyumba Shinyen)* to assign to the selected families of weavers the work of producing particular types of cloths. The same was the case for the dyers' families also. Thirty families were assigned the work to weave different designs of clothes. It is very interesting to know that in the twelfth century AD the Manipuri weavers developed such rich varieties of weaving patterns which were patented with the state. As many as thirty-two different designs of cloth were found. The dyers' families were assigned to produce different colours for clothes, based on the colours of popular flowers. Eight families were assigned to dye specific colours. The *Loiyumba Shilyen* thus projected the picture of a well organized economy of Manipur in which the wet rice agrarian economy was supplemented by the growing handloom and handicraft industries. It was in such a situation that the state had to intervene and regulate the organization of these industries. The people, who were primarily the peasants, had now become artisans. These evidences make it apparent that the weaving prevalent in Manipur was an indigenous one, and the spinning, weaving and dyeing were fairly developed in the state. Later on, the handloom industry was further developed with the introduction of flying shuttle, known as *Pangandem*. It is likely that the flying shuttle might have been introduced in the kingdom by the Muslim immigrants.[39]

Alongside the success in wet rice cultivation and the surplus generation that followed, the industrial activity in metals and scarce goods witnessed slow and gradual changes to meet the basic requirements of the state. Because of the specific importance, the extraction of precious metals like iron, boat building for transport and defence, handloom and handicrafts and all other manufacturing activities received attention of the Meitei kings. Like agriculture, these industries were also dependant on the labour of the *Lallois*. Salt being a scarce commodity, the Meitei state made systematic efforts to indigenously produce this essential article. Salt was mainly obtained from the brines of the salt wells situated in the valley. The principal salt wells were situated at the villages of Ningel, Chandrakhong, Sikhong and Waikhong.[40] The salt wells were considered as property of the king and were worked for his benefit. The men employed in production of salt were remunerated for their labour by setting aside a certain amount of manufactured salt for them. The king collected thirty percent of the produce as revenue and the remaining seventy percent was distributed among the salt manufacturers. Though there were seasonal variations in production, at an average about 150 *maunds* of salt (estimated in 1867-68) were produced per month from these wells. The quantity almost met the requirements of the people of the state. Only a small quantity of salt was occasionally imported in times of scarcity form Burma and Cachar.[41] The wholesale price of salt was rupees six per *maund* in 1873.[42] The Ningel inscription of King Garibniwaz forbade the people from disturbing the salt wells and prescribed heavy punishment for any violation of the royal order. This clearly shows the importance attached to the protection and preservation of the salt wells.[43] The salt indigenously produced from these wells seems to have been of good quality. The villagers employed in the salt manufacturing were mostly from the Loi community and their *Lallup* duty was for six months in a year, i.e., three months of more labour service than that of the common Meiteis. However, the engagement in the *Lallup* service for the longer period was supposed to have been reasonably well remunerated by the state.[44]

The boat building was another important industry under the state supervision. This industry was also sustained by the heavy demand of boats for transportation in the water logged valley region and the easy availability of timber and free labour of the *Lallup*. The local artisans made elegant and imposing boats, both large and small. The officials, called *Hiyangloi Hangjaba* and *Hisaba Hanjaba*, oversaw the whole operation of construction and maintenance of the boats.[45] The boat building technique seems to have been very simple. The locally available tree-trunks were hollowed out until only an outer skin of about an inch and a quarter thick remained. The inhabitants of Hiroi-Lamgang village (a Loi village) in the southern division of the valley made special boats for the kings.[46] Widespread use of boat is also evidenced by the annual boat race competitions, known as *Hiyang Tannaba*, which were regularly held in the month of September every year. As many as seventy rowers occupied one boat in the competition.[47]

It may, however, be observed that the economy of Manipur being basically agrarian, the manufacturing did not emerge as a popular occupation of the common people. The limited industrial activity that developed on the initiative of the state was based on the easy availability of raw-materials and to meet certain basic needs of the state and the people. Being a land of rivers and streams, which intersected the valley like a natural network, the boat making developed out of necessity. The salt manufacturing became an important industry because of its household need as an essential consumer item and the easy availability of the salt brines in the outlying areas. Amongst the few manufacturing items, silk was considered important for the aristocrats and it also constituted an important article of export. Silk manufacturing was an ancient art in Manipur and it was the continuation of a popular tradition till the modern times. The relatively stagnant technology and crude implements were the characteristic features of the silk industry. No scientific or technological change formed part of the eighteenth and nineteenth century historical experience in silk manufacturing. The technology in general was backward. The uneven development of technology over a range of crafts resulted from a semi-tribal economic base, a small quantum of surplus in circulation and the relative scarcity of basic metals like iron in the kingdom.

Peasant Production

The *Lallois*, whose labour service sustained the Meitei state apparatus, were also the peasants and primary producers. While not on active state service, the *Lallois* carried on their subsistence activity mainly by cultivation. Alongside the cultivation of wet rice in the plots allotted by the state, they were also involved in petty production, mainly for domestic consumption. On the slopes of the hills and undulating grounds which were not easily reducible to the plains level, or in the deeply flooded plains, swamps and marshes, the peasants cultivated a wide variety of vegetables and *Anganphou* (early crops) which included *Sanjikhong, Tumai, Kabaw Phou* and *Phouren Anganba* that ripen in three months and was ready for reaping in the month of September every year.[48] This was followed by the cultivation of later varieties of paddy (*Athengphou*). The later crops being transplanted one, the seeds were sown and nurtured in the nursery beds for about two months and then the seedlings were transplanted in June or July to the carefully manured beds, which had been ploughed as many as four or five times till the soil was converted into a fine puddle of clay. The transplantation of the seedlings to the field was mainly done by the women. The harvest was reaped in December every year. Each *pari* of land generally yielded as much as one hundred sixty to two hundred baskets of paddy. The annual average yield per *pari* was about one hundred and fifty baskets and each basket contained about sixty pounds of paddy.[49]

The dry field cultivations included pulses, potato, brinjal, pumpkin, onion, pepper, tobacco of good quality and white sugarcane which contained medicinal property. English vegetables, peas, and English cabbage, cauliflower, and beans were also cultivated in the nineteenth century. A small quantity of opium was also grown by the Muslims.[50] However, the most important crop grown for manufacture was cotton. The cotton plant was generally cultivated in the periphery of the valley and its adjoining hills, more specifically by the tribal people. The small quantities of Indigo, Bixa, Alba, etc., used for dying were also cultivated by the peasants in the vicinity of their villages and homesteads.[51]

The rich variety of garden crops, such as tobacco, opium, several kinds of plantains, vegetables and a few varieties of spices, were grown by the peasants. The richness and variety of the crops grown indicated not only the fertility of the soil but also a secure and settled life enjoyed by the peasants. A number of fruits such as mangoes, plantains, pineapples, apples, peaches, bramble, wild raspberry, jack and guava, etc. were grown in the valley and the hills. Ginger, India corn and pan leaves are widely grown in the hills of Manipur.[52]

Besides these agricultural and horticultural crops, the rich endowment of forest products enabled the peasants to meet their requirements for shelter, fuel, etc. without much effort. The forest provided valuable timbers, chiefly adapted for constructing houses, furniture, boats, etc. The bamboo, which grew abundantly, was utilized by the peasants for their houses, furniture, implements of agriculture, basketry, etc. These crafts constituted the subsidiary occupation of the peasants.[53]

Division of Labour

Though King Loiyumba, in his edict of 1110 AD, had initiated the distribution of economic occupations among various *Yumnaks* (families), the close unity between agriculture and handicrafts was reflected in the distribution of labour. Most of the crafts and artisans services needed by the peasants were satisfied within the households. The handicraft and handloom were among the household activities for the commoners. Therefore, there was no strict division of labour in the society. Except for some Loi villages and few Meitei families, who were assigned specific occupations like pottery making or sword making or weaving and dyeing, there was no sharp division of labour between agriculture and industry. Every peasant or every household built its own huts, grew its own vegetables and tobacco, scoop out its own canoe and weaved its own mats. In most cases, the crafts constituted a subsidiary occupation for the peasant and his family.

Thus, blessed with a favouable ecology and environment the Manipuri peasants could sustain and reproduce themselves without much toil and hardship. The micro-economies of the peasants were largely of subsistence nature. The peasants produced to the extent that their household needs were met and the self-exploitation was minimal. The livelihood in the fertile valley of Manipur did not réquire much labour or prolonged physical exertion. Besides, the lack of incentives for surplus production which was linked to the mode of appropriation and the restrictive nature of state service did not encourage the peasant activity. However, the peasants' enterprises for enhancing productivity of crops by adopting new techniques were lacking, perhaps due to the absence of incentives and compulsions. There was practically no rotation of crops, apart from the system under which the winter rice was followed by pulse or oil seeds. The wooden plough with an iron tipped share, wooden rakes, a rough wooden harrow, sickles, knives, winnowing fan, a large mat and baskets comprised a peasant's tools even by the end of the nineteenth century.[54]

Mode of Appropriation

By the eighteenth century the Meitei sate had evolved

the elaborate and systematic state machinery for the appropriation of surplus. However, the appropriation generally took place in the form of labour services which the *Lalloi* peasants offered to the state in various fields. The cash revenue collection of the state from all sources, including the Kabaw (Kabo) valley compensation which the British government paid to Manipur since 1834, according to an estimate of 1873, was only about twenty-five to thirty thousand rupees annually.[55] The collections in kind were mainly realized from the land grants to the officials in lieu of salary, tributes from the hill chiefs and the income from the brine wells. The revenue in kind was also collected from the Loi villages. The available data are not sufficient for estimating the gross revenue collected under import and export of goods. However, according to an information furnished by the state administration to the British officials, the cash revenue realized from import and export of goods for the year 1868-69 stood at 1,975 rupees, 7 *annas* and 9 *paise* and 3,533 rupees, 1 *anna* and 9 *paise* respectively. The export of silk to Burma accounted for the revenue of rupees one hundred only.[56] The other estimates of revenue from the export and import trade during that period came around rupees twelve thousand per annum.[57]

The tributes paid by the tribes, though very nominal in scale, were also appropriated by the state. The hill tribes, such as the Kabui, Mao, Maram, Tangkhul, Anal, Maring, Khongjai, etc., came annually to the Meitei court bringing with them a number of articles grown in the hills, such as cotton, ginger, pepper and elephant tusks, etc., failing which retributive actions were carried out against them. The exaction from the hill tribe was limited only to the vindication of the Meitei suzerainty. The idea was not so much to collect revenue as it was to bring and keep the indigenous hill tribes under control and to ensure from them some sort of allegiance to the Meitei kings. The annual congregations of the tribal chiefs within the kingdom were regularly held at the palace since 1700 AD. It began during the reign of Charairongba (1697-1709 AD) and later on came to be known as *Mera Haochongba* festival. As R. Brown mentioned: "This festival in October lasts only for one day; it is a gathering of the hill tribes under the Manipur government, and is a curious sight on account of the great number of different tribes assembled, with their curious dress and weapons, differing from each other in feature and language, but all unanimous in one particular, to get drunk as speedily and remain so long, as possible. The hillmen indulge in feats of strength before the Raja, such as carrying heavy weights, etc. They also indulge in war dance and sham fights. The sports of the day conclude with a feast, at which they are regaled with the flesh of cows, buffaloes, dogs, cats, etc., which may have died in the valley. The flesh is dried and preserved for this feat."[58] The organization of such events by the kings helped in bringing about integration among the hill and valley people and also the safety and integrity of the kingdom.

The facts available thus suggest that the extent of appropriation by the Meitei state was not very extensive as compared to the strength of the population and resources. Though the Meitei rulers attempted to exploit all the probable source of revenue available within the region, the royal receipts were comparatively small owing to the cumbrous nature of the system and loose control over the receipts. The number of items of the revenue receipts increased over the years to meet the growing need of resources, especially after Manipur-Burma conflicts, but the amount actually collected under various heads was far less of the potential resources of the state. The allegations were made from time to time about the revenue officials involved in corrupt practices while collecting revenue and in measuring the lands allotted to the peasants. There are also instances of punishment meted out to the officials on charges of bribery.[59]

Trade and Commerce

The mode of appropriation by the state in the form of labour service not only determined the level of production and the development of a marketing network but also eventually determined the level of trade and commercial activity within and outside the state. Because of the limitations imposed by the mode of appropriation, the range of trading activities at various levels was greatly limited. The available evidence suggests that the state not only paid in kind but also received mostly in kind and service. The surplus, therefore, largely took the form of labour rent for direct appropriation by the ruling class. Most of the basic requirements of the peasant and his family for food, clothing, etc. were satisfied within the household. However, the concept of self-sufficiency in its totality appears to be a myth. The minimal surplus production was necessitated by the scarcity of essential items within the state. Theoretically, the production of surplus might sometimes become necessary to utilize the services of the artisans and craftsmen. But in case of Manipur, the division of labour on caste specific profession was yet to emerge.[60] Hence, though the peasants did exchange their products, a substantial surplus production on their part was not necessary. Moreover, the artisans and craftsmen still retained their linkage with agriculture. As the surplus production was minimal, the marketing network and trade that developed were also rudimentary in structure. At local markets, the exchanges were made of scarce products. The private trade not only did not appear in any substantial form, it also does not seem to have been encouraged by the state. It is, however, not presumed that the private trade was totally absent in pre-colonial Manipur. What is suggested is that considering the magnitude of the trade, which was meager, it seems that the private trade was very limited and highly susceptible to the vagaries of the political situation of the day. Besides, most of the traders never cut off their linkages with agriculture which was considered their primary occupation.[61]

The local markets *(Keithel)*, where most of the exchanges took place, served as the main marketing network within the kingdom. The exchanges were mainly intra-local on petty scale and at a peddling level within the limitations of a basically barter and *cowrie* economy. The important marketing centres in Manipur in the pre-colonial period were at Sana Keithel, Kha Keithel, Moirang Keithel, Khuman Keithel, Phaibung Keithel, Chairen Keithel, Nambol Keithel, Konglang Keithel, Andro Keithel and Phayeng Keithel.[62] The markets contiguous to the hill areas were generally frequented by the neighbouring hill tribes. In those markets, where regular trade was carried on between the plains and hill tribes, a variety of goods, mostly perishable, were exchanged. A large number of hill people frequented the main markets, particularly during the winter seasons. Most of the items sold or exchanged in the markets were dry fish, rice, vegetables, *pan*, *supari*, clothes, and ornaments for the hill people and the sweetmeats. One very interesting feature of the markets in Manipur was that these were exclusively run by women. About three thousand women used to assemble in the afternoon *bazaar*. The men, with the exception of the foreigners, were not allowed to enter the market place. The buying and selling was conducted only by the women. The most important essential item which the hill people bought from these markets was salt. They brought cotton, ginger, pepper, baskets, wax, etc. for exchange or sold those for cash. Trade with the hill tribes was also conducted on a small scale. The exchange was carried out mainly on the basis of use value or consumption. It was mostly on personal level that the goods were usually bartered. Though the markets were established by the state since a long time, it appears that the state did not exercise much control over them. [63]

Though sketchy references have been made in the royal chronicle of the long distance trade routes between Manipur and the neighbouring kingdoms, like Tripura, Cachar, Assam and Burma, a fair picture cannot be drawn about the nature and quantum of the trade carried out between Manipur and those countries for want of sufficient data. However, some important items of trade, as suggested by the chronicle, included the elephants and horses. It appears that the elephant trade was exclusively a royal monopoly. About the horses, there is virtually no recorded data on the quantum of trade. The Manipuri silk, which was of fine quality, was said to be in great demand by the Burmese. However, by the eighteenth and nineteenth centuries Manipur's trade and commercial relations with the neighbouring countries, particularly with Burma, were at its lowest ebb as wars frequently broke out between Manipur and her neighbours, especially with Burma. This is vindicated by the recorded fact that in 1873 only a sum of rupees on hundred was collected by the state as export duty for the export of silk from Manipur to Burma.[64] This might explain further that the economy in pre-colonial Manipur continued to be basically agrarian in character. The primary occupation of the common people was agriculture and the land revenue was the main source of income of the state, while the crafts and industries were subsidiary occupations for certain sections of people and the revenue earned by the state on account of those sectors was only nominal.

NOTES & REFERENCES

1. J. B. Bhattacharjee, "Colonialization of Economy in Northeast India" in D. R. Syiemlieh & Manorama Sharma (ed.), *Society and Economy in North-East India*, Volume Three, Regency Publications, New Delhi, 2008, pp. 12-20.
2. B. Hindess and P. Hirst, *Pre-Capitalist Modes of Production*, London, 1975; John G. Taylor, *From Modernisation to Modes of Production*, London, 1979.
3. Jyotirmoy Roy, *History of Manipur*, (Calcutta, 1958); Revised & enlarged edition, Eastlight Book House, Calcutta, 1973.

4. O. Kumar Singh, *Stone Age Archaeology of Manipur*, Imphal, 1997, pp., 101-118. Based on the findings and results of extensive fieldwork, O. K. Singh has drawn a chronological sequence of stone age cultures of Manipur as under:

Culture	*Phase*	*Approximate Age*
Neolithic	Phunan Ware	First Millennium
	Tripod Ware	B.C.1450 B.C.4,460 ± 120
	Corded Ware	years B.P.
Hoabinhian	Late Hoabinhian	Later Mid-Holocene
	Early Hoabinhian	Early Mid-Holocene
Palaeolithic	Late Palaeolithic	Later Late PleistoceneLate
	Early Palaeolithic	Pleistocene

5. *ibid.*, p.126. Regarding the archaeological finds at Napachik the author wrote, "The stone tool assemblage at Napachik suggests the practice of mixed economy based on hunting, fishing and food-production".
6. M. Chandra Singh (ed.), *Poireiton Khunthokpa*, Imphal, 1967, p. 3; M. Narendra (ed.), *Langwol*, Imphal, 1981, p. 1. Such references are also found in the literary and historical texts like *Soubol Lairembi Loutarol* (MS.), *Ningthou Maputhiba* (MS.) and *Soubol Yairel* (MS.).
7. O. Kumar Singh, *op.cit.*, p. 4.
8. M. Narendra (ed), *Langwol*, *op.cit.*, p. 1.
9. M. Chandra Singh (ed.), *Poireiton Khunthokpa*, *op.cit.*, p.3. The first reference to paddy cultivation in Manipur is also found in the texts like *Soubol Lairembi Loutarol* (MS.), *Ningthou Maputhiba* (MS.) and *Soubol Yairel* (MS.);
10. M. Chandra Singh (ed.), *op.cit.*, p.3.
11. L. Ibungohal Singh & N. Khelchandra Singh (ed.), *Cheitharol Kumbaba* (royal chronicle of Manipur), Manipuri Sahitya Parishad, Imphal, 1967 (Reprint 1989), pp. 2-3 and N. Manaoyaima (ed.), *Tutenglon* (an archaic text), Kakching, 2000, pp. 2-38, refers to dredging of Imphal River by Meitei king Taothingmang (264-364 AD) along with his brother Yoimongba.
12. N. Khelchandra Singh (ed.), *Naothingkhong Phambal Kaba,* Imphal, 1968, p. 38.

Shilyen/Shinyen

13. Kh. Chandrasekhar Singh (ed.) *Loiyumba Shinyen,* All Manipur Umanglai Haraoba Committee, Uripok Naoremthong, 1982.
14. *Mashil* is an unpublished Meitei *Puya,* the manuscript is in the custody of N. Khelchandra Singh, Imphal.
15. B. Kullachandra Sharma and Badr-ud-din, *Meitei Pangal Hourakpham,* Imphal, 1991, p.146.
16. O. Bhogeswar Singh & M.A. Janab Khan (ed.), *Nongshamei Puya,* Imphal, 1973, p. 261.
17. *Tutenglon, op.cit,* p. 38; *Cheitharol Kumbaba, op.cit,* p. 38.
18. A person who renders *Lallup* service was known as *Lalloi.*
19. A. A. Howell, *A Short Account of Land Revenue in Manipur,* Imphal, 1907, p.9.
20. Though sketchy, the useful information could be found in the books and accounts left behind by the colonial officials. These accounts were mostly prepared during the nineteenth and early twentieth century. Among these mention may be made of R. B. Pemberton, *Report on the Eastern Frontier of British India,* (Calcutta, 1835) Reprint DHAS, Gauhati, 1966; W. McCulloch, *An Account of the Valley of Munnipore* (Calcutta, 1859), Reprint Gian Publishing House, Delhi, 1980; R. Brown, *Statistical Account of Manipur,* (London, 1874) Reprint Sanskaran Prakahsak, Delhi, 1974; E. W. Dun, *Gazetteer of Manipur,* (London, 1875) Reprint Vivek Publishing Company, Delhi, 1981; B.C. Allen, *Gazetteer of Manipur and Naga Hills,* (Calcutta, 1905) Reprint B. R. Publishing House, Delhi, 1975; A .A. Howell, *A Short Account of Land Revenue in Manipur,* Imphal, 1907; T. C. Hudson, *The Meitheis,* (London, 1911) Reprint Low Price Publications, Delhi, 1989; James Johnstone, *My Experience in Manipur and Naga Hills,* (London, 1896) Reprint B. R. Publishing House, Delhi, 1971.
21. A. A. Howell, *A Short Account of Land Revenue in Manipur, op.cit.,* p.9.
22. *ibid.*
23. *ibid.,* pp. 5-6.
24. *ibid.,* p.4.
25. *ibid.,* pp. 3-4.

+Loiyumba/Loiyamba

26. *ibid.*, p. 8.
27. *ibid.*, pp. 8-9.
28. W. McCulloch, *An Account of the Valley of Munnipore, op.cit.*, p. 37; R. Brown, *Statistical Account of Manipur, op.cit.*, pp.11,13,83; T. C. Hudson, *The Meitheis, op.cit.*, p.31.
29. James Johnstone, *My Experience in Manipur and Naga Hills, op.cit.*, p.14.
30. *ibid.*, pp. 114-15.
31. *ibid.*, p. 115. R. Brown, *op.cit.* pp.83-84. Though the early crops are known as *Anganphou; Anganba* meaning early and *Phou* as paddy there is no Manipuri equivalent term of later variety of paddy. The nearest literal meaning is *Athengphou.* However, it is not in popular vocabulary. Since the paddy crops of the later variety are cut down in the months of late November and early December these are generally known as *Poinulou* as the Meitei month of *Poinu* falls during that period.
32. E. W. Dun, *Gazetteer of Manipur, op.cit.*, p.15.
33. T. C. Hudson, *op.cit.*, p. 2.
34. *Chakpa Khunthok Khunda*, an unpublished Meitei *Puya.*
35. Kshetri Kumar, *Manipurda Chaphu*, Kakching, 1984, p.12.
36. R.K. Sanahal (ed.) *Pangal Thorakpa*, Imphal, 1985, p.xv; B. Kullachandra Sharma & Badr-ud-din (ed.) *Meitei Pangal Thorakpa*, Imphal, 1991, p.27.
37. M. Gourachandra, *Manipurda Yotshung Yotsha* (Traditional Iron Smelting and Forging in Manipur), Kakching, 1997, p.9.
38. *ibid.*
39. Mutua Bahadur, *Traditional Textile of Manipur*, Imphal, 1997.
40. Kh. Chandrasekhar Singh (ed.), *Loiyumba Shinyen*, All Manipur Umanglai Haraoba Committee, Uripok Naoremthong, 1982.
41. R. Brown, *op.cit.*, pp. 9-19.
42. *ibid.*, p. 10.
43. Mutua Bahadur & P. Gunindra Singh, *Epigraphical Records of Manipur*, Imphal, 1986, vol. I, pp. 8-13.
44. T. C. Hudson, *0p.cit.*, pp. 33-36.
45. N. Khelchandra Singh (ed.), *Phamlon*, Imphal, 1987, pp.4,14.

46. T. C. Hudson, *op.cit.*, p. 33.
47. *ibid.*, p. 52.
48. R. Brown, *op.cit.*, p. 86.
49. *ibid*, p. 83.
50. *ibid*, p. 84
51. E. W. Dun, *op.cit.*, p. 57.
52. B. Kullachandra Sharma, *Meiteigi Machugi Manat*, Imphal, 2000, pp.34-41.
53. R. Brown, *op.cit.*, p. 87.
54. *ibid.*

#Kabaw valley/Kabo valley

55. *ibid*, p. 88.
56. *ibid.*
57. *ibid.*
58. E. W. Dun, *op.cit.*, p. 66.
59. *ibid.* pp. 24.
60. *ibidt.*, pp. 24-25. Though majority of the population had been converted to Hinduism in the 18th century under royal patronage, the caste system as practiced in other parts of India was almost absent in case of Manipur.
61. R. Brown, *op.cit.*, p. 86.
62. Gangmumei Kabui, *History of Manipur*, Vol. I, National Publishing House, Delhi, 1991, p. 220.
63. R. Brown, *op.cit.*, pp. 90-91.
64. *ibid.*, p. 86.

10

Touching Upon the Neglected: An Overview of the World of Women in Pre-Colonial Manipur

H. Sudhir

Beginnings

Chada [*Chata*] *Lahui* is the royal metronymic of the Meitei kings of Manipur. Written in archaic *Meiteilon* (Meitei language), it originally span from the reign of Nongda Lairen Pakhangba (33-154 AD) to that of Garibniwaj (1709-1748 AD).[1] The royal *pundits* with the approval of the successor kings subsequently added the genealogies of the respective kings down to the reign of Maharaja Chandrakirti (1850-1886 AD).[2] On the other hand, there are myths of the dignified *lairembis* (female deities) and their being worshipped since the remote days till today. There is a myth saying that Kangla, the seat of the Ningthouja rule, is guarded by four directional female deities viz., *Wangthonbi* (West), *Chinga Lalheibi* (South), *Toknga Lairembi* (North) and *Panthoibi* (East).[3] There are also legends of *Thongak Lairembi*, *Thangkhul Nurabi*, *Haoreima Sambubu* and *Phouoibi* which are revered till these days. One will find the mythical stories of *Panthoibi Khongkul* (*Khonggul*), *Khongchomnupi* (*Khongjomnubi*), *Nongkarol* (*Nonggarol*), etc.[4] Apart from these, Khwairamband Keithel, historically, has been an all-in-all women's actively engaged public space where the right of inheritance (inheritance of market plots) is till now confined to the women only.[5] This market in earlier times was administered by a women's body, called *Lakhong*.

Manipur has been exposed to different intruding cultural waves in different historical timings; yet, a unique intrinsic cultural root appears to be continuously maintaining the women's vibrancy that is glued to its social system in one way or another. All these are not merely mythic narrativisation, but a history in the myths unfolding a pragmatic articulation of a social root. Are all these testimonials evidence of matriliny? There is interestingly a dominant trend of subscribing to the matrilineal root of the Meitei social system. It is said that the autochthonous *Chakpa* people, who constitute a section of the Meitei community, might have been matriarchal based on worshipping of the mother goddess, *Leimaren*.[6] However, finding an accurate answer, for obvious reasons, is certainly a difficult one. In terms of *Chada* [*Chata*] *Lahui* as metronymic, let us remember what Kumkum Roy has, may be in a different context, to say:

> Whether metronymics are indicative of matriliny or not is a more difficult question to answer. It is possible, as has been suggested that the use of metronymics could co-exist with patriliny.[7]

To keep the ball rolling, why was *Chada Lahui* written and maintained? Can we, based on *Chada Lahui*, simply jump to conclude matriliny as the root of Meitei social system? Did matriliny exist in the ancient past? Let us once again listen to what Kumkum Roy says:

> It has been suggested that in a polygynous situation, metronymics were used to distinguish amongst sons born from the different wives of a ruler. They could also have been used to underscore the importance of a specific marital alliance.[8]

This is an area wide open for a rigour of research to explore a plausible answer. However, leaving aside all these historical discourses, what has/had been seen throughout the historical pages is that the women were always in the forefront of social, economic and political activism in Manipur. This is the crucial nucleus that has attracted, more particularly, the outside scholars to come all along to investigate more in details. The paper will examine the world of women in pre-colonial Manipur by way of categorizing two types of women – royal women and common women. In the meantime, the realities of women's lives are also discussed in two fronts - pubic and private.

Problem

Reading the available writings on history of Manipur, either pre-colonial or colonial, without any question is till today by and large the political history. Social and cultural history, in its strict sense, is still quite young, while histories of women or gender are yet to be given birth. The histories of women or gender have been for long a neglected area and even today it continuously seems to be neglected in the upcoming historical writings.[9] Talking about the colonial time, one can see that the writings are all centered around the narrative histories of nothing else but specifically only on the women's protests of 1904 and 1939. An active engagement aimed at exploring the real lives of women deserves a prominence.[10] In case of the pre-colonial period, the area is a wide barren. However, much more stimulating is the fact that there is a mine of precious historical sources on women, may be in myths/legends/folklore/oral traditions, which can certainly be tapped towards a historical reconstruction of women in Manipur. This is what the present paper precisely intends to attempt.

Conceptualization

The timeframe and methodological concept of the paper need to be clearly defined. As is the general trend in case of the history of Northeast India, the history of Manipur follows the periodization model of pre-colonial and colonial periods. The pre-colonial timeframe of the paper, therefore, follows the same model that runs chronologically from the first century AD (more particularly from Nongda Lairen Pakhangba's reign) to the Anglo-Manipur War of 1891. Meanwhile, it may be reminded that Manipur's diplomatic relation with the British had already commenced with the signing of the Chittagong Treaty of 1762.[11] The diplomatic tie was bound together by agreements and engagements entered between the two from time to time. More interestingly, the diplomatic period has been embellished by a package of colonial-administrators' writings which have yielded a perception of the life-world of the Meitei women. Admittedly, the paper may be broadly dissected into two inter-related parts based on the literature so far used by the historians. In the first part, a design is constructed to write the paper primarily based on the contemporary *puyas* though secondary sources too are read towards theoretical or methodological formulations. Secondly, the colonial knowledge of the world of the women is also examined. This is to admit the fact that the paper itself limits only to the Meitei women of the Manipur valley.

Popular Women

Manipur uniquely prides herself of her own indigenous women's enduring socio-economic roles and their inseparable historic experiences significantly with the state's wider political exigencies from time to time, which have always been fascinating to the scholars. They have praised the Manipuri women, yet have failed to thrust upon the other side of the reality. Amidst newness of the area of the study and scant nature of relevant literature, this paper is a humble attempt devised to address the issue based on the framework that combines a theoretical setting with the available sources.

There are undoubtedly cultural remnants in the traditional patrilineal Meitei society that favoured common women to be economically self-reliant and to build up socio-political collective energy. Apart from shouldering the responsibility of familial sustenance, the women, in the productive economic arena, were seen in household industrial enterprises, brunt of agricultural operations and market activities. There are evidences of the common women's collective participation directly or indirectly in political domain in multitude of forms even to that extent of either correcting administrative malaises or shaping the state policies on constitutional framework. What makes the Manipuri women so visible in the public domain? It is quite imperative to dwell upon the governing factors that had bridged the gap between the domesticity and the public domain. Its genesis in a historical setting could perhaps be traced back to the formal inception of the *Lallup* system[12] under which all able bodied adult males transcending barriers, excepting the craftsmen pursuing crafts for the king, were made to render mandatory ten days' military service to the state in every forty days for which were they exempted from the payment of taxes that was inseparably necessitated by the incessant warfare among the chiefdoms and with the neighbouring states.[13] In war free times, they rendered feudal services to the state in the form of state's constructive works. This genesis of regimentalisation and constant abreast in the active state services combined to foster the male folks away from full time household management and to the creation of a required push factor that lifted the women from domesticity to public space. Other prime movers responsible to the question were

'Reign of Terror for seven years (1819-26)[14] while the kingdom was succumbed to the onslaught of Burmese imperialism,[15] which brought a devastating male depopulation considerably changing the sex role in socio-economic and political relationships.

Women were, hence, forced to fulfill the multiple roles ranging from familial sustenance to public lives. Apart from shouldering the family livelihood',[16] massive depopulation of males compelled the women to partake in social gatherings and ceremonies as familial heads. Public production activities and social gatherings, therefore, evolved the construction of an open space for knowledge interaction among the women to the problems of the state, which erupted from time to time. Women's market, amongst the centers of knowledge exchange, was undoubtedly the most unquestioned avenue of political interchanges and collective identity of women. The market women being politically empowered by this contextual cultural root were found visible in a more organized manner in a greater scale attuning to the flowing winds of politics and social transformation in collective voices. Apart from being a potent transaction centre, it was 'non-market function', particularly the political function that has made the women's market a unique place. The economic independence, strong cord of mutual support and collective identity among the women, besides building up a strong 'social force', also helped towards construction of indigenous feminism among the women in the traditional Meitei society.

Royal Women

While the *Cheitharol Kumbaba* is primarily the chronological accounts of the Meitei kings, the *Ningthourol Lambuba*, on the other side, is about the Meitei kings together with the accounts of the queens. These sources inform that in terms of public space the *Maharani* (Chief Queen) used to occupy a centre-stage in *phambaltongba* (royal coronation of the king).[17] Given the royal women's participation in the individual levels in the state's formal administrative and judicial system, it has been a long tradition. To begin, Pakhangba ascended the throne with the wisdom of his mother.[18] This is a popular myth revolving around Pakhangba's accession to the throne. Testimony runs for an all-in- all women's court of justice, called *Kutchu* (*Laishna Kutchu)*, headed by the queen Laishna,[19] wife of the first recorded king of Manipur, Nongda Lairen Pakhangba, handling the autonomous power of jurisdiction over both civil and criminal cases related to a variety of women's issues like adultery, divorce, wife-beating, assault, etc. Laishna[20] earned the credit for her commendable contribution to cement the Ningthouja rule, founded by Nongda Lairen Pakhangba, in the infancy of state formation in the first century AD. *Pacha* is another significant all-in-all women's court. Nakhang Hanjabi, Heerushang Hanjabi and Loikhomshang Hanjabi (who was either mother or maternal aunt of the *Maharani*) were all members of the *Pacha*. The *Ametpa Loisang*,[21] established in the time of Mungyamba (1562-1597 AD), was also headed by the queen.[22] The valour of the queen Laitonkhu, wife of Pengshiba (379-394 AD), to the annexation of a tribal village and the wisdom of the queen Yaoreiba Chanu, wife of Naokhamba (411 -428 AD), to resolve the wars of succession between the two princes – Naophang Ahanba and Naophangba - are recorded in the chronicles. Yaoreiba Chanu has been elevated to the status of *Leishangthem Lairembi* (goddess) and worshipped. The exalted role of the queen Linthoingambi to safeguard successfully the territorial integrity of the kingdom, during the absence of her husband ruler, Ningthoukhomba (1432-1467 AD), who embarked on a warfront at Akla, is another jewel in the crown of a Meitei queen. Queen Linthoingambi disguised herself as her husband king Ninthoukhomba as she donned in kingly attire and deceived the Tangkhul raiders of Tushen led by its chief Hen Puringba. The Tangkhuls prayed for excuse. In return, under queen Linthoingambi's order, wine was served in plenty till they were lost. They were, hence, overpowered.[23] Similarly, the statesmanship of Maharani Kumudini, wife of Gambhir Singh (1821; 1825-34 AD), and of Gomti, another royal women, are well known in the history of Manipur.

In addition to the royal women, there were different categories of women working in different capacities in the palace. Among the common women in the society, they held important social status. The position of *Sanamapi* can be remembered as an example. Their duties were to bring up and look after the new born babies of the queens. They were so close to the queens that sometimes they held the keys of the queens. In the marriage of the princesses, the respective *sanamapis* led the palanquins carrying the princesses. In the *Lai haraoba* dance in their respective places/villages, their high social status was recognized by way of reserving separate seats for them.

The Meitei kings could customarily have five queens. These five queens had their own titles. The eldest queen used to be addressed as '*Leimarenbi/Leima Athoibi/Maharani*; the second one as *Apambi Ahal*; the third as *Apambi Naha*; the fourth as *Leimakhubi Ahal* and the fifth one as *Leimakhubi Naha*. Beyond this prescription, there were as many queens as the kings wanted. It is recorded that Maharaja Bhagyachandra (1759-1761; 1763-1798 AD) had ninety-four queens[24]. One among the reasons that has largely contributed to the royal polygyny was the 'gifts of daughters' by the parents to the kings, obviously for royal relations. The royal relations meant nothing but favours and exemptions from a variety of royal impositions. On the private lives of sexuality, only the *Maharani* had the right to possess a bed earmarked for the king in her apartment. The other queens were not allowed this privilege. The violation of the convention was subject to penalization.[25] The *Maharaja* will go to the *Maharani* but the rest of the queens had to attend the *Maharaja* at his own royal apartment. The sexual life of the *Maharani* with the *Maharaja* was strictly regulated for the auspicious days because it was meant for a baby boy who would be the king of the state some day. It has always been an intense longing for every queen to have her first born child to be a baby boy in the patriarchal kingdom. It is worth noting that there was a special court of nine women councillors to strictly look after the sexual life of the king with his queens. All the related cases are handled by this all-in-all royal women's court.[26] The private life of all the queens was strictly regulated. They were looked after by the *feidas*. Their family members could meet the queen only with prior appointment from the *feida*. It was the duty of the *feida* to lock the bed rooms of the queens at night and open them in the morning.[27] The *feidas* were also selected to look after the administration of the women's market, more particularly at times of any market related crisis. The records mention an earmarked mound amidst an early market, called *feidapung* market.[28] This mound was the space from where the *feidas* transacted market administration.[29]

Colonial Perception

Reading official colonial accounts as well as non-official observations/private diaries/ personal memoirs of the colonial officers, who served or whose relatives spent sometime in this frontier region, had observed their contemporary Meitei women in two different positions. While the Meitei women were praised for their significant politico-economic roles as well as comparatively better off social status, the gray areas in the world of women were also picked up. The women's role in the economic front is captured as follows:

> The most of the work of the country, except the heaviest, is performed by them, and they are consequently the mainstay of the family circle. All the marketing is done

> by the women, all the works of buying and selling in public, and the carrying to and fro of the articles to be sold; whilst at home they are busily employed in weaving and spinning. It would be difficult to find more industrious women in India than the Manipuri.[30]

On the political consciousness of the Manipuri women, the following official account can be glanced at:

> The market women form the vast majority of travelers along our roads, and they are most keen in bringing any grievances to notice. If a bridge is washed away, the first information comes from them, and they are also not backward in reporting a bad piece of road.[31]

Once again, E. W. Dun commented,

> The women of Manipur, married or unmarried, are not confined to zenanas as they are in Bengal or Hindustan; ... neither do they cover their faces before strangers.[32]

Contrarily, his following observation depicted another side of the story:

> With all their industry and usefulness, women hold but a very inferior social position, and are considered more in the light of goods and chattels than as persons to be treated with honour and consideration.[33]

The colonial accounts, in contrast to the industriousness of the Manipuri women, have also screened the 'laziness and indolence' of the male counterpart.[34]

The above observations have shown a meaning on the complex situation of the world of Manipuri women. While the age-old historical roots and the progressive societal attitude positively favoured the women,[35] there are, no doubt, negative markers towards defining their status. Much against their positive roles, they were 'indifferently treated'[36] in the society. Non-existence of typical mainland India's dowry issue or child-marriage[37] have been answered by the practices like polygamy that was very much common among the privileged classes, if not so much in the 'lower orders'.[38] The paradox of the praised role and non-reciprocal social position in the colonial perspective has been partially traced to the 'laxity of marriage rules' and to the 'baneful system of domestic slavery'.[39] Dun writes, "a man can put away his wife without any fault on her part, and if a person of influence, he may do so without its being noticed".[40] He then comments, "women are really the slaves of their husbands; they are sold in satisfaction of their debts, and it is said that men often pawn their wives to purchase some office or even a pony".[41] Though the colonial accounts had hinted some institutional factors, which have disfavoured women, they have shortfalls from developing scholarly engagement to journey a little deeper into the task of excavating the root.

NOTES & REFERENCES

1. While Nongda Lairen Pakhangba was recorded as the first king, it was Garibniwaj who declared the Vaishnavite Hinduism as the royally patronized state religion followed by an aggressive Hinduisation of the Manipuri society.
2 See "*Chada* (*Chata*) *Lahui*", in N Khelchandra (ed), *Ariba Manipuri Sahityagi Itihas*, Imphal, 1969, pp.222-225.
3. Thounaojam Chanu Ibemhal, *Haoreima Shambubi*, Imphal, 2000, p.30.
4. As a student of history, my fundamental concern is towards historicity. I have read myths/ legends/folklores/oral tests, but have cautiously maintained history as quite distinct from them.
5. Customarily, market plots are transferred from mother to daughter-in-laws or daughters. See H. Sudhir, "Women's Market and State", *Proceedings of North East India History Association*, XXIVth Session, Guwahati, 2003, p.234.
6. Saroj Nalini Arambam Parratt, *The Court Chronicle of the Kings of Manipur-The Cheitharon Kumpapa*, Routledge, 2005, p.1.

7. Kumkum Roy, "Gender Relations During the First Millennium: An Overview", in B. D. Chattopadhyaya (ed), *A Social History of Early India, History of Science, Philosophy and Culture in Indian Civilization*, Vol.II, Part 5, p.223.
8. Kumkum Roy, *op. cit.*, pp. 225-226.
9. Almost all the modern historical writings on Manipur are of the men. Women writers are not only very few, even their writings are far distant from histories of Women and Gender.
10. I have, in this line, attempted a humble one. See H. Sudhir, "Gender and Society in Manipur", in Priyam Goswami (ed.), *Changing Patterns of Economy and Society- 19th and 20th Century North East India*, Guwahati, 2007, pp.195-208.
11. It was entered between Haridas Gosain, emissary of Jai Singh and Harry Verelst, Chief of the Chittagong Factory. For authority on this treaty, see Abdul Ali, "Notes on the Early History of Manipur", *Bengal Past and Present*, October-December, 1923.
12. Literally meant war organization (*Lal* = war; *Lup* = organization).
13. H. Sudhir, "Women and Public Domain", *Proceedings of Indian History Congress*, Mysore, 2003, p.926.
14. See Lal Dena (ed.), *History of Modern Manipur*, Orbit Publishers and Distributors, Delhi, 1991.
15. Anglo-Manipur War of 1891 was another factor. An account on the war is available in R. C. Majumdar, "The Manipur Rebellion of 1891", *Bengal Past and Present*, January-June, 1959; Gourchandra, *Manipurgi Aroiba Lan*, Imphal, 1971.
16. E. W. Dun, *Gazetteer of Manipur*, (London, 1886), Reprint Vivek Publishing Company, Delhi, 1981, p. 17.
17. N. Khelchandra Singh, "Meitei Ningthouna Phambal Tongba", in I. R. Babu Singh (ed), *Apunba Wareng*, Imphal, 1986, pp.108-09.
18. L. Ashokkumar Singh, *Ariba Manipuri Sahityagi Paring*, Imphal, 1988, p.17
19. Laishna (Laisna) sister of Poireiton, accompanied her brother (Poireiton) in the immigration journey called *Poireiton Khunthok*. Poireiton was a strong contender against Pakhangba for the vacant throne of Manipur. Poireiton was defeated in the race. Nevertheless, a closer tie was set in by a

matrimonial alliance when Poireiton's sister Laishna married Pakhangba.

20. A little later, queen Yaoreiba Chanu played a crucial role to put Naophangba to the throne. See N. Indramani, *Phamballon*, Imphal, 2009, p.13.
21. Department of Medicine.
22. Gangmumei Kabui, *History of Manipur*, Vol.I, National Publishing House, New Delhi, 1991, p.208.
23. Oinam Bhogeshor Singh, *Ningthourol Lambuba*, Imphal, 1967, pp.228-29.
24. Details may be seen in Ch. Hemchandra, *Meihoubarol Shangai Phammang*, Imphal, 2004, p.71.
25. O. Bhegeshor, *Loina-Shillon*, Imphal, 1976, p.19.
26. The nine royal women councilors were Makhong Hanjabi, Heerushang Hanjabi, Leimakhong Hanjabi, Yendren Hanbi, Keikrun Hanbi, Phiru Hanbi, Phourung Hanbi, Ngarung Hanbi, Thumjaorungbi. Leimakhong Hanjabi has to be the maternal aunt of the *Maharani*. See N. Khelchandra Singh, *Mashin* (unpublished Manuscript) cited in Bimabati, *Manipurgi Ningthoukon Amashung Chatna Lonchat*, Imphal, 2008, p.10.
27. Grateful to Indramani Singh of Imphal for sharing with me the information.
28. For history of the markets, see H. Sudhir, "Women's Market and State", *op.cit.*, pp. 231-233.
29. For a brief account, see H. Sudhir, "Women's Market and State", *op.cit.*, pp.231-239.
30. E.W. Dun, *op.cit.*, p.17.
31. *Administration Report, Manipur, 1895-96*, Manipur State Archives, Imphal, p. 8.
32. E.W. Dun, op. , cit., p.17.
33. *Ibid.*
34. *Ibid.*
35. Wife of Mr. Grimwood, Political Agent in Manipur (1888-91) recollects when she underlines, " The Manipuris do not shut up their women, as is the custom in most parts of India, and they are much more enlightened and intelligent in consequence. As soon as a woman marries she puts back her fringe, but no

other restrictions are laid upon her". See Ethel St. Clair Grimwood, *My Three Years in Manipur* (1891), Gyan Publishing House, New Delhi, 2000, p.45.

36. McCulloch, *Selections from the Records of the Government of India* (Foreign Department), No. XXVII: "Account of the Valley of Munnipore and of the Hill Tribes with a comparative vocabulary of the Munnipore and other languages", Bengal Printing Company Limited, 1859, p.19. Major McColloch, Political Agent in Manipur (1844-62; 1863-67), married a Manipuri lady named Thotpi and had two daughters.
37. Girls generally did not marry until fifteen. Widow re-marriage was permitted but 'not with the deceased husband's brother in the Meitei community. See Grimwood, *op.cit.*, p.45.
38. It records, "the Senaputti was supposed to be the happy owner of nine wives, and the others had almost as many". See Grimwood, *op.cit*, p.43.
39. Dun, *op.cit.*, pp.17-18.
40. *Ibid.*
41. *Ibid*

11

Historiography of Meitei State Formation

Jayati Bhattacharjee & Sarbani Bhattacharjee

Introduction

The state formation study became a popular field of research in the last quarter of the twentieth century, particularly ever since the publication of Henri J. M. Claessen and Peter Skalnik (ed.) *The Early State*[1] which covered a large number of case studies spread over all the geographical and ethnic regions of the world, including two cases from India, namely, the Mauryan State from early Northern India and the Dimasa State from medieval Northeast India, besides a number of serious theoretical essays on the basics of state formations. The origin of this multi-disciplinary field of research is generally attributed to Friedrich Engels' *The Origin of the Family, Private Property and the State*[2] which was published in the last quarter of the nineteenth century. While Engels considered the emergence of private property as the beginning of social stratification and the resultant state formation, Claessen and Skalnik took serious note of a large number of factors of state formations which were identified by the multi-disciplinary researches in the twentieth century.

However, Claessen and Skalnik also observed that the economic factor was the most crucial in state and polity formations. In India, a considerable interest in the field in the ancient Indian context was evoked by Romila Thapar's work *From Lineage to State*[3] which dealt mainly with the Ganga valley or Indo-Gangetic plains but delved into the concepts and issues that are theoretically basic to the social and state formation studies. In case of Eastern India and the Northeast, the major inspiration was the publication of Surajit Sinha's *Tribal Polities and State Systems in Pre-Colonial Eastern and North Eastern India.*[4] In fact, Sinha had already drawn the attention of the Indian scholars to the importance of the state formation studies in his presidential address to Anthropology section of the Indian Science Congress in 1962, which was published in the *Man in India* same year.[5] Thereafter, a good number of scholars took interest in the field, including Hermann Kulke who did an excellent work on the tribal areas of Eastern India.[6]

The study of the emergence of states and polities in Northeast India was largely inspired by the work of Surajit Sinha who established contacts with the local scholars in different areas since 1977 and organized two workshops in Kolkata in 1980 for the preparation of a book on tribal polities and state systems in eastern and north-eastern India. Some of the scholars from the Northeast, namely, Amalendu Guha, J. B. Bhattacharjee, B. Pakem, Hamlet Bareh, A. C. Sinha, B. B. Goswami and R. K. Saha, were involved in that project of Sinha and they contributed studies on the Ahoms, Dimasas, Jaintias, Khasis, Sikkimese, Mizos and Meiteis respectively.[7] Inspired by the Kolkata experience, J. B. Bhattacharjee made a strong plea for the state formation studies in Northeast India while presenting a paper on 'Tripuri State formation' at the third annual session of the North East India History Association (NEIHA) at Manipur University, Imphal, in 1982.[8] He followed up the plea by publishing a special issue of *The NEHU Journal of Social Sciences and Humanities*[9] on state formations and by assigning relevant topics to his doctoral students at the North-Eastern Hill University.[10] The publication of his work entitled *Social and Polity Formations in Pre-Colonial North-East India* in 1991,[11] which is a collection of his own research papers published in various journals and proceedings over a period of ten years, induced a good number of younger scholars to take up studies on the ethnic groups in the Northeast within the framework of the 'Early State Model' of Claessen and Skalnik. Bhattacharjee's *Bhauma-Naraka Legend and State Formation in Pragjyotisha-Kamarupa*,[12] which contains the text of his H.K. Barpujari Endowment Lecture at the twenty-fourth annual session of the North East India History Association at Guwahati in 2003, is another seminal work on state formation in early Northeast India. However, in the instant case of Meitei State formation in particular, the pioneering contribution was from Gangmumei Kamei (Kabui) who presented the first paper on the subject in the same session of North East India History Association as J. B. Bhattacharjee did on the Tripuris.[13]

Basics of State Formation Studies

The state formation study is not just the empirical narrative of where, when and how a state came into existence or it was established, but a critical analyses of the factors and forces which worked towards the emergence of a state or polity in an absolutely non-state situation by stages and degrees of changes and developments. The conceptual framework for such studies owes its origin to Friedrich Engels' *The Origin of Family, Private Property and the State* wherein Engels had observed that "The state has not existed from all eternity. There have been societies which have managed without it, which had no notion of the state or state power. At a definite stage of economic development, which necessarily involved the cleavage of society into classes, the state became a necessity because of this cleavage."[14] The works that came in much later than that of Engels generally accepted his position on correlation between property, class and state. As a matter of fact, these works further strengthened Engels' position on the role of economy in state and polity formations. For example, the German sociologists like L.Gumplovicz[15] and Franz Oppenheimer,[16] who developed the 'conquest theory' to propose that the pastoral groups in the regions combined their organizational strength and striking power to defeat and subjugate the more sluggish agricultural communities and forced them to accept the subordination and to pay tributes to the conquerors, tentatively affirmed that social inequality was one of the factors which further empowered the more powerful to oppress and exploit the subjects and the subjugated. Robert H. Lowie,[17] Richard Thurnwald[18] and D. Westermann,[19] improved upon the 'conquest theory' by their respective case studies, but they also endorsed the view that the social inequality was one of the basic factors of the origin of a state. The 'irrigation theory' of Julian H. Steward[20] and the 'hydraulic state' of Karl A. Wittfogel[21] looked upon the division of labour, intensive cultivation and massive cooperation in the ethnic societies as significantly consequential in the emergence of states. The 'population theory' of Morton H. Fried,[22] Jack Stauder,[23] M. J. Harner,[24] M. A. Bakel,[25] C. P. Kottak,[26] Elman R. Service,[27] Robert L. Carneiro,[28] Steven Polgar,[29] and Marshal D. Sahlins[30] contended that the increase in population, changes in the means of subsistence, and the development of a market economy had substantially influenced the development of states. Finally, Henri J. M. Claessen and Peter Skalnik's *The Early State,*[31] which enumerated a large number of factors for the rise, growth and sustenance of the early states, established reasonably beyond doubt that in spite of the regional variations in contents in specific cases the economic root of state formations remains unquestionable.

It is now generally accepted that the economic change or changes in the mode of production was the commonest of the common factors of state formations in all conditions. However, what causes the economic change or development also cannot be overlooked while enumerating the factors of state formation, because going beyond the 'immediate' is always a logical demand in historical method. Thus, in the process of 'economic development' a consequential factor must have been the technology. The rudiments of technological inventions and innovations, in the form of crude tools and their application, began in the hunting and food gathering stage of the societies. The pastoral societies also required tools and equipments of different sorts. The development of the war materials for conquest, the equipments for irrigation, and the agricultural techniques to augment productivity under compelling pressure of population growth were essentially linked with the improvisation of technology. The advances in technology invariably impacted the economic development of the societies and the economic differentiation within the societies. The uneven economic development due to the emergence of private property, which Friedrich Engels identified as the starting point of social stratification and state formation, is in effect a consequence of the technological development from the crude tools and implements to the sophisticated equipments and machineries. There are, of course, opinions that the technological development in its true sense could take place in an area only after the state had already come into existence. This is because the development of technology required a lot of organizational and financial support which is possible only when the state is already in place. As for example, while discussing the role of technology in *The Early State*,[32] Robert Cohen observed that the formation of early state systems followed in an invariant way the development of improved technology and that remarkable improvements did actually occur in production, transportation, information processing, architecture, and scientific knowledge only in association with the statehood. In his view, the basic tools for production in agriculture and crafts did not show any remarkable systematic improvement in the pre-state situation. The plough and other forms of primitive tools were generally unconnected with the state systems. The state formation occasioned specialization as the society had to be organized economically and politically and the specialists were to be encouraged and supported by the state to ensure an uninterrupted supply of the trained manpower for the large variety of jobs in a growing and expanding system. The capacity for long-distance trade with improved transportation techniques, record-keeping and writing, complex architectural forms and accurate measurement devices developed only when the society had already differentiated and the coordinating managerial bureaucratic offices were in place. The authority system and its bureaucratic officialdom were the true causal agents of later technological improvements for control over large masses of labour to build monuments, roads, bridges, and canals.[33] The technological development in the real sense, therefore, in the opinion of Cohen, was possible only after the formation of the state. However, according to Cohen, only one possible exception was the warfare as some sort of soldiery and war-equipments were necessary for conquest, subjection and subjugation as a step towards initial growth of the states where two non-state polities competed for local control and the superior military technology became crucial in giving victory to one or the other party. This is because the 'conquered states' depended to a great extent upon the military technology of the victors. However, the professional soldiery and sophistication of the equipments were often the results of political centralization after the emergence of the state. Similarly, irrigation also needed some equipments and technical know-how, but irrigation was a special problem which served largely to the intensification of centralization.[34]

Thus, Cohen's main argument is that the technological development in a real sense was possible only with the support of the state system which is possible only after the state has already been formed. Nonetheless, Robert Cohen himself admitted that some sort of technological development in the form of inventions and improvisation - no matter how primitive or crude that may have been - was called for to hasten the state formation process, since technology had a decisive role to play in the surplus generation without which no state could originate.

No wonder, Surajit Sinha's *Tribal Polities and State Systems in Pre-Colonial Eastern and North Eastern India*[35] underlined 'Surplus Generation, Extraction and Redistribution' as the most crucial factor in the state formation processes in the region. The work also clearly emphasized that the surplus generation was possible only by the use of improved technology. Thus, according to Sinha, there was a "significant correlation between the degree of surplus generated through appropriate technological innovations and the level of functional differentiation, stratification and centralization of a polity."[36] His opinion on the role of technology in the pre-state polity becomes more emphatic when he says,

> The Mizo chieftaincies provide a case where polities could not develop beyond the level of petty chiefdoms by depending only on shifting cultivation in the rugged and steeply inclined terrains of Mizoram. In the case of the Siyem chiefdoms in the Khasi hills we do not find either settled plough cultivation or extensive animal herding. The small scale chiefdoms or principalities (Siyems) were sustained by horticulture, intensive hoe cultivation, some shifting cultivation, development of metal-crafts, mineral extraction and trade with the people of the plains. It is important to observe that only when originally shifting cultivator groups like the Jaintia or the Dimasa could command control over the

> plough cultivating rice lands in Sylhet and in the Cachar plains that they were able to develop states of elaborate scale like the Jaintia state of Meghalaya and Sylhet and the Dimasa state of Cachar.[37]

In the same tenor, Amalendu Guha, in his paper in the same collection of Sinha, reflected on the origin of states in tribal situations, means of surplus generation, and the impact of surplus on the state organization.[38] In his words,

> No tribe leaped to statehood while it was still at its pristine stage. Before that it needed a sedentary agricultural population, with a degree of division of labour and social stratification, as the starting point. Statehood emerged only when a community was itself capable of yielding a surplus sufficient for the maintenance of a non-producing public authority, or of systematically appropriating such a surplus in the form of tribute from a neighboring community. Smaller the surplus, less elaborate was its public authority structure.[39]

Finally, it can be observed that the privatization of resources and surplus generation, which resulted in economic differentiation and social stratification, are taken as the initial conditions for state formations. The research is to look into the processes of privatization and methods of generation, extraction and redistribution of surplus and its enlargement by the emerging leadership of the community or ethnic society which would ultimately rule the rest of the community or society. The surplus generation is intrinsically linked with the technological innovations and improvisations without which the productivity would have stagnated at the subsistence level and would not allow any surplus for extraction and appropriation by the public authority. The role of technology in economic change and surplus generation, therefore, needs to be appropriately integrated in the conceptual framework for state formation studies. The origin myths and the role of religion and priestly orders, among other factors, are also important in specific conditions in which a particular state originated.

Glimpses of the Meitei State

The Meitei state in Manipur came into existence in the first century AD and flourished till it was subjugated by the British in the nineteenth century. The state emerged from the Meitei ethnic society which at some point of time consisted of seven clans, namely, Ningthouja, Angom, Luwang, Khuman, Khaba-Aganba, Chenglei, and Moirang, which had migrated to the Manipur valley from Southern China or Burma through the Kabo valley# at different points of time. The migrations were in groups or batches, probably clan-wise, and each one of them settled in an exclusive area that eventually developed into a clan-principality or chiefdom. All of them in course of time came to be known as Meiteis. On the other hand, the autochthonous groups in the valley (Loi, Chakpa, and few other minor ethnic or dialect groups) gradually merged into one group, called Loi. These pre-Meitei autochthonous groups as well as other ethnic groups which had immigrated into the Manipur valley till about the fifteenth century AD were assimilated in the Meitei social fold by adopting the Meitei lineage structure and language through a process of Metei-ization. A new group that emerged from within the Meitei society, called Yaithibi, consisted of those Meiteis who were accused of various offences and excommunicated from the respective clans. They were given penal settlements outside the Meitei villages within the valley. In course of time, the entire valley was divided between the seven clan principalities. These principalities included the settlements of the pre-Meitei inhabitants and the immigrants. The principality of the Ningthoujas, who were possibly the first Meitei clan to immigrate into the valley and who were also the most powerful among the proto-Meitei clans, included the most fertile central valley or the modern Imphal area. Kangla was the seat of authority of the Ningthouja chief.

When the Meitei state finally came into existence by subjugation of the six other clan-principalities, the Meitei kings belonged only to the Ningthouja clan. As informed by *Cheitharol Kumbaba*, the royal chronicle of the Meitei kings, the first Ningthouja king, Nongda Lairen Pakhangba, had a divine origin. This legend deified the Ningthouja chiefs and gave them the legitimacy. The Ningthouja principality thus enjoyed a superior status among the Meitei clan-principalities. In course of time, the Ningthouja chiefs subjugated the Angom, Luwang, Khaba-Aganba, and Chenglei principalities. The Khumans and the Moirangs offered resistance for sometimes. However, in the fourteenth century the Khuman principality was also subjugated. The Ningthouja chief was then proclaimed as the king of the Meiteis. Kangla became the capital of the kingdom. In the fifteenth century, the Moirang chiefdom was also defeated and forced to accept the Ningthouja suzerainty. This last principality was also eventually absorbed in the Meitei kingdom. The king was first called *Lainingthou*. In 1724 AD, the title was formally changed to *Mahârâjâ* and the kingdom came to be known as Manipur. It became a protected state under the British after the Anglo-Burmese War (1824-26) and a princely state after the Anglo-Manipur War of 1891.[40]

The emergence of the Meitei state seems to have been in two distinct phases. The first was a case of indigenous growth from the clan-level institutions to the chiefdoms in which the traditional Meitei religion (*Laining/Sanamahi*) played the role of establishing the seniority or precedence of the Ningthouja chiefs through the beliefs and practices of the traditional ancestor worship. The myth of the divine origin of the legendary founder of the Ningthouja dynasty, namely, Nongda Lairen Pakhangba, deified the Ningthouja chiefs. In the second phase, the state assumed its final form as a kingdom of the pan-Indian Brahmanical model after the

Meitei society was Vaisnavised at the initiative of the Meitei kings. However, the state had already emerged much before the advent of the Vaiṣṇava preachers and the immigration and settlement of the Brahmins. The ancestor worship (*apokpa khurumjaba*) continued to be the most important ritual practice for each Meitei household. This ritual served the twin purpose of ensuring the loyalty of the people to their ancestors and legitimizing the superior status of the Ningthouja chief over other chiefs on the basis of seniority. The integration of the non-Meitei groups into the Meitei lineage structure further strengthened the position of the Ningthouja chief in the enlarged Meitei society. The king looked after the defence of the kingdom and the maintenance of law and order, while the religious and social matters were taken care of by the *Pandit Laisong* which was the highest body of the Meitei literati. Nonetheless, the external influences also considerably reinforced the state-building processes. The word *'pandit'* or *'pundit'* is in all likelihood of Indo-Aryan root. Moreover, a copper-plate inscription of the Meitei king Khongtekcha (8th century AD) mentioned about the worship of '*Hari*, *Ganesha*, *Śiva* and *Devi*', among other deities. The next ruler, Kyamba (1467-1508) built a temple for Viṣṇu at Bishenpur. These happened much before the Vaisnavisation of the Meitei society. Charại Rongba (16th century AD) was the first Meitei king to be formally initiated to Vaisnavism. King Gareebniwaz (1709-48 AD) declared Vaisnavism as the state religion. Finally, *Mahârâjâ* Bhagyachandra or Jai Singh (1759-98 AD), who was initiated to the Gauḍiya Vaisnavism, popularized Gauḍiya Vaisnavism among the masses and persuaded the *Pandits* to accept the new faith. However, the Meiteis continued to practice the traditional rites and rituals, including ancestor worship, even after the mass conversion of the community to Vaisnavism. The *lai haraoba*, which pronounce the social hierarchy on the basis of origins of the clans, was declared to be the annual state festival. Similarly, when the Meitei kings gradually established their control over the chiefs in the surrounding hills, a dance performance by the tribes in the palace, called *haochongba*, became an important annual festival like the *lai haraoba* of the Meiteis. Alongside these internal changes and efforts towards universalization of indigenous culture, the authority of the kings was further strengthened by external relations with Cachar, Tripura, Bengal, Assam, etc., in the west and the Shan states, Burma, etc., in the east. The Meitei princes and princesses were married in the ruling families of the neighbouring states. There were also commercial and diplomatic relations with those states.[41]

The most consequential material factor towards the formation of the Meitei state seems to be the quality of the land under occupation of the various groups. The Meitei clans as well as the Yaithibis and the autochthonous Lois had their own chiefs at the level of the clan or community. The conflicts over occupation of the more fertile agricultural lands in the valley commenced almost with the advent of the Meiteis. The Ningthoujas gradually pushed the Lois to the less fertile peripheral areas in the foothill region and then subdued and subordinated their chiefs. The Loi and other indigenous groups were then structurally integrated into the Meitei society through the lineage system. The next major step was the assignment of specific occupational or functional roles to the selected Meitei as well as Meitei-ized lineages by the Ningthouja chiefs. This dispensation not only expanded the size of the principality and increased its population but also brought the artisan and service-groups within the principality. The Lois and the Yaithibis were mainly assigned such works which were generally despised by the common Meiteis. The Brahmins, Bishnupriyas and Pangans (Muslim), who immigrated into the valley from across the western hills (*i.e.*, Barak-Surma valley) in the 15th-16th century AD, maintained their respective ethnic, caste and religious identities within the larger Manipuri society, but they also adopted the local language and culture and they immensely contributed to the economic and cultural development of the kingdom. The Bishnupriyas were given settlement in the marshy lowlands, while the Pangans, who were the prisoners of war from Bengal (Northeast Bengal/Barak-Surma valley), were settled in the riverbanks as they were expert agriculturists who introduced the method of paddy transplantation in Manipur. The prosperity of the valley attracted some sections of the Kukis and Nagas in the neighboring hills to descend down to the plains. They were allotted land in the marshy region for settlement and were recruited in the police force of the chiefs. The immigrant communities held specified tracts of land and within the tracts different clans laid their own villages. The Brahmins were initially settled in the central valley, but they were later on dispersed to the Meitei villages throughout the valley as their services were required by all the Hinduized Meiteis as priests, preceptors and educators. The kings made generous gifts to the Brahmins and the temples. The principal wealth of the king or the state was the land. The chief of a clan or an ethnic group was earlier considered as the owner of the land under the control of that clan or group, but after the establishment of the kingship the Meitei king became the theoretical owner of all land within the state.[42]

The Meitei chiefs took several initiatives for generating surplus out of the natural and human resources of the principality. The incentive to immigration and the assimilation of the new-comers in the Meitei society led to population growth and the proliferation of occupational groups — artisans, craftsmen and other specialists — in the territory. Similarly, the assignment of specific occupations and functions to families or lineages resulted in the hereditary division of labour. In fact, the skilful land management, technological improvisation, division of labour and intensive labour utilization by the kings contributed to the economic prosperity of the kingdom. They developed the productivity level in the marshy lowlands by draining out excess water through excavated canals and by constructing dykes and dams for irrigation and watering the agricultural fields. The successful water management contributed positively to the agricultural productivity, besides reclamation of fallow lands and expansion of settlements. On the other hand, the acceleration of economic development caused increasing social differentiation among the people due to uneven distribution of natural resources between the geographical divisions within the state. Firstly, the valley dwellers were more prosperous than those in the hills, because the valley land was more suitable for agriculture. The hill people depended on horticulture and shifting cultivation, whereas in the valley wet rice cultivation was practiced. Secondly, within the valley also there was economic differentiation on the basis of the yielding capacity of land. The Meiteis and the Brahmins in the most fertile northern plains and the central valley were wealthier than any other group. The surplus generating central valley constituted the prime economic zone of the state. The dominant status of the Ningthoujas among the seven Meitei clan-principalities was also the result of their control over larger portion of the most fertile tracts of land. The six other Meitei clans, who shared the rest of the fertile parts of the northern plains amongst themselves, were better off than the dwellers of the foothills and the marshy regions, but the Ningthoujas were ahead of them. Thirdly, the agricultural income of almost all the groups in the valley was supplemented by handloom which was almost a household occupation for the Meiteis and the tribal groups in Manipur. It was considered as a respectable craft and almost every household owned a loom of its own. The cocoanut and betel-nut were grown almost in every compound in the valley, besides the vegetables and fruits. The Pangans grew large quantity of vegetables in the riverine belt, besides practicing agriculture in which they were indeed the specialists. Fourthly, the agricultural yield of the foothills region was not enough for subsistence of the dwellers, since it was least fertile and often inundated by flood. Therefore, the Lois resorted to horticulture, rearing goats, fowls and swine, liquor distillation, poultry farming, pot-making and producing salt and charcoal, and also worked as palanquin bearers for the members of the royal family and the officials. However, the ecology of the foothills region favoured certain crafts and industries in which the Lois specialized. The salt wells were mostly situated in that region, and salt-manufacturing was an important industry for the Lois. The best quality clay for pottery was available only in the Loi area and the potters' villages were also located in that area. Fifthly, the Bishnupriyas and the Yaithibis, who inhabited the less fertile and flood-prone marshy lands, had to supplement their agricultural income by fishing, carpentry and basketry, salt-manufacturing, lime-making, iron-work, pottery and such other professions which the Meiteis of the northern and central valley refused to perform. The Lois and the Yaithibis specialized in sericulture and in growing cotton and fibre plants, which gave a boost to handloom and textile. Finally, the social stratification accrued from the economic differentiation based on productive quality of land in each ethnic or clan division as agriculture continued to be the mainstay of economy of the state. However, in the matter of generation of surplus all the regional and ethnic components of the state contributed, either through agriculture or craft and manufactures, or by labour.[43]

Alongside the development of agricultural productivity, the Meitei society passed through a process of professional specialization and the institutionalization of social stratifications on the basis of occupations and professions. Agriculture and handloom were common occupations for almost all the ethnic groups in Manipur, but the professional specializations emerged in the society in course of time on the basis of hereditary occupations and the localized availability of raw-materials. King Loiyamba (1094-1122 AD) formally recognized the occupational status of certain groups, villages and lineages by issuing a *Shinyen* (royal edict). This was further expanded and sophisticated by the later kings, namely, Kyamba (1467-1508 AD), Khagemba (1597-1652 AD), and Garibniwaz (1709-1748 AD). The *Loiyamba Shinyen* assigned social and economic functions to various families (*yumnak*) and held selected families responsible for maintenance of the shrines of various deities (*umanglai*). The weavers were divided into two categories, *viz.*, weavers and dyers. Thirty families were identified for weaving and eight families were given the duty of dying. Fifty-five families were allotted the duty of maintenance of the religious shrines, and the selected families of priests made responsible for worship of various deities. One hundred and one families of priests and priestesses were to cure diseases by herbal medicines and ritual sacrifices. A state department was created for propitiating the guardian spirits for protection of the king. Ten officials were appointed for the management of land.[44] The social status of the families thus became identical with occupations and professions and the type of service one was to render to the king and his subjects. The king was himself entitled to three types of services from the people, *viz.*, *fandom* (honourable / prestigious services), *lallup* (essential services) and *laipot* (manorial services). The chiefs, priests and selected favourites of the king enjoyed the privilege of personal servants (*loi-il*) and services of the families (*yuj-tinnaba*) assigned to them, and the villagers were engaged to carry their luggage while on tour (*pothang*). The Meitei commoners were divided into four *panas*, each under a *pana hazari*, and were required to provide *lallup* service to the king. The *Lallup* system provided that every able-bodied male between 16 and 60 years should be enrolled as soldier (*lalmee*), while in peace time they should serve the king by rotation for ten days in every forty days. The peace time service included those of personal attendants, cultivation of land under direct control of the king, construction of houses and roads and bridges, collection of construction materials, and looking after the horses, ponies and cattles. In course of time, the *Lallup* system became the backbone of the economy of the state. The elements of forced labour and rudiments of slavery were noticed in this system. The war captives and the captives from the neighbouring areas were also used as slaves by the kings and high officials. Some of the kings possessed 1,200 to 1,500 such personal servants and attendants. The degraded Meiteis (ostracized for social offences), the immigrants (who were settled in marshy lowlands), and the Lois and Yaithibis (who formed the degraded groups) were required to render the *laipot* services. They had to do such works which were despised by the common Meiteis. The manufacturing of salt, iron and silk-thread, distilling liquor, fishing, making wooden posts, beams and canoes, collection of grass for the royal stable, gardening in the palace compound, etc. were considered as low works which the respectable people should not do.[45] All these are suggestive of the fact that specified families, clans or communities and villages specialized in certain art, craft and professions on hereditary lines.

Another important factor of economic development and surplus generation was the development of technology. The technological advancement of the state can be gleaned from the fact that the war-materials, including swords and shields, and bows and arrows, were locally manufactured. The Meitei kings issued commemorative coins in gold and silver of various denominations, which were minted locally, while the huge quantities of extant bell-metal coins of smaller values are supposed to be pointers to the monetization of economy. The goldsmiths, blacksmiths, carpenters and the brass and bell-metal workers emerged from the ranks of the Meitei society. The market linkages with the neighboring areas might have influenced the technological innovations and refinements. One of the chronicles mentioned that a person managed to visit Tripura and stay there for a long time to specialize in iron technology and on his return there was virtually a revolution in iron-manufacturing in Manipur. Certain arts and crafts might have been introduced by the immigrants who were also assimilated in the Meitei society. The raw-materials like gold, silver, brass, bell and other metals were possibly imported from outside. The cattle-powered plough was used for cultivation. Weaving was more or less a household occupation for the Meiteis and the tribal communities of Manipur. Elephant-catching by lassoing was an act of chivalry for the royalty. The horse and boat races and martial arts were popular in the state. Manipur is known as the homeland of polo game. The canoes or country-boats were widely used in local lakes and streams and on festive occasions. Some of the sub-clans specialized in tailoring different types of garments. The kings exercised strict control over crafts and manufacturers, and there were restrictions on the use of certain garments and jewelries by the commoners.[46] Despite checks and hindrances, there is no doubt that the technology made some advances and contributed to the economy of the state.

The remains of palaces, buildings, temples and other works of art and architecture and the pomp and grandeurs of the palace life and the life-style of the aristocracy suggest that the Meitei state generated considerable surplus. The kings extracted surplus in the form of taxes and tributes as well as labour. The king was the theoretical owner of all land in the kingdom. One third of the total land seemed to have been under direct control of the king, while another one-third in possession of the members of the ruling family, the priests and the soldiers. The kings granted rent-free land to the priests, temples, officials and other favourites in fixed proportions either permanently or for specified periods. The land for the king was cultivated by the *lallup kabas,* for which each individual was entitled to cultivate for his own support one *pari* (2.5 acres) of land. The commoners were required to pay a land tax generally at the rate of twelve baskets of paddy for each *pari* per annum. The demand used to be higher during the wars and other emergencies. The demand on the relatives of the kings, priests, soldiers and other favourites, who were not required to pay any tax for fixed proportions of land and paid a nominal tax for land in excess of the proportions in normal times, used to be as high as twenty-four baskets during wars and emergencies. Only the Meiteis were allowed to establish new villages in reclaimed lands on payment of usual taxes, although the labour for reclamation was extracted mostly from the degraded Mieteis and the non-Meiteis. The Lois, Yaithibis and non-Meiteis not only rendered *laipot* or manorial services but also paid a portion of the produces as tributes to the king. The salt-manufacturers and the fishermen had to handover a fixed portion of whatever they produced or gathered. The hill chiefs paid tributes in weaved clothes and forest produces. They were also required to provide food and attendants for the officers who visited the hills for the collection of tributes. King Charairongba (1698-1709 AD) introduced the annual dance performance (*haochongba*) by the tribes in the palace during which the kings offered food and drink to the tribal chiefs and received from them gifts and tributes. The kings also generated some income by exercising control over markets and external trade.[47]

The redistribution of surplus was in the form of public welfare activities by the kings. They constructed temples, roads and bridges, canals and dykes, provided relief to the people at times of distress, and patronized the temples and priests. They also extended patronage to the scholars and the court poets who produced literary works, including the chronicles. The draining out of water from the marshes and the construction of dams and dykes enhanced agricultural productivity. King Khyamba opened routes to Assam, Cachar, Tripura and Burma which gave a fillip to trade and commerce. Khungasba improved the markets, reclaimed forests, constructed dams and repaired the channels. Jai Singh introduced land surveys and developed the salt wells. During the sixteenth to eighteenth century AD there were several famines due to cyclones, floods and draughts when the kings provided relief and rehabilitation to the victims and granted tax exemptions to the affected people. They used the *lallup kabas* to clear the water channels and to drain out the floodwater, and performed rituals and offered *pujas* to propitiate the nature against calamities. These redistributive measures enhanced the popularity and strengthened the authority of the kings.[48]

The long story of the rise of the Meitei state may be summarized to say that it was one of emergence of a political society by integration and assimilation of large number of ethnic groups into a larger society with a common language under the leadership of the chief of one of the original groups. The Meiteis had immigrated into the Manipur valley from Southeast Asia in the hoary past over a long period of time in several waves and groups. The Southeast Asian root was common and they were possibly ethnically kindred to each other, but each group possibly had different dialect and group identity and own leader or chief. Among the Southeast Asian racial kindred or proto-Meitei groups, the Ningthoujas (originally perhaps called Mangang) were the earliest to arrive and to settle in the most fertile portion of the valley, and it can be presumed that they were numerically the largest and militarily the most powerful. They gradually pushed the autochthonous or earlier settlers (Loi, Chakpa, etc) out of the central part of the valley to expand their own settlement. The other kindred ethnic groups, who followed the

Ningthoujas one by one, also settled in different parts of the valley and joined the Ningthoujas in further pushing the autochthones to the least fertile foothill and marshy regions. Originally only the Ningthoujas seem to have been called the Meiteis, but gradually Meitei became the common identity and language for all the kindred immigrant groups. The ancestor worship was the common religious practice, and the ancestor of the Ningthoujas came to be recognized as the senior-most among the Meitei ancestors since he was the first to arrive in the valley. The ancestors of all the groups or clans came to be identified or named with a place each within the Manipur valley, perhaps where the group had originally landed. The seniority of the clans or groups among the Meiteis became accepted on the basis of the antiquity of arrival of the ancestors. The conflicts and reconciliation towards adjustment seem to have gone hand in hand towards the development of a settled life in the valley. When the Meitei kindred groups were laying settlements and expanding those, despite mutual conflicts and wars for occupation of better lands, the autochthones were pushed to the walls by the might of the immigrants. In their struggle for survival, the autochthonous groups also gradually found a common identity under the name Loi. However, before long, these Lois were also culturally and linguistically influenced by the Meiteis. Some of the tribal clans, who descended from the neighbouring hills and settled in the plains, became part of the process of assimilation. It seems that at some point of time in history the entire valley became dotted with innumerable settlements under respective chiefs with the potential of growing into autonomous principalities and chiefdoms. The wars and conflicts for elimination loomed large. It was at this juncture that there was the advent of Longda Lairen Pakhangba who was endowed by myths and legends with a divine origin to establish the Meitei Kingdom (and he was variously known as God-king, Dragon-king, Serpant-king, etc.). He occupied Kangla, the seat of the Ningthouja chief and laid foundation of the Ningthouja dynasty. It was for the first time in the history of the Meiteis that there was a coronation ceremony when Pakhangba formally ascended the throne at Kangla (supposedly in the first century AD). The divine origin of Pakhangba and the sacredness of Kangla, besides his military power, might have played wonder in favour of Pakhangba to make the beginning for the unification of all the political entities in the Manipur valley into the single Meitei state. He inspired and effected the regrouping of all the proto-Meitei groups into only seven clans, namely, Ningthouja, Angom, Luwang, Khuman, Khaba-Aganba, Chenglei, and Moirang, each of which developed into principalities and chiefdoms in course of time and maintained tributary relationship with the Ningthouja King. There were conflicts and wars during the reigns of the later kings, but by the fifteenth century AD all six other principalities were subjugated and subordinated by the Ningthouja chief to complete the unification of the Meitei Kingdom. Moirang maintained a kind of tributary-cum-autonomous status for some times, but it was also eventually absorbed into the Meitei Kingdom like five other proto-Meitei principalities.

The seven units of the proto-Meiteis of the valley created at the time of Pakhangba came to be recognized as seven principal Meitei clans (*salai*) and the groups which were absorbed within the seven clans became sub-clans (*sagei/ yumnak*). Pakhangba also initiated the settlement of the immigrants within the principalities and admission of the non-Meiteis into the Meitei social fold. The stray or sporadic infiltrations might have continued from various directions for a long time, either recorded or unrecorded in historical sources, but the strangers became unidentifiable in the Meitei midst as they adopted the land and culture of the valley as their own to merge into the Meitei milieu in course of time. The Bishnupriyas, Brahmins and Pangans who immigrated as late as the fifteenth century AD were also assimilated in the same process. This Meitei-ization or cultural assimilation with a common language and common social identity concretized the political edifice and ensured a very long lease of life for the state.

The foundation of the Meitei state lay in the fact that the Ningthoujas were endowed with a dominant position among the clan principalities of the proto-Meitei entities by virtue of the occupation of the most fertile region in the valley. They were the first to arrive and to occupy the best space. The concept of seniority rooted in the practice of ancestor worship made their chief the natural leader in designing the future of the peoples in the valley. The position of the Ningthouja chief was strengthened further by the more wealthy nature of his principality or chiefdom than others. The God-king Pakhangba belonged to the Ningthoujas. He was the first king and the founder of the Nongthouja dynasty. He enjoyed an unenviable position of dictating terms to others because of his divine origin and his military and economic might. His successors received tributes from others. The Ningthouja territory included most part of the Loi inhabited areas which was important as the source of raw-materials and for the supply of work force to the entire kingdom. The initiative for economic development of the valley came from the Ningthouja chiefs. They began the work of dredging of the river and opening new channels for draining out the stranded water and reclamation of land for agriculture and settlement. The inventions and innovations of technology for agriculture and crafts and industry are also credited to the Ningthouja chiefs. The division of labour by assigning social and economic functions to families and lineages on hereditary basis and through the *Lallup* system began in the Ningthouja principality and became the model for all the principalities and the entire Meitei society. This *Lallup* system was the backbone of the economy of the kingdom. The kings were the owners and givers of land. They supposedly looked after the protection and welfare of the people. It was their natural right to collect taxes and tributes and to demand manorial service from the people. However, the society and economy in the Meitei Kingdom was under total control of the state. The land, forests, mines and minerals, agriculture, industry and craft, including dress and ornaments of the people, were absolutely regulated by the kings. As a result, natural and human resources were not fully explored, technology remained backward and the economy could not develop to its full potentials. The control exercised by the rulers on every aspect of the life of the state did not allow any initiative on the part of the people, particularly those who had the skill and capability, to introduce reforms or new techniques and methods for improvement of the material conditions in general interest of the state.

Studies in Meitei State Formation

The Meitei Kingdom in Manipur, if the evidence of the chronicles, like *Cheitharol Kumbaba*, is to be accepted, is one of the longest surviving kingdoms (from ancient to modern periods) not only in the Northeast but also in the entire Indian sub-continent. The origins of the kingdom goes back to the first century AD and it remained in existence till subjugated by the British colonialism in the nineteenth century AD. During this long period the kingdom was ruled by a single dynasty, namely, the Ningthouja Dynasty. It is, therefore, but natural that the scholars would be interested in studying this kingdom in the format of the formation of early states since the state formation study became a popular field in social sciences in the last quarter of the last century. A brief survey of the studies in the past decades on the Meitei state formation in Manipur reveals that the interest in the subject was perhaps generated by Gangmumei Kabui (Kamei)'s paper entitled "A brief note on *Loiyamba Shilyen**: A Royal Edict on social distribution of economic and administrative functions" presented at the third annual session of the North East India History Association at Manipur University, Imphal, in 1982.[49] This seems to have been the first paper on the subject. Later on, the issue of this royal charter or edict by King Loiyamba in the beginning of the twelfth century AD has been described by J. B. Bhattacharjee as a crucial step in formalizing the social differentiation and stratification on hereditary occupational and professional basis which, according to him, provided the objective preconditions for the development of the chiefdom into statehood. According to Bhattacharjee, the *Loiyamba Shinyen* was issued by a king of the Ningthouja dynasty (namely, King Loiyamba) at a time when almost two-third of the Manipur valley and possibly five of the seven Meitei clan-principalities were already under the domination of the Ningthoujas. The reforms and innovations introduced by Loiyamba through this *Shinyen*, therefore, became a model for the rest of the valley and the principalities which subsequently came under the Meitei kings. The principle of specific functions or occupations for specific families was a major step in inducting the practice of professional specializations on hereditary basis. The king was already the owner of land, and the introduction of the institutions for the management of land ensured protection of land, regular flow of revenue and the king's control over the people as the giver of land. As the state expanded and matured further, the later kings inducted additions and modifications to the *Shinyen* to take care of the emerging needs and to further sophisticate the state machinery.[50]

In the meantime, a technical paper on Meitei state formation entitled "State Formation among the Meitei in Manipur" was contributed by R.K. Saha in the volume edited by Surajit Sinha.[51] An anthropologist by training, Saha not only followed the tools and techniques of his own discipline but also used the secondary sources like the pre-colonial local chronicles and the gazetteers and accounts of the colonial times for historical data to go into the past and to delve into the root. Beginning with the land and the people like conventional anthropologists, he focused on the ecological and the ethnic texture of the geographical space of Manipur, village formations, segmentary structure of the Meitei society, assimilation of the non-Meiteis into the Meitei social fold, development of political organizations, religious institutions of the Meiteis and the impact of Vaisnavism, the relations of the Meitei rulers with the hill people in Manipur and the neighboring states, and finally concluded that "the authority which was inherent in the segmentary structure itself gave rise to the chieftaincy and the particular valley ecology provided the economic prop and the mythology provided the charter for state formation."[52] Saha particularly emphasized that,

> instead of introducing a rigid Varna-Jati body-politic of the Meitei state, the Vaisnavite Brahmans, with their notion of purity and pollution mainly strengthened the centralized authority of the state. The hierarchy which was inherent in the genealogical structure itself developed into a sort of a centralized political order under the favourable ecological condition of the valley. Although there was an attempt to remodel the state in the form of Hinduised states by exogenous factor, namely, the introduction of the value of purity and pollution by the Brahmin priestly groups, it was not successful because the social ecology, specially the uniethnic nature of the villages, and the distribution of the various groups in varying ecological setting was not favourable. So the exogenous factor could only strengthen the existing hierarchy. Autocracy is the feature of the smallest unit uni-clan village, intermediary phase chieftaincy and of the superstructure of kingship.[53]

Saha's solitary contribution to the study of the Meitei state formation is indeed path breaking in the sense that he related the polity formation to the ethnic roots and social processes, identified the origin of the state in the hierarchical social order of the Meiteis which zealously maintained the genealogies and guarded the concept of seniority of the clans at various levels of social organization through ancestor worship, and concluded that social stratification was imbedded in the segmentary structure of the Meitei society itself. This paper of R. K. Saha has been extensively used by J. B. Bhattacharjee in his later works.[54]

Nonetheless, a real boost to the study of the Meitei State Formation was the inspiring presidential address to the eighth annual session of the North East India History Association at Kohima (1987) by Gangmumei Kabui, entitled "State Formation: An Enquiry into the Process of the Emergence of States with special reference to North East India", in which he outlined the emergence of early states in Northeast India, including the Meitei State in Manipur, and made a rapid survey of the state formation studies to drive home to the researchers in the region that there is indeed an excellent opportunity to pursue the theme in the specific context of the Northeast.[55] Kabui followed up his presidential address by presenting another paper at the next session of the North East India History Association at Guwahati (1988) on 'Nongda Lairen Pakhangba' who was the founder of the Ningthouja dynasty of Manipur.[56] In the same session, L. Basanti Devi also presented a paper on the 'Moirang Principality' of Manipur.[57] The subsequent sessions of the North East India History Association witnessed the presentation of a large number of papers by the scholars from Manipur which were directly or indirectly related to the rise and growth of the Meitei kingdom. Among the scholars who contributed on the subject were M.C. Arunkumar,[58] L. Basanti Devi,[59] L. Kunjeswori Devi,[60] L. Sanajaobi Devi,[61] M. Shantirani Devi,[62] Mahmoodah Khannam,[63] B. Kulachandra,[64] Rena Laisram,[65] C. Priyaranjan,[66] M.

Ranjana,[67] K. Ratan,[68] H. Nilkant Singh,[69] M. Jitendra Singh,[70] M. Lokendra Sing,[71] N. Nilkant Singh,[72] R. K. Jhalajit Singh,[73] Lokendra Arambam,[74] Kh. Ranendrajit[75] and others. The most recent rounding up of the theme is by Gangmumei Kamei (Kabui) himself, who delivered the seventh H.K. Barpujari Endowment Lecture at the thirtieth session of the North East India History Association at Nagaon (Assam) in November 2009 on 'Meitei State Formation'.[76]

The survey of literature attempted in this paper, no doubt very brief in nature, does make it clear that the Meitei state formation as a viable research field has already caught the imagination of a good number of scholars who have contributed papers on different aspects of the subject in various journals and proceedings during the last three decades. The *Proceedings of North East India History Association*, between the volumes, contain some invaluable presentations which are contextually relevant to Meitei state formations, as they do in various other aspects of the history of Manipur and other areas of the Northeast. The scholars of Meitei state formation studies contributed their research to other publications as well. For example, Gangmumei Kabui's *History of Manipur*[77] contains detailed discussion on the origin and growth of the Meitei Kingdom in the early period. In fact, this book provides interesting information on geographical setting and historical ecology, autochthonous and pre-Meitei settlers, proto-Meitei groups, Meitei immigration, pre- and proto history of Manipur, political and religious institutions, ethnic consolidations, land reclamation, technological inventions and innovations, agriculture, craft and industry, taxes and tributes, economic change, social development, and many such details that are useful in state formation studies. Similarly, Amal Sanasam's contribution[78] on the sociology of settlement pattern is very informative and useful for understanding the dynamic of the evolution of the Meitei society by commingling and acculturations of the indigenous and immigrant ethnic elements with respective skills and technologies which were contributory factors for the state formation. A paper on the economic dimension of the Meitei state formation and another on a royal edict by J. B. Bhattacharjee addressed the basics of the interdisciplinary discourse on the formation of early states.[79] There must be some more studies in other publications which we have not been able to survey for the limited purpose of this paper to profile the trends and directions in studying the formation of the Meitei state in pre-colonial Manipur. Our survey of literature has also been limited to the publications in English only, although we are aware that there are some good scholarly works in Manipuri language.

Critique

It may be evident from this brief survey that there is a fairly good number of research papers published in journals, proceedings and collections, particularly in different volumes of the *Proceedings of North East India History Association*, the contents of which are directly or indirectly relevant to the history of Meitei state formation in Manipur. The critical review of the papers, however, suggests that most of these studies are empirical in nature and only a few of them are genuinely in the format of state formation studies. As already said in the beginning, one is expected to appreciate that the state formation study is not just profiling the history of a state or kingdom or the rise and growth of the political systems and institutions but a critical probe into the roots or the factors responsible for the emergence and growth of the states involving the ideology and structure, apparatus of surveillance, means of sustenance, mode of production, the role of technology, the labour process, the surplus - generation, extraction and redistribution, etc. To begin with, the researcher has to be clear about the concepts and issues involved in such studies and the quality of data available for the specific case study, and develop a conceptual framework for the instant discourse. It is also important to note that the state formation studies are concerned only with the 'early states' which gradually and spontaneously emerged from the indigenous ethnic social roots over a long period of time through a process of social stratification which is based on economic differentiation, and that the 'early states' are different from the 'modern states'. This division of states between 'early' and 'modern' is on the basis of the level of development, since the 'early states' are simple, non-industrialized and pre-capitalistic and the 'modern states' are complex, industrialized and capitalistic.[80] As observed by Henri J.M. Claessen and Peter Skalnik, "the early state is the organization for the regulation of social relations in a society that is divided into two emergent social classes, the rulers and the ruled."[81] They also identified the population growth and population pressure, war, threat of war, conquest, surplus generation, ideology, and the influence of the already existing states as among the major factors for the rise of early states, and the territory, population, sovereignty, citizenship, productivity, hierarchy, and legitimacy to be the major components of such states.[82] Therefore, an early state is supposed to have a territory of its own, the size of the population within that territory must have been sufficient to facilitate social categorization, stratification and specialization, the citizenship had to be determined by birth or residence in the territory, the ruling stratum or the government must have been centralized with sovereign authority to maintain law and order and to prevent separatism and must have the capacity to defend its integrity against external or internal threats, the productivity or the level of development of the productive forces must have been developed to such a degree so as to ensure a regular surplus for the maintenance of the state organization, the population must have shown a degree of social stratification to the extent that the emergent social classes (rulers and ruled) could be clearly distinguished, and the legitimacy of the ruling stratum must have been based on a common ideology.[83] Whether or not the Meitei state in Manipur fulfilled all the requirements to be identified as an 'early state' (or pristine, primitive or primary) is not evident from the studies covered in this paper. In fact, this aspect of the characterization of the state has not been touched upon by the scholars whose studies have been surveyed for this paper.

As a matter of fact, only R. K. Saha, Gangmumei Kamei (Kabui), and J. B. Bhattacharjee seem to have addressed some of the basic concepts and issues involved in state formation studies in the context of the Meitei state. Bhattacharjee confined his enquiry to the economic dimension,[84] while Kamei emphasized the lineage factor and the role of the origin myths in Meitei state formation.[85] R.K. Saha's contribution indeed remains unique for his critical analysis of the genealogy of the various Meitei lineages and for relating the state origin to the social structure of the Meiteis. He is, in deed, emphatic about the structural relations between the ethnic configurations and the evolution of the state. Unfortunately, neither Saha is known to have pursued the theme by more contributions on the subject nor do we come across scholars, other than J. B. Bhattacharjee, who referred to Saha's important paper in their works. However, Bhattacharjee seems to have extensively and approvingly used Saha's paper in his later works.[86]

It is indeed a fact that the early history of Manipur has by and large remained empirically unexplored due mainly to the limited nature of the source materials, whereas the enquiry into the formation of early states requires specific evidence on specific issues. The main source of information for the history of Manipur in the pre-colonial period is only a set of local chronicles (*Puyas*) the most of which are generally datable to the late-medieval period, precisely fifteenth to nineteenth century AD. The history of the earlier periods is generally conjectured on the basis of these later literary sources. Of these chronicles, *Cheitharol Kumbaba*,[87] the royal chronicle, is the most detailed and it has been extensively used by the historians while writing on Manipur. This chronicle, which is in the nature of a dairy of the Meitei kings, claims to have recorded the major events since 33 AD, although even the early part of the text cannot be dated earlier than the fifteenth century AD. N. Lokendra Singh has, therefore, questioned the historicity of the documentation of *Cheitharol Kumbaba* and pointed out several instances of contradictory nature of information provided by this royal chronicle.[88] Gangmumei Kamei, who made liberal use of the chronicles, also observed that some of these chronicles are mere compendiums of myths and legends.[89] As Rena Laisram says, "A study of the *Puya*s encounters the vexing problem of separating the myths from facts and locating the historical in the myriad of legends, traditions, folklore and narratives. Notwithstanding the existence of reliable historical material alongside mythical narrative, the problem has been the treatment of the *Puya*s by majority of scholars as authentic historical records *per se*."[90] The epigraphic, archaeological and numismatic materials are very few and also far between, besides being relevant only to the later period of history of the Meitei kingdom. Thus, the research in the history of Manipur remains dependant on the literary sources, locally called *Puyas*, which the scholars have been liberally using, even without content analysis. Whereas the *Puyas* constitute a very rich treasure of source material, the use of those sources without criticism or verification to ensure authenticity is likely to cause methodological problems. Rena Laisram seems right when she says that 'the treatment of the *Puyas* by majority of scholars as authentic historical records'[91] has been the problem in historical research in Manipur. The critical and impartial use of the *Puyas* in her recently published work,[92] besides fairly rigorous documentation and classified bibliography with essential details, is henceforth expected to positively impact historical research in Manipur. The analytical and interpretative approach might help the critical appreciation of the *Puyas* as reliable sources of history. Till then, the dearth of historical data specifically required for state formation studies remains an insurmountable predicament for the scholars to critically study the Meitei state formation processes in early Manipur.

Nonetheless, the historical writings by the scholars so far have undoubtedly introduced the Meitei state formation as a significant theme around which the pre-colonial history of Manipur intrinsically revolved and they have also indicated the availability of data as well as the dearth of those. It is, therefore, expected that the theme shall be perused by many more scholars. This will also be helpful in focusing on the totality of the history of Manipur, because the methodology of state formation studies reflects on the every aspect of change and development in the given space and society. However, what seems to be most important for future research in the subject is to conceptualize the theme and to develop a framework for study in the specific context of Manipur.

NOTES & REFERENCES

1. Henri J. M. Claessen & Peter Skalnik (ed.), *The Early State*, Mouton Publishers, The Hague, 1978.
2. Friedrich Engels, *The Origin of Family, Private Property and the State*, First published 1891, Reprinted with an Introduction by Eleanor Burke Leacock, Lawrence and Wishan, London, 1972.
3. Romila Thapar, *From Lineage to State– Social Formations in the Mid-First Millennium B.C. in the Ganga Valley*, Oxford University Press, Bombay, 1984.
4. Surajit Sinha (ed.), *Tribal Polities and State Systems in Pre-Colonial Eastern and North Eastern India*, Centre for Studies in Social Sciences/K .P. Bagchi & Company, Calcutta, 1987.
5. Surajit Sinha, "State Formation and Rajput Myth in Tribal Central India", *Man in India*, Vol. 42, no.1, January-March, 1962, pp.35-80.

6. Hermann Kulke, "Early State Formation and Royal Legitimation in Tirbal Areas of Eastern India", in R. R. Moser & M. K. Gautam (ed.), *Aspects of Tribal Life in South Asia I: Strategy and Survivals*, Bersenia, 1978.
7. Surajit Sinha (ed.), *op.cit*, pp.143-176, 177-212, 243-260, 261-306, 329-366, 307-328, 213-242.
8. J. B. Bhattacharjee, "Tripuri State Formation in Mediaeval Tripura", *Proceedings of North East India History Association* (hereafter, *PNEIHA*), IIIrd Session, Imphal, 1982, pp.57-72.
9. *The NEHU Journal of Social Sciences and Humanities* , Vol. II, no. 3, July-September, 1984. This special issue, edited by J. B. Bhattacharjee, contained seminal papers on state formation in the Northeast by J. B. Bhattacharjee (on Dimasa State), B. Pakem (on Jaintia State) and A. C. Sinha (on Sikkim).
10. "The Village Formations among the Angami Nagas" by Visier Sanyu, "Ahom State Formation in Assam" by Ramesh Buragohain and "Polity Formation among the Wars of Shella" by Elizabeth Laitflang Warjri, for example.
11. J. B. Bhattacharjee, *Social and Polity Formations in Pre-Colonial North-East India*, Har-Anand Publications/Vikas Publishig House, New Delhi, 1991.
12. J. B. Bhattacharjee, *Bhauma-Naraka Legend and State Formation in Pragjyotisa-Kamarupa, NEIHA*, Shillong, 2004.
13. Gangmumei Kabui, "A brief note on Loiyamba Shilyen: A Royal Edict on social distribution of economic and administrative functions", *PNEIHA*, IIIrd Session, Imphal, 1982, pp.31-36; J. B. Bhattacharjee, "Tripuri State Formation in Mediaeval Tripura", *PNEIHA*, IIIrd Session, Imphal, 1982, pp.57-72.
14. Friedrich Engels, *op.cit.*, p.232.
15. L. Gumplovicz, *The Outlines of Sociology*, American Academy of Political and Social Science, Philadelphia, 1899.
16. Franz Oppenheimer, *Der Staat, Frankfurt*, 1909, referred to by Claessen & Skalnik, *op.cit.*, p.8.
17. Robert H. Lowie, *The Origin of the State*, Harcourt, Brace and World, New York, 1927.
18. Richard Thurnwald, "Die menschliche Gesellschaft" (1935), referred to by Claessen & Skalnik, *op.cit.*, p.8.

19. D. Wesremann, Geschichie Afrikas, etc., (1952), referred to by Claessen & Skalnik, *op.cit.*, p.9.
20. Julian H. Steward, *Theory of Culture Change*, University of Illinois Press, Urbana, 1955.
21. Karl A. Wittfogel, *Oriental Despotism: A Comparative Study of Total Power*, Yale University Press, New Haven, 1957.
22. Morton H. Fried, *The Evolution of Political Society*, Random House, New York, 1967.
23. Jack Stauder, "Anarchy and Ecology: Political Society among the Majangir", *Southwestern Journal of Anthropology*, Vol. 28, 1972, pp.153-168.
24. M. J. Harner, "Scarcity, the Factors of Production, and Social Evolution" in Steven Polgar (ed.), *Population, Ecology and Social Evolution*, Mouton Publishers, The Hague, 1975, pp.123-138.
25. M. A. Bakel, *Population Pressure and Cultural Evolution* (1976), referred by Claessen & Skalnik, *op.cit.*, p.11.
26. C. P. Kottak, "Ecological Variables in the Origin and Evolution of African States", *Comparative Studies in Society and History*, Vol. 14, 1972, pp.351-380.
27. Elman R. Service, *Primitive Social Organization*, Norton Press, New York, 1974.
28. Robert L. Carneiro, "A Theory of the Origin of the State", *Science*, 169, 1970, pp.733-738.
29. Steven Polgar, "Population, Evolution, and Theoretical Paradigms" in Steven Polgar (ed.), *Population, Ecology and Social Evolution*, Mouton Publishers, The Hague, 1975, pp.1-25.
30. Marshal D. Sahlins, *Stone Age Economics*, Aldine Press, Chicago, 1972.
31. Henri J. M. Claessen & Peter Skalnik, *op.cit.*, pp.603-606.
32. Robert Cohen, "State Origin: A Reappraisal" in Claessen & Skalnik, *op.cit.*, p.61.
33. *ibid.*
34. *ibid.*, p.62.
35. Surajit Sinha (ed.), *Tribal Polities and State Systems in Pre-colonial Eastern and North Eastern India*, Calcutta, 1986. This collection included eleven case studies, and six of these,

namely, 'Ahom', 'Dimasa', 'Meitei', 'Jaintia', 'Khasi' and 'Mizo' are from Northeast India.

36. *ibid.*, p.xiv.
37. *ibid.*, p. xv.
38. Amalendu Guha, "The Ahom Political System: An Enquiry into State Formation in Medieval Assam, 1228-1800", in Surajit Sinha (ed.), *op.cit*, pp.43-76.
39. *ibid.*, p.144.

Kabo valley/Kabaw valley

40. Saroj Nalini Arambam Parratt (tr. & ed.), *The Court Chronicle of the Kings of Manipur: The Cheitharon Kumpapa*, Routledge, New York, 2005; L. Joychandra Singh, *The Lost Kingdom– Royal Chronicle of Manipur*, Prajatantra Publishing House, Imphal, 1995; R. K. Saha, "State Formation Among the Meiteis of Manipur" in Surajit Sinha (ed.), *op.cit.*, pp.213-242; Jyotirmoy Roy, *History of Manipur*, Eastlight Book House, Calcutta, 1958, pp.15-43; L. I. Singh, *Introduction to Manipur*, Imphal, 1963, pp.23-65; J. B. Bhattacharjee, *op.cit.*.
41. Jyotirmoy Roy, *op.cit.*, pp.78-112; R. K. Jhalajit Singh, *A Short History of Manipur*, O. K. Stores, Imphal, 1965, pp.67-96; R. K. Saha, "State Formation Among the Meiteis of Manipur" in Surajit Sinha (ed), *op.cit.*, pp.214-224; J. B. Bhattacharjee, *op.cit.*
42. Amal Sanasam, "Sociology of Settlement Pattern in Manipur Valley", *The Insight*, Vol. I, No. I, January-June 2006, pp.71-90; J. B. Bhattacharjee, "Economic Dimension of the Meitei State Formation", in F. A. Qadri (ed.), *Society and Economy in North-East India*, Volume 2, Regency Publications, New Delhi, 2006, pp.58-76; L. Ibungohal Singh & N. Khelchandra Singh (eds.), *Cheitharol Kumbaba*, Manipuri Sahitya Parishad, Imphal, 1967; R. Brown, *Statistical Account of Manipur*, (London, 1874) Reprint Sanskaran Prakashak, Delhi 1975, pp.39-55; E. W. Dun, *Gazetteer of Manipur*, London, 1875, reprint Vivek Publishing House, Delhi, 1981, pp.63-115; T. C. Hudson, *The Meitheis*, London, 1911, reprint B. R. Publishing House, Delhi, 1981, pp.37-49; L. Basanti Devi, "Ancient Meitei Military Organization", *PNEIHA*, XIth Session, Imphal, 1990, pp.128-129; Gangmumei Kabui, "Nongda Lairen Pakhangba and the Establishment of the

Ningthouja Dynasty of Manipur", *PNEIHA*, IXth Session, Guwahati, 1988, pp.33-34; L. Kunjeswori Devi, "Ancient Discoveries in Sekta, a village in Manipur", *PNEIHA*, XIIth Session, Jagiroad, 1991, pp.120-123.

43. R. K. Saha, *op.cit.*, pp.214-224; J. B. Bhattacharjee, *op.cit.*; Amal Sanasam, *op.cit.*, pp.71-86; R. Brown, *op.cit.*, pp.39-55; E. W. Dun, *op.cit.*, pp. 63-85; Gangmumei Kabui, *op.cit.*, pp.33-34; L. Basanti Devi, "Origin, Growth and Fall of the Moirang Principality in South Manipur Valley", *PNEIHA*, IXth Session, Guwahati, 1988, pp.45-91; L. Kunjeswori Devi, *op.cit.*; M. Shantirani Devi, "Relics of Kangla (Old Palace}", *PNEIHA*, XIIth Session, Jagiroad, 1991, pp.124-128; Saroj Nalini Arambam Parratt (tr. & ed.), *op.cit.*, L. Joychandra Singh, *op.cit.*; Gangmumei Kabui, *History of Manipur*, Volume One , National Publishing House, New Delhi, 1991, pp.95-146; Quazi Hamid Ali, *The Manipuri Muslims*, Banskandi, 1979.

44. Gangmumei Kabui, "A brief note on Loiyamba Shilyen: A Royal Edict on social distribution of economic and administrative functions", *PNEIHA*, IIIrd Session Imphal, 1982, pp.31-36; J. B. Bhattacharjee, "Loiyamba Shinyen: A Landmark in Meitei State Formation in Manipur", *Proceedings of Indian History Congress*, Mysore, 64th session, December, 2003, pp.123-32; J. B. Bhattacharjee, "Economic Dimension of the Meitei State Formation", F. A. Qadri (ed.), *Society and Economy in North-East India*, Volume 2, Regency Publications, New Delhi, 2006, pp.58-76.

45. R. K. Saha, *op.cit.*; M. Jitendra Singh, "Slavery in Pre-British Manpur: A Historical Survey", *PNEIHA*, Vth Session, Aizawl, 1984, pp.79-84; Jyotirmoy Roy, *op.cit.*, pp.67-135; R. K. Jhalajit Singh, *op.cit*, pp.67-96; J. B. Bhattacharjee, *op.cit.*

46. *ibid.*, pp.231-236; R. Brown, *op.cit.*, pp.10-13.

47. *ibid.*; H. Nilkant Singh, "Meitei Village Community", *PNEIHA*, XVIth Session, Silchar, 1995, pp.85-89; R. K. Jhalajit Singh, *op.cit.*, pp.59-60 ; R. Brown, *op.cit.*, p.14.

48. R. B. Pamberton, *Report on the Eastern Frontier of British India*, (Calcutta, 1835) Reprint DHAS, Gauhati, 1966, pp.136-149; K. Ratan, "Myths and Rituals in Laiharaoba", *PNEIHA*, XVIth Session, Silchar, 1995, pp.90-97; K. Ratankumar Singh, "Genesis of the Lai Haraoba in Meitei Society", *PNEIHA*,

XIIIth Session, Shillong, 1992, pp.136-140; M. Jitendra Singh, "Famines in the Valley of Manipur as recorded in *Cheitharol Kumbaba*", *PNEIHA*, VIIth Session, Pasighat, 1986, pp.48-52; E. W. Dun, *op.cit*, p.10; T. C. Hudson, *op.cit.*, pp.107-110; L. Kunjeswori Devi, "Ancient Discoveries in Sekta, a village in Manipur", *PNEIHA*, XIIth Session, Jagiroad, 1991, pp.120-123; M. Shantirani Devi, "Relics of Kangla (Old Palace}", *PNEIHA*, XIIth Session, Jagiroad, 1991, pp.124-128; Saroj Nalini Arambam Parratt (tr. & ed.), *op.cit.*; L. Joychandra Singh, *op.cit.*; Gangmumei Kabui, *History of Manipur*, Volume One , National Publishing House, New Delhi, 1991, pp.95-146; J. B. Bhattacharjee, *op.cit.*

**Shilyen/Shinyen*

49. Gangmumei Kabui, "A brief note on *Loiyamba Shilyen*: A Royal Edict on social distribution of economic and administrative functions", *PNEIHA*, IIIrd Session, Imphal, 1982, pp.31-36.
50. J. B. Bhattacharjee, "*Loiyamba Shinyen*: A Landmark in Meitei State Formation in Medieval Manipur', *Proceedings of the Indian History Congress*, 64th Session, Mysore, 2003, pp.362-368.
51. R. K. Saha, *op.cit*, pp. 213-242.
52. *ibid*, p.239.
53. *ibid.*
54. J. B. Bhattacharjee, "Economic Dimension of the Meitei State Formation",in F. A. Qadri (ed.), *Society and Economy in North-East India*, Volume 2, New Delhi, 2006, pp.58-76.
55. Gangmumei Kabui, "Presidential Address", *PNEIHA*, VIII th Session, Kohima, 1987, pp.1-32.
56. Gangmumei Kabui, "Nongda Lairen Pakhangba and the Establishment of the Ningthoujas Dynasty of Manipur", *PNEIHA*, IXth Session, Guwahati, 1988, pp.33-44.
57. L. Basanti Devi, "Origin, Growth and Fall of the Moirang Principality in the South Manipur Valley", *PNEIHA*, IXth Session, Guwahati, 1988, pp.45-51.
58. M. C. Arunkumar, "Towards Hypotheses to the Decline of the Meitei Kingdom", *PNEIHA*, XIIIth Session, Shillong, 1992, pp.141-148.

59. L. Basanti Devi, "Ancient Meitei Military Organization", *PNEIHA*, XIth Session, Imphal, 1990, pp.128-129.
60. L. Kunjeswori Devi, "The Bearing of the Inscriptions on the History of Manipur", *PNEIHA*, XIth Session, Imphal, 1990, pp.17-19; "Ancient Discoveries in Sekta, a Village in Manipur", *PNEIHA*, XIIth Session, Jagiroad, 1991, pp.120-123.
61. L. Sanajaobi Devi, "First Muslim Settlement in Manipur", *PNEIHA*, IXth Session, Guwahati, 1988, pp.155-158.
62. M. Shantirani Devi, "Relics of Kangla (Old Palace)", *PNEIHA*, XIIth Session, Jagiroad, 1991, pp.124-128; "Meitei Military System", *PNEIHA*, XIVth Session, Jorhat, 1993, pp.108-111.
63. Mahmoodah Khannam, "Economic Contribution of the Muslims to Manipur", *PNEIHA*, XIth Session, Imphal, 1991, pp.212-215.
64. B. Kulachandra, "Prehistoric and Proto-historic Man of Manipur", *PNEIHA*, XIVth Session, Jorhat, 1993, pp.32-39.
65. Rena Laisram, "The Social Reality of Pre-Hindu Religion of the Meiteis of Manipur", *PNEIHA*, XXIInd Session, Tezpur, 2001, pp.302-304; "Genealogy as a source of Meitei History", *PNEIHA* , XXVth Session, Shillong, pp.100-104.
66. C. Priyaranjan, "Differentiation among the Peasantry: Historical Roots and Emerging Relations in Manipur", *PNEIHA*, XIIth Session, Jagiroad, 1991, pp. 283-89.
67. M. Ranjana, "Ethnic Groups of Moirang Principality", *PNEIHA*, XIXth Session, Kohima, 1998, pp.100-103; "Mera Haojongba: A Meitei Policy of National Integration", *PNEIHA*, XXIst Session, Tezpur, 2001, pp.382-385.
68. K. Ratan, "Myths and Rituals in Lai Haraoba", *PNEIHA*, XVIth Session, Silchar, 1995, pp.90-97.
69. H. Nilkant Singh, "Meitei State Formation: A Preliminary Study", *PNEIHA*, XIIth Session, Jagiroad, 1991, pp.175-184; "Meitei Village Community", *PNEIHA*, XVIth Session, Silchar, 1995, pp.85-89; "Lallup System", *PNEIHA*, XVIIIth Session, Aizawl, 1996, pp.129-134.
70. M. Jitendra Singh, "Slavery in Pre-British Manipur: A Historial Survey", *PNEIHA*, Vth Session, Aizawl, 1984, pp.79-84; "Famines in the Valley of Manipur as recorded in *Cheitharol Kumbaba*", *PNEIHA*, VIIth Session, Pasighat,

1986, pp.48-52; "The Origin of the Meitei: An Overview", *PNEIHA* , Xth Session, Shillong, 1989, pp.249-252.

71. M. Lokendra Singh, "Divine Kingship in Manipur", *PNEIHA*, Xth Sesion, Shillong, 1989, pp.253-260.
72. N. Nilkant Singh, "Loiyamba's Statecraft", *PNEIHA*, XXth Session, Dibrugarh, 1999, pp.209-211.
73. R. K. Jhalajit Singh, "The Immigration of Brahmins and its Impact on the Culture of Manipur", *PNEIHA*, IIIrd Session, Imphal, 1982, pp.84-88.
74. Lokendra Arambam, "Manipur: A Ritual Theatre State", *PNEIHA*, VIIth Session, Pasighat, 1986, pp.221-238.
75. Kh. Ranendrajit, "The Chakpa of Manipur: A Brief Historical Account", *PNEIHA*, XXVIth Session, Kokrajhar, 2005, pp.299-313.
76. Gangmumei Kamei, 'From Tribalism to Feudalism: Evolution of the Meitei State in Pre-Colonial Manipur' (to be published by *NEIHA*).
77. Gangmumei Kabui, *A History of Manipur, Vol.1 (Pre-Colonial Period)*, Delhi, 1991, pp.35-66.
78. Amal Sanasam, "Sociology of Settlement Pattern in Manipur Valley", *The Insight*, Vol. I, No.I, January-June 2006, pp.71-90.
79. J. B. Bhattacharjee, *op.cit.*; "Loiyamba Shinyen: A Landmark in Meitei State Formation in Medieval Manipur', *Proceedings of the Indian History Congress*, 64th Session, Mysore, 2003, pp.362-368; *Bhauma-Naraka Legend and State Formation in Pragjyotisa-Kamarupra, op.cit*, see "Early State Model", Appendix-C, pp.80-84.
81. Henri J. M. Claessen & Peter Skalnik (ed.), *op.cit*, p.21.
82. *ibid.*
83. *ibid.*
84. J. B. Bhattacharjee, "Economic Dimension of the Meitei State Formation", in F. A. Qadri (ed.), *Society and Economy in North-East India*, Volume 2, New Delhi, 2006, pp.58-76.
85. Gangumei Kamei (Kabui), "Nongda Lairen Pakhangba and the Establishment of the Ningthouja Dynasty of Manipur", *PNEIHA*, IXth Session, Guwahati, 1988, pp.33-44. However, we have not been able to go yet through the text of his H.K.

Barpujari Endowment Lecture (2009) which might have dealt with the subject more comprehensively.

86. J. B. Bhattacharjee, "*Loiyamba Shinyen*: A Landmark in Meitei State Formation in Medieval Manipur', *Proceedings of the Indian History Congress*, 64th Session, Mysore, 2003, pp.362-368; "Economic Dimension of the Meitei State Formation", in F. A. Qadri (ed), *Society and Economy in North-East India,* Volume 2, New Delhi, 2006, pp.58-76; *State and Wealth: The Early States in Northeast India*, DVS Publishers, Guwahati, 2010.

87. Saroj Nalini Arambam Parratt (tr. & ed.), *op.cit.*

88. N. Lokendra Singh, "A Historical Study of Some Aspects of *Cheitharol Kumbaba*', *PNEIHA*, IXth Session, Guwahati, 1988, pp.52-59.

89. Gangmumei Kamei (Kabui), "Nongda Lairen Pakhangba and the Establishment of the Ningthouja Dynasty of Manipur", *PNEIHA*, IXth Session, Guwahati, 1988, p.35.

90. Rena Laisram, *Early Meitei History – Religion, Society & The Manipur Puyas*, Akansha Publishing House, New Delhi, 2009, p.xi.

91. *ibid.*

92. Rena Laisram, *Early Meitei History – Religion, Society & The Manipur Puyas*, Akansha Publishing House, New Delhi, 2009.

Select Bibliography

A. A. Howell, *A Short Account of Land Revenue in Manipur*, Imphal, 1907.

Abdul Ali, "Notes on the Early History of Manipur", *Bengal Past and Present*, October-December, 1923.

Alexander Mackenzie, *History of the Relations of the Government with the Hill Tribes on the North-East Frontier of Bengal*, Bengal Government Press, Calcutta, 1884.

Atombapu Sharma, *Manipuri Itihas*, Imphal, 1942.

____________ (ed.), *Pakhangba*, Imphal, 1952.

Amalendu Guha, "The Ahom Political System : An Enquiry into State Formation in Medieval Assam : 1228-1800", in Surajit Sinha (ed.), *Tribal Polities and State Systems in Pre-Colonial Eastern and North Eastern India*, Centre for Studies in Social Sciences/K P Bagchi & Company, Calcutta, 1987.

Amal Sanasam, "Sociology of Settlement Pattern in Manipur Valley", *The Insight*, Vol. I, No.I, January-June, 2006.

Barrie M. Morrison, *Political Centres and Cultural Regions in Early Bengal*, (Arizona, 1976) Indian Reprint, Rawat Publishing House, Delhi, 1980.

B. D. Sharma, C. L. Anand & J. B. Bhattacharjee (ed.), *History of Science*, The NEHU Publications, Shillong, 1984.

B. Hindess & P. Hirst, *Pre-Capitalist Modes of Production*, London, 1975.

B. Kulllachandra, "Prehistoric and Proto-historic Man of Manipur", *Proceedings of North East India History Association* (hereinafter *PNEIHA*), XIVth Session, Jorhat, 1993.

B. Kullachandra Sharma, *Meiteigi Machugi Manat*, Imphal, 2000.

B. Kullachandra Sharma & Badr-ud-din (ed), *Meitei Pangal Hourakpham*, Imphal, 1991.

____________*Meitei Pangal Thorakpa*, Imphal, 1991.

Ch. Hemchandra, *Meihoubarol Shangai Phammang*, Imphal, 2004.

____________(ed.) *Thunkhonglon*, Imphal, 2004.

Chitrasen (ed.), *Leiron Tengtha*, Imphal, 1996.

Ch. Manihar Singh (tr. & ed.), *Naothingkhong Phambal Kaba*, Manipur University, Imphal, 1986.

C. P. Kottak, "Ecological Variables in the Origin and Evolution of African States", Comparative *Studies in Society and History*, vol. 14, 1972.

C. Priyaranjan, "Differentiation among the Peasantry : Historical Roots and Emerging Relations in Manipur", *PNEIHA*, XIIth Session, Jagiroad, 1991.

D. G. E. Hall, *History of Southeast Asia*, London, 1968.

Edward Gait, *A History of Assam*, (London, 1906) 3rd Revised & Enlarged Edition, Thacker Sprink & Co., Calcutta, 1963.

Elman R. Service, *Primitive Social Organization*, Norton Press, New York, 1974.

Ethel St. Clair Grimwood, *My Three Years in Manipur*, (London, 1891) Reprint Gyan Publishing House, New Delhi, 2000.

E. W. Dun, *Gazetteer of Manipur*, (London, 1875) Reprint Vivek Publishing Company, Delhi, 1981; Manas Publications, Delhi, 1992.

F. Pridmore, "The East India Company's bell metal coinage for Manipur", *Seaby's Coin and Medal Bulletin*, No. 652, London, 1972.

Friedrich Engels, *The Origin of Family, Private Property and the State*, First published 1891, Reprinted with an Introduction by Eleanor Burke Leacock, Lawrence and Wishan, London, 1972.

Gangmumei Kabui (Kamei), "A brief note on *Loiyamba Shilyen* : A Royal Edict on social distribution of economic and administrative functions", *PNEIHA*, IIIrd Session, Imphal, 1982.

____________, "State Formation in North East India : A Review", Presidential Address, *PNEIHA*, VIIIth Session, Kohima, 1987.

____________,"Nongda Lairen Pakhangba and the Establishment of the Ningthouja Dynasty of Manipur", *PNEIHA*, IXth Session, Guwahati, 1988.

____________, *History of Manipur*, Volume One (Pre-Colonial Period), National Publishing House, Delhi, 1991.

Gourchandra, *Manipurgi Aroiba Lan*, Imphal, 1971.

H. D. Sankalia, *Pre and Proto history of India and Pakistan*, Pune, 1974.

__________, *Indian Archaeology Today*, Delhi, 1979.

Henri J. M. Claessen & Peter Skalnik (ed.), *The Early State*, Mouton Publishers, The Hague, 1978.

H Nilkant Singh, "Meitei State Formation : A Preliminary Study", *PNEIHA*, XIIth Session, Jagiroad, 1991.

________ "Meitei Village Community", *PNEIHA,* XVIth Session, Silchar, 1995.

________"Lallup System", *PNEIHA,* XVIIth Session, Aizawl, 1996.

Hermann Kulke, "Early State Formation and Royal Legitimation in Tribal Areas of Eastern India", in R. R. Moser & M. K. Gautam (ed.), *Aspects of Tribal Life in South Asia I : Strategy and Survivals*, Bersenia, 1978.

H. Sudhir, "Women's Market and State", *PNEIHA*, XXIVth Session, Guwahati, 2003.

_________, "Women and Public Domain", *Proceedings of Indian History Congress*, Mysore, 2003.

__________, "Gender and Society in Manipur", in Priyam Goswami (ed.), *Changing Patterns of Economy and Society - 19th and 20th Century North East India*, Guwahati, 2007.

Irom Amubi Singh (ed), *Nunglon*, Ningthoumacha Manisana Keibung, Imphal, n.d.

Irom Mangi, *Yelhoungei Manipurda Phi Shabagi Lam*, Imphal, 2002.

International Encyclopedia of Social Sciences, vol. 15, New York, 1997.

I. R. Babu Singh (ed), *Apunba Wareng*, Imphal, 1986.

Janakinath Basak, *Manipur Prohelika*, Kolkata, 1891.

James Johnstone, *My Experience in Manipur and Naga Hills*, (London, 1896) Reprint B. R. Publishing House, Delhi, 1971.

J. B. Bhattacharjee, "Tripuri State Formation in Mediaeval Tripura", *PNEIHA*, IIIrd Session, Imphal, 1982.

________________, *Social and Polity Formations in Pre-Colonial North-East India*, Har-Anand/Vikas Publishing House, New Delhi, 1991.

________________, *Bhauma-Naraka Legend and State Formation in Pragjyotisha-Kamarupa*, NEIHA, Shillong, 2004.

________________, "*Loiyamba Shinyen* : A Landmark in Meitei State Formation in Medieval Manipur', *Proceedings of the Indian History Congress*, 64th Session, Mysore, 2004.

________________, "Economic Dimension of the Meitei State Formation", in F. A. Qadri (ed), *Society and Economy in North-East India*, Volume 2, Regency Publications, New Delhi, 2006.

________________, *State and Wealth: The Early States in Northeast India*, DVS Publishers, Guwahati, 2010.

Jack Stauder, "Anarchy and Ecology: Political Society among the Majangir", *Southwestern Journal of Anthropology*, vol. 28, 1972.

J. P. Singh & Nishar Ahmed (ed.), *Coinage And Economy of the North-Eastern States*, Varanasi, 1980.

Jyotirmoy Roy, *History of Manipur*, Eastlight Book House, Calcutta, 1958.

John G.Taylor, *From Modernisation to Modes of Production*, London, 1979.

Julian H. Steward, *Theory of Culture Change*, University of Illinois Press, Urbana, 1955.

Karl A. Wittfogel, *Oriental Despotism : A Comparative Study of Total Power*, Yale University Press, New Haven, 1957.

K. B. Singh (ed), *An Introduction to Tribal Language and Culture of Manipur*, Manipur State Kala Academy, Imphal, 1993.

K. Dhono, *Meitei Puya Wari Machang*, Imphal, 1974.

Kh. Chandrashekhar Singh (ed.), *Loiyamba Shinyen*, All Manipur Umanglai Haraoba Committee, Uripok Naoremthong, Imphal, 1982.

Kh Ranendrajit, "The Chakpa of Manipur : A Brief Historical Account", *PNEIHA*, XXVIth Session, Kokrajhar, 2005.

Kh. Ibungoyaima, *Manirpugi Pisha Lonsa Amasung Hourakpham*, Imphal, 1997.

Kh. Yaima (ed.), *Poireiton Khunthokpa*, Imphal, 1971.

________ (ed.) *Pakhangba Phambal*, Imphal, 1987.

K. Ratan, "Myths and Rituals in Laiharaoba", *PNEIHA*, XVIth Session, Silchar, 1995.

K. Ratankumar Singh, "Genesis of the Lai Haraoba in Meitei Society", *PNEIHA*, XIIIth Session, Shillong, 1992.

K. Sobita Devi, *Traditional Dress of the Meiteis*, Manipur State Museum, Imphal, 1984; Reprint 1998.

Kshetri Kumar, *Manipurda Chapu*, Kakching, 1984.

Kumkum Roy, "Gender Relations During the First Millennium: An Overview", in B. D. Chattopadhyaya (ed), *A Social History of Early India, History of Science, Philosophy and Culture in Indian Civilization*, Vol.II, Part 5, New Delhi, 2005.

L. Ashokkumar Singh, *Ariba Manipuri Sahityagi Paring*, Imphal, 1988.

Lal Dena (ed.), *History of Modern Manipur*, Orbit Publishers and Distributors, Delhi, 1991.

L. Basanti Devi, "Origin, Growth and Fall of the Moirang Principality in South Manipur Valley", *PNEIHA*, IXth session, Guwahati, 1988.

__________, "Ancient Meitei Military Organization", *PNEIHA*, XIth session, Imphal, 1990.

L. Chandramani, *Manipur Itihas*, Imphal, 1970.

Lewis Henri Morgan, *The Ancient Society* (Cleveland, 1877) Indian reprint, K P Bagchi & Co., Calcutta, 1982.

L. Gumplovicz, *The Outlines of Sociology*, American Academy of Political and Social Science, Philadelphia, 1899.

L. Ibungohal Singh, *Introduction to Manipur*, Imphal, 1963.

L. Ibungohal Singh & N Khelchandra Singh (ed.), *Cheitharol Kumbaba*, Manipuri Sahitya Parishad, Imphal, 1967.

L. Joychandra Singh, *The Lost Kingdom – Royal Chronicle of Manipur*, Prajatantra Publishing House, Imphal, 1995.

L Kunjeswori Devi, "The Bearing of the Inscriptions on the History of Manipur", *PNEIHA*, XI [th] Session, Imphal, 1990.

__________, "Ancient Discoveries in Sekta, a village in Manipur", *PNEIHA*, XIIth Session, Jagiroad, 1991.

__________, *Archaeology in Manipur*, Rajesh Book Depot, Delhi, 2003.

Lokendra Arambam, "Manipur : A Ritual Theatre State", *PNEIHA*, VIIth Session, Pasighat, 1986.

L. Sanajaobi Devi, "First Muslim Settlement in Manipur", *PNEIHA*, IXth Session, Guwahati, 1988.

Mahmoodah Khannam, "Economic Contribution of the

Muslims to Manipur", *PNEIHA*, XIth Session, Imphal, 1991

Manipur State Kala Academy (MSKA), *Sagai Salairol,* Imphal, 1994.

Marshal D Sahlins, *Stone Age Economics*, Aldine Press, Chicago, 1972.

M. C. Arunkumar, "Towards Hypotheses to the Decline of the Meitei Kingdom", *PNEIHA*, XIIIth Session, Shillong, 1992.

M. Chandra Singh (ed.), *Poireiton Khunthok,* Manipuri Sahitya Parishad, Imphal, 1979.

M. Chandrasing, *Lai-Haraoba and Ras,* Imphal, 1963.

M. Gaurachandra, *Manipurda Yotshung Yotsha* (Traditional Iron Smelting and Forging in Manipur), Kakching, 1997.

M. J. Harner, "Scarcity, the Factors of Production, and Social Evolution" in Steven Polgar (ed.), *Population, Ecology and Social Evolution,* Mouton Publishers, The Hague, 1975.

M. Jitendra Singh, "Slavery in Pre-British Manipur : A Historial Survey", *PNEIHA*, V^th Session, Aizawl, 1984.

__________, "Famines in the Valley of Manipur as recorded in *Cheitharol Kumbaba*", *PNEIHA*, VIIth session, Pasighat, 1986.

__________, "The Origin of the Meitei : An Overview", *PNEIHA* , X^th Session, Shillong, 1989.

M. Lokendra Singh, "Divine Kingship in Manipur", *PNEIHA*, X^th Session, Shillong, 1989.

M. Narendra (ed), *Langwol*, Imphal, 1981.

M. Manaoyaima (ed), *Tutenglon*, Kakching, 2000.

Morton H. Fried, *The Evolution of Political Society*, Random House, New York, 1967.

M. Ranjana, "Ethnic Groups of Moirang Principality", *PNEIHA*, XIXth Session, Kohima, 1998.

__________, "Mera Haojongba : A Meitei Policy of National Integration", *PNEIHA,* XXIst Session, Tezpur, 2001.

M. Shantirani Devi, "Relics of Kangla (Old Palace}", *PNEIHA*, XIIth Session, Jagiroad, 1991.

__________, "Meitei Military System", *PNEIHA*, XIVth Session, Jorhat, 1993.

Mutua Bahadur, *Traditional textile of Manipur*, Imphal, 1997.

__________, *Meitei Phizet Leiteng*, Imphal, 1998.

Mutua Bahadur & P. Gunindro Singh, *Epigraphic Records of Manipur*, Imphal, 1986.

____________________, *Khangabok Coins Hoarding*, Imphal, 1985

Mutua Museum , Bulletin No.1, *Coins of Manipur*, Imphal, 1981; Bulletin No. 2, *Sculptures of Manipur*, Imphal, 1982; Bulletin No. 3, *Temple Architecture of Manipur*, Imphal, 1983; Bulletin No. 5, *Manipur Rock Carvings and Inscriptions of Manipur*, Imphal, 1985; Bulletin No. 6, *Forts and Monuments of Manipur*, Imphal, 1987; Bulletin No. 7, *Jewelleries of Manipur*, Imphal, 1988; Bulletin No. 8, *Cane and Bamboo Crafts of Manipur*, Imphal, 1994.

Nandalal Sharma, *Meitrabak*, Imphal, 1960.

N. Ibobi, *Manipur Administration*, Imphal, 1976.

N. Indramani, *Phamballon*, Imphal, 2009.

N. G. Rhodes, *The Coinage of North-East India*, Kent, 1994.

Ng. Kullachandra (ed) , *Chakpa Khunda Khunthok*, Imphal, 1993.

Ng. Kullachanra Singh (ed.), *Sading*, Imphal, 1982.

N. Lokendra Singh, "A Historical Study of Some Aspects of *Cheitharol Kumbaba*', *PNEIHA*, IXth Session, Guwahati, 1988.

N. Khelchandra Singh, *Manipuri to Manipuri and English Dictionary*, Imphal, 1964.

______________, *Chada Lahui*, Imphal, 1966.

______________, *Ariba Manipuri Sahityagi Itihas*, Manipuri Sahitya Parishad, Imphal, 1969.

______________ (ed.), *Naothingkhong Phambal Kaba*, Imphal, 1968.

______________ (ed.), *A Catalogue of Manipuri Manuscripts*, Manipuri Sahitya Parishad, Imphal, 1984.

______________ (ed.), *Phamlon*, Imphal, 1987.

N. Nilkant Singh, "Loiyamba's Statecraft", *PNEIHA*, XXth Session, Dibrugarh, 1999.

O. Bhogeshwor Singh (ed.), *Ningthourol Lambuba*, Imphal, 1967.

______________, *Loina Shillon*, Imphal, 1976.

O. Bhogeshwor Singh & M. A. Janab Khan (ed.), *Nongshamei Puya*, Imphal, 1973.

O. K. Singh, "Archaeological Research in Manipur", *East Himalayas*, 1970.

________, "Toll Gazing at Tharon: Did Austroloids Once Inhabit Manipur?", *Resistance*, Imphal, 30 Dec. 1980.

_________, *Manipurgi Meihourol*, Yeningtha, Imphal, 1980.

_________, *Report of the State Archaeology Department*, Govt. of Manipur, 1983.

_________, *Archaeology in Manipur (series-1):Napachik, A Stone Age Site in Manipur valley*, Imphal, 1984.

_________, *Pre-historic Archaeology of Nongpok Keithelmanbi*, Imphal, 1986.

_________, *Archaeology in Manipur*, State Archaeology, Arts and Culture Department, Govt. of Manipur, Imphal, 1988.

_________, *Stone Age Archaeology of Manipur*, Imphal, 1997.

P. Chandrasekhar (ed.), *Yellon*, Imphal, 1998.

P. C. Choudhury, *History of the Civilisation of the People of Assam till Twelfth Century AD*, DHAS, Gauhati, 1959.

P. K. Bhattacharya, "An Interesting Coin of Manipur", *Journal of the Numismatic Society of India* (*JNSI*), Vol. XXXV, Varanasi, 1977.

Quazi Hamid Ali, *The Manipur Muslims*, Banskandi, 1979.

R. B. Pamberton, *Report on the Eastern Frontier of British India*, (Calcutta, 1835) Reprint DHAS, Gauhati, 1966.

R. C. Majumdar, "The Manipur Rebellion of 1891", *Bengal Past and Present*, January-June, 1959

R. Brown, *Statistical Account of Manipur*, (London, 1874) Reprint Sanskaran Prakashak, Delhi, 1975.

Rena Laisram, "The Social Reality of Pre-Hindu Religion of the Meiteis of Manipur", *PNEIHA*, XXIInd Session, Tezpur, 2001.

_________, "Genealogy as a Source of Meitei History", *PNEIHA*, XXVth Session, Shillong, 2004.

________, *Early Meitei History – Religion, Society & The Manipur Puyas*, Akansha Publishing House, New Delhi, 2009.

R. K. Jhalajit Singh, *A Short History of Manipur*, O. K. Stores, Imphal, 1965.

________ "The Immigration of Brahmins and its Impact on the Culture of Manipur", *PNEIHA*, IIIrd Session, Imphal, 1982.

R. K. Saha, "State Formation Among the Meitei of Manipur" in Surajit Sinha (ed), *Tribal Polities and State Systems in Pre-Colonial Eastern and North Eastern India*, Centre for Studies in Social Sciences/K P Bagchi & Company, Calcutta, 1987.

R. K. Sanahal (ed.), *Pangal Thorakpa*, Imphal, 1985.

Robert H. Lowie, *The Origin of the State*, Harcourt, Brace and World, New York, 1927.

Robert L. Carneiro, "A Theory of the Origin of the State", *Science*, 169, 1970.

Romila Thapar, *From Lineage to State*, Oxford University Press, Bombay, 1984.

Ronald Cohen & E. R. Service (ed.) *Origin of the State: the Anthropology of Political Evolution*, Philadelphia, 1978.

R. Sarma, *Political History of Tripura*, Calcutta, 1986.

Saroj Nalini Arambam Parratt (tr. & ed), *The Court Chronicle of the Kings of Manipur: The Cheitharon Kumpapa*, Routledge, New York, 2005.

S. K. Bose, "Intriguing Manipur' : The Views of a 19th Century Trader", *PNEIHA*, XXVIIth Session, Aizawl, 2006.

__________, "Sel Coinage of Manipur", *Coin – 2007*, Numismatic Society of Calcutta, Kolkata, 2007.

S. N. Pandey (ed.), *Sources of the History of Manipur and Adjoining Areas*, National Publishing House, Delhi, 1985.

S. P. Basu, "A Rare Gold Coin of Manipur", *JNSI*, Vol. XXVII, pt. I, Varanasi, 1965.

Steven Polgar, "Population, Evolution, and Theoretical Paradigms" in Steven Polgar (ed), *Population, Ecology and Social Evolution,* Mouton Publishers, The Hague, 1975.

Surajit Sinha, "State Formation and Rajput Myth in Tribal Central India", *Man in India*, vol. 42, no. 1, January-March, 1962.

________ (ed.), *Tribal Polities and State Systems in Pre-Colonial Eastern and North Eastern India*, Centre for Studies in Social Sciences/K P Bagchi & Company, Calcutta, 1987.

T. C. Hudson, *The Meitheis*, (London, 1911) Reprint B. R. Publishing House, Delhi, 1981; Low Price Publications, Delhi, 1989.

Thounaojam Chanu Ibemhal, *Haoreima Shambubi*, Imphal, 2000.

W. Marsden, *Oriental Coins*, British Museum, London, 1825.

W. McCulloch, *An Account of the Valley of Munnipore* (Calcutta, 1859) Reprint Gian Publishing House, Delhi, 1980.

APPENDIX

Participants of the Workshop

1. Professor J. B. Bhattacharjee, Chairman, Institute of Northeast India Studies, 13/A Udayan Abasan, Udayrajpur, Madhyamgram, Kolkata – 700129.
2. Professor Gangmumei Kamei, Retired Professor of History, Manipur University, Imphal – 795003.
3. Professor N. Joykumar Singh, Department of History, Manipur University, Imphal – 795003.
4. Professor M. Jitendra Singh, Department of History, Manipur University, Imphal – 795003.
5. Dr. (Mrs) Salam Irene, Associate Professor, Department of History, Manipur University, Imphal – 795003.
6. Dr. (Mrs) L. Kunjeswori Devi, Associate Professor, Department of History, Manipur University, Imphal – 795003.
7. Dr. Ch. Priyaranjan Singh, Associate Professor, Department of Economics, Manipur University, Imphal – 795003.
8. Mr. H. Sudhir, Assistant Professor, Department of History, Manipur University, Imphal – 795003.
9. Mr. K. Touthang, Research Scholar, Department of History, Manipur University, Imphal – 795003.
10. Mr. Ksh. Rajesh Singh, Research Scholar, Department of History, Manipur University, Imphal – 795003.
11. Mr. M. Dominic, Research Scholar, Department of History, Manipur University, Imphal – 795003.

12. Mr. Jangthang Haokip, Research Scholar, Department of History, Manipur University, Imphal – 795003.
13. Mr. S. Tejbanta, Research Scholar, Department of History, Manipur University, Imphal – 795003.
14. Dr. C. Mathew, Assistant Professor, Department of History, Manipur University, Imphal – 795003.
15. Mr. Dominic D. Golmei, Lecturer in History, Maram College, Maram, Senapati Dist., Manipur.
16. Mr. L. Bishwajit Singh, Research Scholar, Department of History, Manipur University, Imphal – 795003.
17. Bhabananda Takhellambam, Lecturer in History, C.I. College, Bishanpur, Manipur.
18. M. Rantan Kumar Singh, Lecturer in History, S.K. Women's College, Nambol, Manipur.
19. Ms. Ng. Jayshree, Lecturer, Kanandevi Modern College of Education, Pangei, Manipur.
20. Dr. (Mrs)) Priyadarshni M. Gangte, Lecturer in History, Dambei Christian College, Motbung, Senapati Dist., Manipur.
21. Ms. Ningthoujam Sangita, Research Scholar, Department of History, Manipur University, Imphal – 795003.
22. Ms. Chandam Ragini Devi, Research Scholar, Department of History, Manipur University, Imphal – 795003.
23. Mr. Pritam Hanjabam, Research Scholar, Department of History, Manipur University, Imphal – 795003.
24. Mr. Gongthouri Pamir, Research Scholar, Department of History, Manipur University, Imphal – 795003.
25. Mr. Khangembam Rabichandra, Research Scholar,

Department of History, Manipur University, Imphal – 795003.

26. Mr. Nangchin Christopher, Research Scholar, Department of History, Manipur University, Imphal – 795003.

27. Mr. Khwairakpam Tiken Thangmeiband, Research Scholar, Department of History, Manipur University, Imphal – 795003.

28. Mr. Pureshwor Nameirakpam, Research Scholar, Department of History, Manipur University, Imphal – 795003.

29. Mr. Moirangtham Tomba Singh, Research Scholar, Department of History, Manipur University, Imphal – 795003.

30. Mr. Phoomei Lantholengou, Research Scholar, Department of History, Manipur University, Imphal – 795003.

31. Mr. Yankhaibam Brajakumar Singh, Research Scholar, Department of History, Manipur University, Imphal – 795003.

32. Dr. N. Debendra Singh, Research Associate, Centre for Manipur Studies, Manipur University, Imphal – 795003.

33. Dr S. Amal Singh, Research Associate, Centre for Manipur Studies, Manipur University, Imphal – 795003.

34. Dr. Oinam Ranjit Singh, Guest Lecturer, Department of History, Manipur University, Imphal – 795003.

35. Mr. Jacob Luiram, Assistant Professor, Department of History, Manipur University, Imphal – 795003.

Index